THE NEW WOMEN'S MOVEMENT
Feminism and Political Power in Europe and the USA

THE NEW WOMEN'S MOVEMENT

Feminism and Political Power in Europe and the USA

edited by

Drude Dahlerup

SAGE Modern Politics Series Volume 12
Sponsored by
the European Consortium for Political Research/ECPR

SAGE Publications
London ● Beverly Hills & Newbury Park ● New Delhi

SAGE Publications Ltd
28 Banner Street
London EC1Y 8QE

Sage Publications Inc
275 South Beverly Drive
Beverly Hills, California 90212
2111 West Hillcrest Drive
Newbury Park,
California 91320

SAGE Publications India Pvt Ltd
C-236 Defence Colony
New Delhi 110 024

British Library Cataloguing in Publication Data

The New women's movement: feminism and
    political power in Europe & the USA.—
    (Sage modern politics series; v. 12)
    1. Feminism—History—20th century
    I. Dahlerup, Drude
    305.4'2'091812   HQ1154

Library of Congress Catalogue Card Number 86-061922

ISBN 0-8039-8010-8
ISBN 0-8039-8011-6 Pbk/

Phototypeset by Sunrise Setting, Torquay, Devon
Printed in Great Britain by J.W. Arrowsmith Ltd, Bristol

Contents

Preface

This book developed from a workshop on the impact of the new women's movement which took place in 1983 during the session in Freiburg of the European Consortium for Political Research (ECPR). At this meeting we decided to publish the papers and also to include contributions from some countries that did not take part in the workshop. At that time we were blissfully ignorant of the amount of work and the many revisions that lay ahead.

Most of the authors are sociologists or political scientists. A list of contributors and their designations is to be found on pages 253–4.

We have chosen to write this book in English. It follows that only a few of the authors have written in their native language. Sonja Eld is responsible for revising the language of several of the articles. I also wish to thank her for many valuable comments on the manuscript. Thanks also to Sue Appleton Hughes, the copy-editor, who has done an excellent job, and to Rosemary Nixon, Sage, who managed to keep everything under control in handling the contributions from eleven different coutries.

Drude Dahlerup
Aarhus, 1986

Introduction

Drude Dahlerup

'How was it possible for small bands of women to have such enormous impact, to change our thinking so radically in so short a period of time?' asked the sociologist Jessie Bernard after the first years of the new women's movement had passed.

Later, the small bands of women began to look like a mass movement. In Italy, the new movement at its peak was able to gather 50,000 women in the streets in one day. In the USA the new feminist organization, NOW, has reached a membership of 250,000.

In the late 1960s and the early 1970s, when the new women's movement emerged, one could hear people say that this was a fad that would soon die away. Today, after more than fifteen years of an unorthodox, norm-shaking, radical and chaotic movement, no one doubts that this has been one of the most important social movements of the postwar period.

Most people in the Western world have an opinion of the new women's movement, whether they detest these bra-burning, man-hating, rabid, outrageous women or feel elevated by these norm-breaking, creative, courageous, vital avant-garde women — or maybe place themselves somewhere in between these two poles.

After more than fifteen years of the new women's movement, it is time to ask what impact it has had, and in which ways the movement itself has changed. Today some people are wondering whether the new women's movement is dead, whereas others maintain that it is as vital as ever.

This book presents the development of the new women's movement in eleven countries: Italy, Ireland, the Netherlands, France, Britain, USA, Iceland, Finland, Turkey, Spain and Denmark; each chapter is devoted to one country. Since the book spans so many countries, it offers a unique context for a comparative study of the new women's movement. Because of the many striking similarities in style, and in the actions and ideas of the new women's movement in the various countries, one may overlook the differences in history and influence of the movements. The feminist movement never had the same opportunities in all Western countries. Consequently, this study illustrates how various political systems respond to protest movements. The focus of the book is on the new women's movement as a *social movement*, its actions, ideas, strategies, organization, recruitment, alliances and in general the interaction between the protest movement and its surroundings.

A social movement is a conscious, collective activity to promote social change, representing a protest against the established power structure and against the dominant norms and values. The commitment and active participation of its members or activists constitute the main resource of any social movement. The story of the women's movement in the eleven countries of this book challenges the notion that a decentralized, non-professional, flat, grass-roots structure is a barrier to political influence. On the contrary, it is suggested that the group-oriented structure, based on the idea that 'the personal is political', in fact was the main reason why it was possible for the new women's movement to release so much energy and to present a radical new way of thinking about women which has influenced public opinion as well as public policy. One could call this the strength of being 'outside the system'.

The book presents several approaches to the study of the women's movement, and deals with several major aspects: the organizational and ideological development, the policy impact, the interaction between the movement and the political parties, and the fundamental question of why the movement emerged at the time it did. Each of the authors was asked to include a description of the various branches of the movement in her country. Finally, all chapters include a discussion of the author's view of the impact of the movement.

The book is divided into three parts, according to the focus of the essay. These sections discuss three main issues in the study of the women's movement:

— Part I: Challenging the establishment: the case of abortion.
             Italy, Ireland, the Netherlands, France.
— Part II: Movement strategies: inside or outside the 'system'.
             Britain, USA, Iceland, Finland.
— Part III: The rise and change of the new women's movement.
             Turkey, Spain, Denmark.

Second- or third-wave feminism
The new women's movement that arose in the late 1960s and early 1970s in most Western countries was not the first feminist movement in history. The term 'second-wave feminism' has been attached to the new movement to indicate that we are witnessing the second peak of a feminist movement that has existed for more than 100 years, ever since the second half of the nineteenth century.

The first wave of feminism is best known for the suffrage campaign, although the vote for women was seldom the first demand put forward by the early women's movement. Second-wave feminism simply indicates a new impetus to this movement which has experienced periods of bloom, strength and visibility alternating with periods of more quiet dogged struggle to better women's position in a male-dominated society.

The women's movement as a collective activity by women to better women's position and change the male dominance of society started in the USA in the 1840s, in England in the 1850s, in France and Germany in the 1860s and in the Scandinavian countries in the 1870s and 1880s, to mention just a few.

Women's studies scholars continuously dig out forgotten or even suppressed knowledge about revolts by women in earlier times (for instance, during the French revolution or the Renaissance). We may eventually find out that all male-dominated cultures have experienced some kind of revolt by women. However, here we limit the discussion to the women's movement of the last 100 to 150 years.

Alice Rossi, the US sociologist, states that the present wave of feminism is not the second wave, but in fact the third wave of feminism. She identifies three peaks of feminist political activity and public visibility in US history: the first, from the 1840s to the 1860s, starting with Seneca Falls; the second, from 1900 to the passage of the Suffrage Amendment in the 1920s; and the third, from the 1960s onwards. Rossi suggests that there may be a generational dialectic involved in this historical ebb and flow, since these three waves are separated by roughly fifty years or two generations (Rossi, 1973, see also McGlen and O'Connor, 1983).

In Denmark, to mention another example, it is also possible to identify three peaks of the feminist movement, but they do not follow the same generational pattern: the first peak occurred in the 1880s during a general rising against the ruling conservative forces, the second lasted from 1905 to the first world war (the suffrage campaign) and the third started in the late 1960s. So the generational aspect, no doubt important for an understanding of the ups and downs of the feminist movement, must be complemented with other factors, such as changes in the general political climate.

It is an interesting task to study the historical periods of expansion, activity and strength of the women's movement. It is, however, no less important to study the less visible feminist movement to be found between the peaks. During its long history the women's movement has been declared dead many times, for example during the interwar period. However, a closer study reveals that in most countries many women still fought collectively for equality and justice for women, although now in a more dogged, less visible fight, partly in the autonomous women's movement and partly in the political parties, the trade unions or the state bureaucracy.

Recent research has provided material for a revision of our image of the 1930s as a bleak period in the history of feminism. One example is Susan Ware's (1981) book on women in Roosevelt's New Deal. Her study has shown the existence of an influential network of women in the administration of the New Deal, a network that was rooted in that generation's common experience in the suffrage campaign.

Such historical studies of the periods following the peaks of the feminist movement may help us understand what is happening to the movement today. Equipped with this knowledge, we should be able not just to understand and observe the changes, but also to act in order to influence the course of history.

Cycles of protest

The many new social movements that emerged in the Western world in the 1960s, 1970s and 1980s restored the theoretical interest in the concept of cycles of protest. An individual movement has its own life-cycle: growth, peak, decline, maybe new growth. But movements do seem to emerge many at a time, creating what Zald (1979) calls a whole 'social movement sector'. In certain historical periods social movements abound, while other periods are more quite. In this way, every society experiences cycles of social movements (Tarrow, 1983).

From Karl Marx on, scholars have discussed whether cycles of protest occur at regular intervals. Historical studies, however, reveal no such regularity. Michael Harrington argues that at any rate time has speeded up in the more volatile twentieth century (in Freeman, 1983:ix). He also rightly states that in the late twentieth century social movements have become more self-conscious and self-analysing, and this might be one of the reasons why we will probably not have to wait fifty years or more for the next period of general protest.

Social movements emerge out of social conflicts. But conflicts exist all the time. The resource mobilization approach to the study of social movements has rightly added that the possibility of mobilization of new resources is crucial to the expansion of movements. Cycles of protest may be more frequent because today more resources are available to challenging groups, and also because self-conscious movements will learn from other movements in a process of collective learning. On the other hand, this may be true only for the more resourceful middle-class-based movements like the ones of the 1960s and 1970s.

The fact that movements emerge in blocks indicates some common causes. These may be fundamental social changes of a given historical period, or of the 'opportunity structure' of society — for instance, the extent to which political authorities are open to reforms. The general amount of resources available for mobilization is important, too, and so is the inspiration from one country to another, particularly in these days of worldwide mass communication.

To this list of more fundamental common incentives, Jo Freeman (1975) adds the practical one that resources mobilized by one movement may be used by new movements. In this way the US new women's liberation movement made use of the resources of the New Left: they created a women's network within the New Left, met at New Left conferences, made use of the many underground papers and simply used the duplicators of the New Left organizations.

Throughout history, the emergence of new waves of feminism in most countries has occurred in periods of general protest and mobilization. Or, instead of saying 'general' (which often refers to men's activities), perhaps I should express it like this: new waves of feminism seem to occur side by side with other social movements. These social movements are often linked together through ideological and personal ties, and may share a protest against the establishment and against traditional values.

Women's experiences in other movements have often given an impetus to revolt on their own behalf; for example, the discrimination and degradation women felt from men when working together for a common cause made women form their own autonomous organizations to fight for the equality of the sexes. This happened when women in the US anti-slavery movement were denied the right to campaign side by side with men. The same thing happened to the women who were deeply engaged in the national and liberal risings in Europe in the nineteenth century. Women in the labour movement have told of similar experiences that made them form women's groups within the labour movement or join the autonomous women's movement.

As in the nineteenth century, the discrimination that women felt within the New Left in the late 1960s and early 1970s became one of the factors that triggered off the new movement. When fighting for equality and justice and participatory democracy 'in general', women became tired of just making tea for the revolution, sleeping with the leaders and typing their manuscripts.

What is feminism?
Confusion persists as to the terms 'women's movement', 'feminism', 'women's liberation movement', 'social feminism', 'radical feminism' and so on. During the first years of the new women's movement one could hear the term 'feminism' used very narrowly as an invective for those in the movement who — according to their opponents — did not put enough emphasis on the class struggle in contrast to the gender conflict. The older socialist women's movement, which remained a part of the labour movement, also tended to use the term

'feminism' in a negative sense, as a label for the autonomous women's rights movement, which they considered bourgeois. This did not prevent many of these organizations from considering themselves part of 'the women's movement' at large (Dahlerup, 1973).

Richard Evans defines feminism as 'the doctrine of equal rights for women, based on the theory of the equality of the sexes' (Evans, 1977:39). Gerda Lerner defines (US) feminism as 'any struggle designed to elevate their [women's] status, socially, politically, economically, and in respect to their self-concepts' (Lerner, 1971: 236). David Bouchier states that 'feminism includes any form of opposition to any form of social, personal or economic discrimination which women suffer because of their sex' (Bouchier, 1983:2). Janet Radcliffe Richards supports a very broad definition of feminism, not limited to the autonomous women's movement, as 'a very general belief that society is unjust to women' (Richards, 1982:15). In this discussion a further problem is that many languages do not have a proper word for 'feminism'.

I prefer a broad definition of 'feminism' as an ideology whose basic goal is to remove the discrimination and degradation of women and to break down the male dominance of society. It is in fact easier to define what feminism is against than to describe positively the common denominator for the visions of all factions of the women's movement, which state as their goal equality, liberation, equal worth or something else.

Feminism is an *ideology*, a doctrine. The women's movement comprises the conscious, collective *activities* of women fighting for feminist goals.

The women's movement is sometimes identified with the autonomous movement and its followers. A broader definition of the women's movement includes feminist activities by women in, say, women's committees in the political parties, trade unions, public institutions or other social movements. Most chapters in this book, including this Introduction, use the more narrow definition of the women's movement.

In empirical research, one should ask the following interesting questions. First, who actually works for feminist goals, no matter in which context? Second, how many of these women consider themselves part of the women's movement? The answers will vary from time to time, and from country to country. It is characteristic of any social movement that the boundaries between the movement and its surroundings are never clear and are constantly changing.

Most chapters of this book focus on the autonomous women's movement, while a few have chosen a broader perspective. But all chapters contain a study of the impact of the new women's movement of the 1960s–1980s on political parties and other major political actors.

Within the women's movement at large several branches have developed, and new groupings are emerging all the time. The two main branches of contemporary western feminism are the women's rights movement and the women's liberation movement.

Women's rights and women's liberation

The new women's movement, which started in most Western countries in the late 1960s and early 1970s, was a protest by a new generation of women against male-dominated or 'patriarchal' society, as it became common to call it. Ideological and strategical differences divided the movement into two major branches.

The branch of the movement usually called the *women's rights movement* works predominantly for political reforms by means of traditional pressure group tactics. These tactics require a national organization and a certain degree of professionalization. Consequently, it becomes an aim to be acknowledged and respected by the political establishment. This kind of feminism has long historical roots going back to the suffrage movement and the successful campaigns for women's access to education, to qualified work and to legal majority.

The new wave of feminism in the 1960–1980s also created new women's rights organizations, notably in the USA, but also in France and Britain. In some countries, for example the five Nordic countries, the old women's rights organizations from the nineteenth century are still at work, but they seldom expanded during the 1960s–1980s.

The core of the new wave, however, was a totally different kind of feminism, usually labelled the *women's liberation movement*. This was a radical, left-wing, often socialist, feminism, which rejected the idea of equality with men. Instead, the movement advocated the liberation of all oppressed people. The women's liberation movement was rooted in the New Left, and seems to have flourished the most where the New Left was strongest.

Political reform, that is reform effected through the political establishment, has never been the main strategy of the women's liberation movement. Its main focus was and is on *women*, not the state. The goal is to change people's way of thinking and acting. Revaluation of womanhood, not the adaptation of women to men's roles, is the basis of the new ideology. It is considered essential to make women work collectively for common goals, instead of competing with each other, to the benefit of patriarchal society only. 'Sisterhood is powerful!' The movement's flat, decentralized organizational structure was from the start considered essential to developing a new consciousness among women. Consequently, no national organization of any duration has ever been established by the women's liberation movement in any country.

While the main strategy of the women's rights movement has been to seek influence through integration, the women's liberation movement follows a different strategy. When engaged in campaigns directed specifically at the political institutions, for example in the abortion campaign, this branch of the movement prefers extra-parliamentary tactics to traditional pressure group tactics. But the main activities of the women's liberation movement consist of:

1. consciousness-raising groups;
2. experiments in new ways of living;
3. creating a counter-culture, e.g., feminist literature, feminist theatre, music bands, women's festivals;
4. creating alternative institutions, e.g., crisis centres, women's centres, self-help clinics.

'The personal is political', one of the slogans says. Through its activities, the women's liberation movement has become one of the best examples of the statement by Gerlach and Hine (1970: xvi) that a successful movement is the point of intersection between personal and social change.

The two kinds of feminism, women's rights and women's libera-tion, have come to exist side by side in most countries, but the balance between them varies from country to country — and, moreover, has shifted during the last fifteen years. Even the first feminist wave in the nineteenth century included both kinds of feminist activities, although the reform strategies were more dominant, except in the early socialist women's movement.

Although the new wave of feminism started in the USA, inspiring women all over Western Europe, the new US women's movement differs from the European pattern. In the USA both a women's rights kind of feminism and a women's liberation kind of feminism emerged and still flourish. Jo Freeman (1975) has labelled these two branches the 'older or conservative' branch, including the National Organi-zation of Women (NOW), founded in 1966, and the 'younger or radical' branch, the small-group-based women's liberation movement. Only in the USA did the women's rights movement expand during this period. In her chapter in this book, Virginia Sapiro concludes that today there are not just two branches of the US movement, but many branches. Membership overlap has become considerable, and a division in goals and strategies is now found within the larger organizations.

Also, the European new women's movement has changed, and consequently the gap between the new women's liberation movement and the traditional women's rights movement has diminished. New coalitions and new splits have occurred. But tension remains between the professional feminism focusing on the state level, and grass-roots feminism preferring activities in the local community.

Studying the impact of the new women's movement

After fifteen to twenty years of the new women's movement, we should be able to start evaluating the impact and influence it has had so far. This is no easy task, however. The character of the movement makes an evaluation difficult. It is much easier to analyse the effects of a single-issue movement than the impact of a movement with such a comprehensive project as that of the women's movement, namely, a complete restructuring of the social relations and the power structure of society.

We should not forget that the most important achievement is that the protest of the original small bands of women developed into a *movement*; that lots of women joined in as movement activists; that many groups, organizations and centres emerged; that the movement spread geographically; that sympathizers and followers began to be found in many circles of society outside the original movement organizations — in short, that collective activities by women with the aim of challenging the male dominance of society spread all over the Western world. Studies of the rise of the new women's movement have made important contributions to the social movement theory in relation to the emergence of protest movements (Freeman, 1975; McGlen and O'Connor, 1983).

The chapters in this book on Ireland, Turkey and Spain illustrate some of the barriers that might prevent a movement from emerging. In Spain the women's movement did not emerge until 1975, after the death of Franco. In Ireland the dominant Catholic and conservative forces have given the women's movement little room to develop. And in Turkey a feminist movement did not unfold until very recently. It is Sirin Tekeli's conclusion that the oppression of women in Turkey is so severe that women — although they have all reasons to revolt — are deprived of the very resources necessary to do so.

In some countries the women's movement provoked an anti-feminist movement. The campaign for abortion on demand, in which the women's movement played a major role, was important for the rise of anti-feminist sentiments. Because it wanted to speak on behalf of all women, the many women in the anti-feminist movement constituted a threat to the position of the women's movement. From their point of view, the anti-feminist women feel that the women's movement represents a threat to their traditional way of life, and to the protection they feel they need from men in order to fulfil their preferred role as housewives and homemakers (Rowland, 1984).

Is it a sign of strength or weakness on the part of the women's movement that an anti-feminist movement has developed? One of the largest anti-feminist movements arose in the USA following the emergence of the New Right. This counter-movement would not have arisen had the feminist movement not been considered a serious threat to traditional values. In this way, the emergence of an anti-feminist movement shows the success of the feminist movement in challenging old norms. However, in the Scandinavian countries no counter-movement emerged. The long feminist tradition, together with the new feminist movement, seems to have been too influential for an open anti-feminist or even an anti-abortion movement of any considerable size to develop in Scandinavia, with the exception of the more religious Norway. The conclusion is that a contextual analysis is needed to interpret the relations between the strength of the feminist movement and the development of an anti-feminist movement.

The abortion issue
The issue of abortion on demand was to the new women's movement of the 1970s what the suffrage issue had been to the feminist movement around the turn of the century. Free abortion on demand became one of the most central, if not the central, demands of the new women's movement of the 1970s. It became a catalyst, a mobilizing factor for the women's movement. Free abortion on demand was an end in itself, but it also became a symbol of women's fight against patriarchal society and the establishment. Moreover, it was a clear issue, one to which the political system was able to respond with a clear solution: legislation that gave women the sole right of decision and hence control over their own bodies.

Two extremes are presented in this book: the Italian and the Irish abortion campaigns. In her chapter on Italy, *Eleonore Eckmann Pisciotta* writes that the growth of the Italian movement into a mass movement in the first half of the 1970s and its later disappearance as a mass movement went hand in hand with the abortion issue. This issue made the Italian women's movement one of the most impressive in Europe, especially when one considers what it was up against: a strong Catholic church allied with the governing Christian Democratic Party.

When the Italian parliament passed a new abortion law in 1978, giving women the right to decide but doctors and nurses the right to 'conscientious objection', many activists withdrew from the movement or turned to other issues. The encounter with the political institutions had been a frustrating experience for many of them. When the new abortion law later was subject to a referendum, in which it was upheld, the political parties had conquered the scene.

In Ireland, also a Catholic stronghold, the result was much less successful — in fact, it was disastrous for the women's movement. The abortion law was not liberalized; rather, it was made more difficult than ever to liberalize it through the 1983 amendment to the constitution forbidding abortion. *Pauline Jackson* states that the resistance to abortion and to most other feminist demands was so ovewhelming that no strong women's movement was able to emerge. She concludes that the referendum on abortion was a defeat for the new women's movement. Nevertheless, it taught women a lesson that might prove important for a future mobilization of women in Ireland.

Why did the issue of abortion become a catalyst for the women's movement? *Anne Batiot* argues in her chapter that it stems from the character of the issue. Abortion is a choice that all women, potentially at least, may have to make. It is a non-reversible choice. And it is an experience exclusively specific to women. Batiot states that, by posing the issue in terms of choice and responsibility, feminists forced the state and public opinion to acknowledge for the first time in history 'not only the specificity of women's condition of existence, hitherto ghettoized into "the family", but also the fact that women are not objects'.

It was, however, not the first time in history that the women's movement succeeded in forcing through a new definition of women as independent subjects. The strong and intense opposition that met the first demands for votes for women in the nineteenth century proves that suffrage was indeed a radical demand. As Ellen Dubois (1975) states, it was a radical demand because it bypassed women's oppression within the family or private sphere, and demanded instead their admission to citizenship and the public arena. In fact, female suffrage was so radical a demand that in most countries the women's movement, although it wanted the vote, did not dare write this into its programme until around the turn of the century. In the 1970s the new women's movement never showed such reluctance or caution, perhaps because it was stronger and had more followers, and perhaps because in the nineteenth century it involved more serious personal costs to be a feminist.

In all Western countries, abortion reached the political agenda during the 1970s and early 1980s. In some countries, for instance Scandinavia and the Netherlands, the demand for a more liberal abortion law had been brought forward by progressive doctors and social workers for decades. But between 1975 and 1985 new abortion laws were passed in most countries after a period of intense and emotional debate.

Women's right to abortion on demand was the outcome in

countries like the USA (by a decision of the Supreme Court in 1973), Denmark (1973), Norway (1978), Sweden (1975), France (1978) and Finland (1974).

In another group of countries, women can have an abortion only on certain conditions. In the Netherlands (since 1984) women must go through a five-day period of 'rethinking', and the consent of the doctor is required. In Iceland also (1975) the consent of a doctor is needed. But in both of these countries the practice is very liberal. In Italy (1979) the clause of conscientious objection makes it very difficult to get an abortion in the southern parts of the country. In West Germany the law of 1976 allows abortion only on certain conditions: in case the mother's life is endangered, in case of rape, in case of risk of malformation of the foetus and on certain social grounds. A doctor's consent is always needed, and today there is a liberal practice in the cities, but not in the countryside. The Spanish abortion law of 1984 permits abortion, but only on a limited number of conditions. In 1983 a new abortion law was introduced in Turkey permitting abortion within the first twelve weeks, but only with the consent of the husband.

In Ireland, the foetus's right to life was written into the constitution in 1983 in order to make it even more difficult to ever liberalize abortion.

In her chapter, *Joyce Outshoorn* applies and further develops the agenda-building approach to the study of the life-cycle of the abortion issue in the Netherlands. Her conclusion is that the main contribution of the women's movement was to redefine the issue of abortion, from a medical and technical problem into a question of women's right to control their own bodies ('Baas in eigen Buik'). Using the broader framework of discourse analysis, *Anne Batiot* also argues that the strength of the feminist movement was its ability to change the fundamental concept of womanhood. In the case of abortion in France, the feminist discourse, according to Batiot, was far more radical than other discourses, refuting the notion of women's 'natural function' and replacing it with that of 'the free and unconditional choice of women'. Contrary to this, the weak Irish women's movement did not succeed in defining the issues of the abortion campaign. Abortion was in Ireland defined mainly as a religious or medical issue.

In all of these countries, with the exception of Turkey, the women's movements were the main actors in the pro-choice campaign. In summing up, the influence of the movement did not come through an involvement in the decision-making process in the political institutions. The new women's movement did not seek integration — nor were they invited to. In the abortion case the strength of the movement was, first, to bring the issue from the back streets into the open and raise it to public discussion; second, to redefine the issue into one of women's right to choose; third, by its insistent campaign, to put pressure on the political parties and the governments to take a stand and to act on the issue.

Although the new women's movement in most countries thus had a major impact on the change in abortion laws since 1973, the whole campaign left many feminist activists frustrated and disillusioned, as the chapters on Italy and the Netherlands, for example, show. This was partly a consequence of the fact that in most countries the new legislation on abortion did not meet all feminist demands. But the frustrations and anger were also a consequence of this — often very first — encounter between the new protest movement and the established political system.

The strength of being outside
Especially during its first years, the new women's movement in most countries defined itself as being 'outside the system'. The implications of that statement, however, have constantly been subject to dispute. In a way, all social movements are by definition outside the system: they are marginal, and are neither part of routine politics nor part of the dominant ideology. But differences of degree exist, following variations in the movement's own strategy and in the political structure it is up against.

The new women's movement has had a considerable impact on Western societies, even if in most countries it has remained a locally based grass-roots movement, only loosely structured and often chaotic and fluctuating.

The women's movement has been able to develop what is here called the strength of being outside. Social movement theory should not overlook this kind of power, even if the most powerful political forces are those forming an integral part of the system, and even if many protest movements do not succeed in gaining any power from being outside.

Many political observers will argue that the decentralized, small-group-based, grass-roots structure of new social movements is well suited to mobilizing activists and members, but that it impedes the movement's influence on the political system. The lack of a well functioning and permanent organization, and a lack of leadership, makes it almost impossible for protest movements to reach the political authorities.

The new women's movement itself has basically looked at this problem the same way. The women's liberation branch of the feminist movement was never willing to pay the price of seeking integration. In accordance with its radical criticism of the elitist character of the political system, the liberation movement has always feared that interaction with the establishment would lead to a de-radicalization of the movement, as has happened to so many previous movements. Contrary to this, the women's rights movement has chosen to build a more or less professional, national organization; to follow the rules of the political game in order to gain influence by traditional pressure group tactics. Actually, the gap between the two branches of the feminist movement has narrowed somewhat, but differences and tension remain.

But does a grass-roots structure in fact hinder political influence? The experience of the new women's movement seems to contradict the theory of a necessary dilemma between recruitment and mobilization on the one hand and influence on the other.

Instead, a theory of the strength of being outside is presented here. This theory rests, first, on a broad definition of political influence, and, second, on an understanding of the actual interaction between those 'outside' and those 'inside' which goes beyond the way in which most movement activists themselves have conceived this delicate relation.

One of the most important results of the new women's movement is its success in changing many women's (and also many men's) way of thinking about women. The movement has also encouraged women to use each other as a collective resource, instead of competing against each other. Consequently, new women's groups have been set up and old ones strengthened. This represents an important political influence.

For all social movements whose constituency is a whole segment of society, until now oppressed and degraded, the change of consciousness and self-esteem is essential. From her study of the US women's movement, Carol Mueller (1983) concludes that the most successful outcome of any social movement is the development of a collective consciousness among its constituency.

The new women's movement challenged the traditional concept of politics by stating that the personal is political. The movement wanted first and foremost to reach *women*, not the state. The focus on consciousness-raising, on experiments in ways of living, on new non-oppressive relations between men and women at home and elsewhere in society and on creating a counter-culture and alternative institutions — all of these represent a deliberate attempt to develop new ways of doing politics.

The movement was not just a means, but also an intersection between personal and social change. In this new way of doing politics, the grass-roots structure of the movement was essential, and was certainly not a barrier. The new women's movement could not have brought forward so much wrath and anger and untied so much energy without the group-based structure, the principle of rotation and the notion that each woman has something important to contribute.

In a recent article, Jane Jenson (1985) concludes that the women's movement, in altering the universe of the political discourse about women, has developed a new collective identity of women. In general, the largest impact of the new women's movement is in the socio-cultural field, to use Habermas's term. The movement's grassroots structure, and its focus on new ways of doing politics, was and is conducive to this aim.

But the women's movement has also influenced the political institutions and the policy outcomes, even though its major strength lies in the socio-cultural field. In some countries, notably the USA, the movement directly addresses the political decision-makers. In most other countries, its influence on the political system has been exercised indirectly by 'the strength of being outside'.

The argument is this. The women's movement managed to make a radical new way of thinking about women heard, even in the political assemblies and bureaucracies. The movement raised new issues, hitherto taboos, and succeeded in redefining old issues. A radical new perspective can probably develop only outside the logic of established institutions. All institutions more or less draw their members into a certain established way of thinking and behaving. It is the historical task of social movements to raise new perspectives from the outside. If successful, the movement will leave an impact on the established institutions and ideologies; but in this process the movement itself will change.

The interaction between the challenging movement and those working inside the political system is crucial to the strength of being outside. To mention one example, free abortion on demand would never have been carried through at the time it was had it not been for the radical, norm-shaking actions by the women's movement, which managed to redefine the issue and press for a solution. Conversely, the new legislation on abortion would not have been passed in parliaments, had it not been for all those women, and some men, who, working inside the political parties, placed the bill on the agenda, discussed and compromised over the paragraphs and watched the implementation. So both movements needed each other, even if many movement activists would dissociate themselves from the political compromises, and even if most politicians considered the new movement much too radical and outrageous. In conclusion, being outside is probably a condition of radical new thinking; but this redefinition must be absorbed by some inside the system in order for the movement to influence public policy.

In her chapter on Iceland, *Audur Styrkársdóttir* argues that the flat, small-group-based structure of the Icelandic women's movement never kept it from dealing *directly* with the political institutions. The Icelandic movement has always been oriented towards the political system, Styrkársdóttir argues, first as a protest movement, and later when it developed into a Women's Party. The Women's Party successfully ran in the local and parliamentary elections of 1982 and 1983, but at the same time worked hard to keep its movement character. The fact that the government was leftist when the movement, itself left-oriented, was young shaped its attitude to the political system, Styrkársdóttir concludes. One might add to this that the small size of the country probably made direct interaction with the authorities more natural, even for locally based small groups.

The interaction with established politics
In this book, the actual interaction between the women's movement and established politics is discussed on the basis of experiences from the Western countries. Movement activists tend to focus on the fate of the movement organizations, which they have worked so hard to build. However, the question of the influence of the movement must be studied in a broader perspective. Three signs of interaction and influence between the movement and the established political system will be discussed here.

1. The ideas of the movement become absorbed by society or important sections of it.
2. The leaders of the movement are coopted into the mainstream of politics and society.
3. The former marginal group (here, women) succeeds in gaining access and influence.

The present discussion is limited to the reaction of the political system, but the same line of argument could be applied to the study of movement impact on social, economic and religious systems.

1. The ideas of the movement become absorbed by society
The interaction between the autonomous women's movement and the political parties is an important subject in this book. What impact did the movement have on the political parties? The conclusion seems to be that the new women's movement has influenced the *programmes* of all the political parties in all the Western countries. The most positive response has come from the political parties on the left — the communist, left-socialist and social democratic parties. The outspoken opponents are to be found on the far right of the political spectrum. The political parties on the left, and to some extent in the centre, have absorbed some part of the movement's new perspective on women. These political parties have placed several of

the more concrete demands of the movement on the political agenda, and, depending on their power and will, have pushed them through the political institutions.

The frustration of many movement activists arose because the political parties in this process altered feminist demands and used them for their own purpose. Sometimes the political parties even took over certain issues from the women's movement, as is described by *Eleonore Eckmann Pisciotta* in the case of the Italian referendum on abortion. In Sweden, the relatively progressive equality policy of the governing Social Democratic Party anticipated the new women's movement, which never reached the strength of its Danish and Norwegian sister movements (Dahlerup and Gulli, 1985). Even if de-radicalization has often been the consequence, the absorption of the movement's demands by the political parties in fact represents a sign of influence and partial success, especially in Europe.

In most cases, it was the women in the political parties who took up the new feminist challenge and translated it into programmes and paragraphs. Studies of the decision-making process in the parties reveal that a party's support for some of the new feminist demands usually has been due to hard work by women and women's committees within that party. Today, these women are willing to admit that the existence of a radical women's movement gave them new ideological perspectives. Also, the pressure by the women's movement and the general debate stirred by its presence seem to have strengthened the position of feminist women within the parties.

During the 1970s and 1980s, a new 'state machinery' has been established in most Western countries with the purpose of promoting equality between the sexes. Examples are the Equal Status Councils in the Nordic countries, the Equal Opportunity Commission in Britain and USA, the Ministry for Women in France and the Women's Rights' Institute in Spain. This represents a first in-stitutionalization of the gender conflict. It is a modest recognition that equality between women and men is now the responsibility of the state. The women's liberation movement has seldom been campaigning for these new institutions, sometimes named 'state feminism'. Those actors directly involved have been women within the political parties and the women's rights organizations. But again, in a complicated interaction between inside and outside forces, this new state machinery has been created as the official answer to the general feminist mobilization of the period.

2. *The leaders of the movement are coopted*

In his study of the strategy of protest movements, William Gamson (1975) discusses the important question of cooption of the leaders of a protest movement into the mainstream of politics and society. For some, cooption of the leaders of a protest movement is considered a symbol of success and a chance to influence, but for others — notably members of revolutionary and radical movements — cooption of the leaders is seen as a step towards the de-radicalization and eventual decline of the protest movement. What has happened to the (informal) leaders of the new women's movement?

Some of the leading activists of the new women's movement have eventually joined a political party, notably left-wing parties or the new green parties. A Women's Party has even been established in Iceland (with success) and in Spain (unsuccessful so far). Other leading feminists today work hard for feminist goals within their trade unions. With their coming of age, many feminists have got jobs in the public sector, ranging from the state bureaucracy to the many local women's centres or councils, often initiated by the movement and now publicly funded. This development recalls the story, told by Susan Ware (1981), of the many women in Roosevelt's New Deal, whose political experience was rooted in the suffrage campaign; only present-day feminists in public employment seem to be more numerous and more committed to feminist goals — to work 'in and against', as British feminists call it. Still many movement activists choose to remain 'outside the system'. But the fact that so many of the most active feminists now work with one foot in the movement and one within the 'system' has contributed to a change in the new women's movement.

3. The former marginal group succeeds in gaining access and influence
Have women as a group obtained access to and influence in the political system and society at large? It was an important goal of the new women's movement to change the whole power structure of society. The overall picture is that women today still remain marginal economically and politically. However, some important improvements have taken place in the political sphere.

Today women are very active in all the new social movements, for example the peace movement, the environmental movements and the movement against nuclear power. In fact, available data indicate that the new social movements constitute the first channel of political influence in which men and women work side by side in equal numbers. Many activists from the women's movement have joined these other movements (Peterson, 1985), and many other young women are also active here; today's young radical women seem to enter the peace movement, the environmental movements and so forth, rather than the women's movement itself.

Women's political representation has increased rapidly during the 1970s and 1980s, especially in countries where the electoral system is based on proportional representation. The record is held by the five

Nordic countries, in which women now occupy between one-fourth
and one-third of the seats in parliament and in the local councils
(Haavio-Mannila et al., 1985).

The relations between the women's liberation kind of feminism
and the many new women politicians have been marked by
ambivalent feelings. A new debate has started: can women in politics
make a difference? Three conditions seem to be crucial for women
politicians to be able to fight a feminist way through: first, a large
number of women inside the political institutions (at least a critical mass); second, efficient women's organizations, whether
autonomous or working within the political parties, to support and
criticize the women politicians and to work as experts on feminist
policies; third, a large and radical women's movement, one not
engulfed by the logic of existing institutions. Whenever some part of
the feminist ideology and some part of the movement activists are
absorbed by the political system — which in itself is a sign of the
impact of the movement — a new movement must emerge to
challenge the establishment with new and radical visions.

Structural differences
Why did the US feminist movement develop so differently from the
ones in Western Europe, where the women's liberation type of
feminism was and is the dominant trend? Anne Costain (1982) argues
that the new US feminism in fact has developed from a social
movement into a pressure group. In her chapter on the USA,
Virginia Sapiro describes how the feminist movement has reacted to
the Reagan presidency ('the most explicitly anti-feminist administration in memory'). The lack of response from the Reagan administration does not seem to have isolated the US women's movement. On
the contrary: the large and expanding reform wing of the movement,
unique from a European point of view, has grown into professional
pressure groups, capable of influencing big-time politics.

In her chapter, *Joyce Gelb* compares the reformist US movement
to the British movement, which is decentralized, localized and anti-
elitist. She argues that what she calls Britain's highly traditional,
centralized and bureaucratic political system tends to isolate the
women's movement as well as all other 'promotional' groups. All
these groups lack influence, resources and the necessary expertise,
and consequently remain without much influence.

Since the new women's movement in most Western countries
emerged and developed as a decentralized group-based liberation
movement, Gelb's argument should be valid for all Western Europe.
No doubt, the US political system is more open to the formation of
new pressure groups, and this fact has influenced the trends of the US
women's movement. In general, it is easier for new US groups to find

funding and gain direct access to decision-makers than it is in most European countries. This, however, should not be confused with influence. Gelb states that in Britain the political parties and the trade unions have pre-empted the demands of the women's movements. But since the political parties and trade unions in most of Europe still represent a major political force, this 'pre-emption' or absorption (although in a moderate form) of the movement's demands might in fact indicate a greater influence on outcomes than the ability to form visible pressure groups and to be successful in fund-raising.

In Western Europe, the interaction between the movement and the political parties is crucial to the understanding of the development and the influence of the women's movement, as pointed out earlier. The much weaker position of political parties in the US political system and the ideological composition of the parties explain many of the differences between the US and European movements.

A large reformist wing of the feminist movement could be said to exist in Europe as well, side by side with grass-roots feminism. But in Europe the reformist wing is to be found within the political parties and the trade unions, as a consequence of the central position of these organizations in European politics.

In her chapter on Finland, *Riitta Jallinoja* studies the crucial question of independence or integration of the women's movement. She concludes that, for both first- and second-wave feminism, the starting point was independence and autonomy. Only when they are autonomous may women develop feminist perspectives and collective power. However, despite this ever-present aspiration, both the old and the new women's movement in Finland in fact developed close ties to the political parties, and splits in the party system were usually followed by splits in the women's movement. The same is true in most other countries, but particularly in countries with strong party systems.

The changes of the women's movement

Some people argue that the new women's movement reached its peak in the 1970s and is now in decline. The conclusion to be drawn from this book is that the movement is still alive and active, but that it certainly has changed since the first enthusiastic period of the late 1960s and early 1970s.

The different stories of the eleven countries remind us of the fact that the new women's movement did not develop at the same time or with the same strength everywhere. *Sirin Tekeli* relates that in Turkey a feminist movement has not begun to unfold until now. When the New Left flourished in Turkey the only absentee was feminism, which did not start until after the military intervention and the suspension of democracy. The structural explanation for the late rise of feminism in Turkey, according to Tekeli, is the under-development of Turkish capitalism and the strong position of the family.

In Spain, the new women's movement did not develop until after the death of Franco in 1975. It arose as part of the mobilization and enthusiasm of the new Spanish democracy. In Ireland, the women's movement has so far managed only to raise a relatively weak voice against the strong oppression of women. In the other countries included in this book, the new movement started in the late 1960s or the early 1970s. The international character of the movement has helped spread the movement from one country to another, but not simultaneously.

All social movements are constantly changing, and so is the women's movement. It seems to be general that the first period of the movement was characterized by direct, disruptive actions, great enthusiasm, intense ideological debates and organizational and personal experiments. That stage is past and has been replaced by a proliferation, fragmentation and specialization of the movements. It has spread to ever-widening circles in each country. In many countries the ideas of the movement have also reached institutions bearing some policy impact.

Obviously, the movement could not continue to live on enthusiasm. It was necessary to create some kind of institutional resources, for example in crisis centres, in women's studies, in art galleries or in new organizations. Further, the 'strength of being outside' probably lasts only temporarily for a particular movement; it is the strength of a new social movement in its first phases. If influen-tial, although not successful in promoting fundamental changes, the interaction between the movement and the establishment will eventually change the character of the movement.

Organizational and generational explanations must be added. The loose, small-group-based structure that was a success in untying energy and developing new radical perspectives in fact resulted in a large turnover of activists and a lot of unsuccessful initiatives. Most movement activists did not stay long, but moved on. The simple fact that the participants grew older has also contributed to today's situation where many movement activists work for feminist goals whenever possible, whether in parents' organizations or health movements or at their workplaces.

In their chapter on Spain, *Angeles Duran* and *Teresa Gallego* identify three periods in the short history of the new feminist movement in that country: the period of expansion, 1975–9; the period of scattering and decline, 1979–82; and the present period, in which feminism has reached the institutions, but unfortunately has lost its strength as an organized movement because it has split into micro-organizations. It is worth noticing that in only ten years Spain has managed to change most of the old discriminatory laws from the fascist period and to improve women's legal status — an effort that took other countries many decades.

In my own chapter on Denmark, I discuss whether or not the new women's liberation movement is dead. My conclusion is that a radical, left-wing-oriented, small-group-based feminism still exists, challenging patriarchal society. I identify three stages of the new women's movement: stage 1 (1970–4), a period of direct actions and extensive ideological discussions; stage 2 (1974–80), a period of proliferation of the movement and successful attempts to create a new feminist counter-culture; and stage 3 (1980–now), which is characterized by the decline of the original movement organizations, the emergence of new centres and the occurrence of further special- ization and to some extent professionalization. The economic crisis and the decline of the New Left have contributed to this change of the movement.

The changes in the *ideas* of the new women's movement are subject to discussion in some of the chapters of this book, although not exten- sively. A common element seems to be changes in the vision of womanhood/femininity.

Audur Styrkársdóttir states that, in the first period of the Icelandic new women's movement, the similarities between the sexes were stressed, while in the second period, in which the Women's Lists were formed, the differences between men and women were emphasized (women are more peaceful and more concerned with social issues than men). In my own chapter I state that the women's rights organ- izations in the sex role debate of the 1960s stressed the equality between women and men, whereas the new women's liberation movement focuses on a re-evaluation of womanhood.

The equality argument was a reaction to the widespread prejudice that women could not match men in mathematics, logical thinking, physical strength and staying power — and why had there been no women geniuses in music, art or physics? The new trend, a re-evalu- ation of womanhood, is a parallel to the reaction to the US civil rights movement by the black movement, which stated that 'Black is beaut- iful'. The goals are consequently different: equality versus 'different but equal'.

Hester Eisenstein (1984) talks about a third phase in the development of contemporary feminism: a shift from a focus on sex roles and androgyny (phase 1) to a woman-centred perspective (phase 2) to a new and potentially reactionary concept (phase 3), namely, the belief in the intrinsic moral superiority of women, implicitly attributed to physiological causes. In this way sections of the movement seem to forget the original insight into the differences between women by class, race and culture.

In her brilliant book about 150 years of feminist movement in Germany, Herrad Schenk (1983) in a similar way identifies a 'neue Weiblichkeitsmythos' (a new myth of femininity) in recent feminism. What is extremely interesting is that she is able to demonstrate that, even during the first wave of the feminist movement, the focus in the same way shifted from equality to positive evaluation of the differences between women and men, stressing women's special role as mothers. Schenk shows that, during the interwar period in Germany, this trend turned into a reactionary and biodeterministic direction.

These remarkable shifts in the goals of the feminist movement throughout history need further investigation. Advocates of each of these different goals can in fact be found within the feminist movements of any time, but the general emphasis seems to change from time to time. Maybe each individual feminist experiences a similar shift and tension during her own life-cycle between showing that 'we women are able to do what men can do' and a wish to re-evaluate womanhood and a search for the femininity of our foremothers.

All social movements change. However, the way they change and the marks they leave vary, and that is the important aspect. The eleven chapters of this book show both considerable variations and considerable similarities in the history of the new women's movement. The movement, especially in Europe, never created national organizations, and today it is more widespread than ever. Some would see this as a sign of decline — and certainly, a large powerful women's movement is missing in most countries during this economic crisis when it is most needed. But on the other hand, this spread of the movement also symbolizes that the movement today is reaching out not only to the institutions, but also to every organization, group and individual. If the drive by women collectively to challenge the patriarchal society disappears, then the movement is dead. This has not happened; in fact, more women have more resources than ever, and also a willingness to use those resources for feminist goals. But we are in the midst of a kind of feminist struggle that is different from the enthusiastic first years of the new movement.

Many feminists say that resistance to feminism is growing. They feel a colder wind blowing against feminism. In many countries that is probably true compared with the mid-1970s. However, compared with the resistance that the feminist movement encountered in the 1920s, not to speak of the 1890s, today's reaction is not overwhelming. We must remember that opponents of the women's movement throughout history have wishfully declared the movement dead, and yet the movement has now been fighting for more than 100 years. I hope that this book about the contemporary women's movement will prove helpful when we continue the work to change the course of history.

References

Bouchier, David (1983)   *The Feminist Challenge. The Movement for Women's Liberation in Britain and the United States.* London: Macmillan.

Costain, Anne N. (1982) 'Representing Women: The Transition from Social Movement to Interest Group', pp. 19–37 in Ellen Boneparth (ed.), *Women, Power and Policy.* New York: Pergamon.

Dahlerup, Drude (1973)   *Socialisme og kvindefrigørelse i det 19. århundrede.* Grenå: GMT Publishers.

Dahlerup, Drude and Brita Gulli (1985)   'Women's Organizations in the Nordic Countries: Lack of Force or Counterforce?' in Haavio-Mannila et al. (1985).

Dubois, Ellen (1975)   'The Radicalism of the Woman Suffrage Movement'. *Feminist Studies*, 3(1/2): 63–71.

Eisenstein, Hester (1984)   *Contemporary Feminist Thought.* London and Sydney: Unwin.

Evans, Richard (1977)   *The Feminists. Women's Emancipation Movement in Europe, America and Australasia 1840–1920.* London: Croom Helm.

Freeman, Jo (1975)   *The Politics of Women's Liberation.* New York: Longman.

Freeman, Jo (ed.) (1983)   *Social Movements of the Sixties and Seventies.* New York: Longman.

Gamson, William A. (1975)   *The Strategy of Social Protest.* Homewood, Ill.: Dorsey Press.

Gerlach, Luther P. and Virginia H. Hine (1970)   *People, Power, Change.* Indianapolis and New York: Bobbs-Merrill.

Haavio-Mannila, Elina, et al. (1985)   *Unfinished Democracy. Women in Nordic Politics.* Oxford: Pergamon Press.

Jenson, Jane (1985)   'Struggling for Identity: the Women's Movement and the State in Western Europe', *West European Politics*, 8(4): special issue on women and politics in Western Europe.

Lerner, Gerda (1971)   'Women's Rights and American Feminism'. *The American Scholar*, 40(2): 235–48.

McGlen, Nancy E. and Karen O'Connor (1983)   *Women's Rights. The Struggle for Equality in the Nineteenth and Twentieth Centuries.* New York: Praeger.

Mueller, Carol (1983)   'Women's Movement Success and the Success of Social Movement Theory'. Working paper, Wellesley College, Mass.

Peterson, Abby (1985)   'The New Women's Movement — Where Have All the Women Gone? Women and the Peace Movement in Sweden'. *Women's Studies International Forum*, 8(6): 631–8.

Richards, Janet Radcliffe (1982)   *The Sceptical Feminist.* Harmondsworth, Middx: Penguin.

Rossi, Alice S. (1973)   *The Feminist Papers: From Adams to de Beauvoir.* New York: Columbia University Press.

Rowland, Robyn (1984)   *Women Who Do and Women Who Don't — Join the Women's Movement.* London: Routledge & Kegan Paul.

Schenk, Herrad (1983)   *Die feministische Herausforderung.* 150 Jahre Frauenbewegung in Deutschland. Munich: C. H. Beck.

Tarrow, Sidney (1983)   'Resource Mobilization and Cycles of Protest: Theoretical Reflections and Comparative Illustrations'. Paper read to ASA meeting, Detroit.

Ware, Susan (1981)   *Beyond Suffrage. Women in the New Deal.* Cambridge, Mass.: Harvard University Press.

Zald, Mayer N. (1979) 'Macro-Issues in the Theory of Social Movements'. University of Michigan, CRSP Working Paper no. 204.

I
CHALLENGING THE ESTABLISHMENT: THE CASE OF ABORTION

1

The strength and the powerlessness of the new Italian women's movement: the case of abortion

Eleonore Eckmann Pisciotta

Introduction

The new women's movement became the biggest and most important social movement in Italy in the 1970s. It grew rapidly in the first half of the decade, reached its peak by 1976–7 and almost vanished from the public eye after 1978. The movement's growth into a social *mass* movement and its subsequent disappearance as a mass movement went hand in hand with the abortion issue. This issue attracted women to the campaign against the then existing anti-abortion law, and led them to withdraw from the movement or to turn to other issues and/or activities once a law regulating abortions had been passed in June 1978.

The abortion issue had been the touchstone of the new women's movement. For this reason, this chapter will focus on the interconnection between the movement's life history and the political Odyssey of the abortion issue. It will show the movement's power in bringing a taboo issue into the public arena, but also its ultimate powerlessness to carry through what women of the movement wanted.

To a great extent, the abortion issue also led to changes in the character of the movement, most of which occurred during the 1970s and especially after the abortion law had been passed. The feminist movement had set out in the early 1970s to work for 'the radical transformation of the entire system'. It included as one of its main objectives a transformation of 'the way of making politics'. In the first half of the decade a large part of the movement nurtured hopes about its impact on the political system, because all the political parties became involved in the abortion question and had to accept it as a political issue. These hopes crashed in the second half of the 1970s, when the movement witnessed the parliamentary handling of the abortion issue, in which the feminists had no say. The disillusion following its weak impact caused many women of the 'hard core' feminist movement to withdraw completely from the political scene, while others chose a more institutionalized way, adopting a more reformist and pragmatic approach.

The physiognomy of the movement
The new women's movement can be divided roughly into four branches:

1. the autonomous feminist movement;
2. the feminists of the New Left;
3. the Movimento di Liberazione della Donna (MLD), or woman's liberation movement;
4. the Unione Donne Italiane (UDI) (see list of abbreviations at end of chapter).

Prior to the rise of the new women's movement, there were women's sections of the political parties. Their role, however, was rather peripheral politically and was confined to attracting women as new party members, to teaching women 'politics' and to helping the political parties attract women's votes in the election campaigns. There were also the two big women's organizations: the UDI (Unione Donne Italiane), a typical women's emancipation movement, and the CIF (Centro Italiano Femminile), a typical Catholic women's organization. While the UDI was ideologically linked to the traditional left (communist and socialist, but mainly the former), the CIF was connected with the Christian Democrats and the Church. Even in the 1970s, the CIF retained its traditional role of emphasizing the importance of the family and the woman's role as wife and mother, adding, however, more importance to women's role in society. Unlike the CIF, the UDI was largely influenced by the new women's movement, especially in the second half of the 1970s. This led to a renewal of the UDI in terms of issues and members, making it an active and important part of the *new* women's movement.

The existence of these two big women's organizations reflects very accurately the political and cultural split in Italy into two forces, one working for the protection of traditions, the other for reforms. These two forces have always coexisted in Italy. But, whereas up to the late 1960s the conservative forces were clearly in the majority and could especially count on women, this changed during the 1970s to a more favourable climate for the left-wing forces. Nevertheless, it has not led to a governing alternative. Up to now — and this is probably the most outstanding fact of the Italian political system — the Christian Democrats (DC) have never ceased to govern, thanks to the lay parties and to the Italian Socialist Party (PSI). Unlike other EC countries, there has been little space for the lay forces; their principal role has been to keep the DC in government in (often fragile) coalitions and to give the DC a hand in excluding the Communist Party (PCI) from cabinet positions. In this context, we can understand first the women's movement's general distrust of traditional politics and second its expectations from the PCI and the New Left as the only political organizations capable of bringing about change.

The autonomous feminist movement

The autonomous feminist movement evolved from the student movement of 1968, from which its first groups sprang. But soon the women discovered that, even where egalitarian principles were preached, they were reduced to a subordinate level and were de facto excluded from the political decision-making process. This led to the creation of autonomous groups. The feminist movement therefore represented, in the first period, nothing short of an answer to the contradictions within the student movement, and consisted mainly of young intellectual women of the middle and upper classes.

One of the first groups to plead decisively for autonomy and separatism, and one that had a great influence on the contents of the evolving movement, was Rivolta Femminile (Female Revolt), which emerged in 1970 in Rome and Milan and soon spread to other cities. From it new groups developed, such as the Collettivo Femminista Romano (Roman Feminist Collective, later Pompeo Magno) and other feminist collectives, as well as Lotta Femminista (Feminist Struggle). Other groups carrying the name Lotta Femminista were quickly formed in a number of cities, especially in the north. The Gruppi per il Salario al Lavoro Domestico (Groups for Wages for Housework) developed out of a part of Lotta Femminista and included new women as well.

The number of new groups formed in the first half of the 1970s is incalculable, since the names of the groups changed and new groups developed out of 'old' groups. The principle of autonomy, and the large numbers of consciousness-raising groups meeting in private houses, make it impossible to give an exact number, which probably goes into the thousands.

The experience within the student movement greatly influenced the theoretical and practical political concepts of the feminist movement. Although radical criticism of patriarchy and sexist structures increasingly formed the theoretical background, some Marxist ideas, Marxist methodology and the consciousness of living in a class society were never abandoned and formed 'the two souls of feminism'. In the course of time feminists stressed the analysis of sexist structures and pleaded for the autonomy of their evolving movement from political parties or groups and from pre-established theories. To this prime principle of *autonomy*, other important elements must be added. For the organizational structure there was the *separatism* from men, as well as the refutation of the principle of delegation and hierarchies; instead, the emphasis was on *full participation*, which was put into practice through the formation of small consciousness-raising groups. For the theoretical structure, two elements were of primary importance. First, there was the development of a new understanding of politics which recognizes the private as political, as is expressed in the slogan, 'The personal is political'. This was also very important in the theoretical handling of the abortion issue. Second, there was the deliberate use of the term 'liberation' instead of 'emancipation', to distinguish the movement clearly from the UDI and also from the historical women's rights movements.

It is the connection of these criteria that distinguished the new feminist movement from women's organizations and groups that, for instance, claim their autonomy and/or separate organization while keeping hierarchical structures and the practice of delegation. The very rigid definition of these principles at the beginning of the movement is peculiar to the Italian feminists. It kept the different branches of the women's movement apart and impeded common action. In the first half of the 1970s the autonomous feminists despised the 'emancipationists'.

With the growth of the new women's movement, feminist thought stressed the diversity of women as a positive value. Accepting differences in thought and political action, the movement lost more and more its radical and in part 'elitist' aspects. But the heterogeneity made it increasingly difficult to speak any longer of 'the' feminist movement. In the first place, once it became 'popular', feminism was watered down. Everyone felt herself a 'feminist', and everyone gave a different meaning to the word. Second, the interests of the feminists became still more diversified. After the year-long battle against the anti-abortion law, many were disillusioned by the outcome and began to concentrate on 'culture' in the broadest sense; they did not want to be involved with politics any more. Others concentrated on practical projects, such as working in the gynaecological counselling services, opening a feminist book store or making films. Still others took up new courses of study; some joined the political parties, in particular the PCI. Many are now working in the peace movement.

A part of the feminist movement came to engage in a new struggle, that of changing the law on sexual violence, which was passed during fascism and which considered sexual violence as 'crimes against the public morality and morals' rather than against the person. The issue had in fact been taken up in the mid-1970s, but had not caught the public eye, because the abortion issue then engaged all of the public's attention. From the issue of violence many new initiatives developed, such as the 'Tribunale 8 marzo', initiated in 1980 by women of different political and cultural backgrounds. This is a kind of Russell tribunal of women which collects and publishes testimonies and holds public 'sessions' on violence, dedicating itself each year to a particular aspect. Up to 1984 the following aspects had been covered: (1) health; (2) justice; (3) domestic violence; (4) discrimination in the world of labour.

The most important feminist development, however, is the emerging autonomous women's peace movement, which puts itself in the broader perspective of fighting the 'culture of violence', of which nuclear armament is only one extreme expression.

The feminists of the New Left

The growth of autonomous feminist movement also influenced the groups of the New Left, especially the women in these groups. The history of these women in the three major groups — Avanguardia Operaia (Worker's Vanguard), Lotta Continua (The Fight Continues) and Manifesto-PdUP (Party of Proletarian Unity for Communism) — is surprisingly similar and can be summed up in three major stages.

First, women in the New Left began to develop a feminist consciousness within their political organizations, starting with the recognition of the importance of the struggle for women's liberation. This struggle was still seen as being necessarily allied to worker's organizations to ensure a higher efficiency of the struggle. Herein lay the main difference between them and the autonomous feminists. This first stage, however, was followed by the recognition of the importance of a separate space for women, and the need for an autonomous analysis about women's social conditions tied to neither a Marxist analysis nor the party line. In this they differed from their sisters in New Left organizations in other countries. The feminists of the Italian New Left started to build separate women's collectives within their political groups, in which women not belonging to the party could also participate. Complementary to this, many of them took part in autonomous feminist groups or started their own consciousness-raising groups, thus creating the phenomenon of a 'double militancy'.

The 'male character' of the political groups, and the women's increasing interest in feminist analysis and practice, made many of them feel a split between their commitment to the party and to women's issues. The second stage, therefore, entailed their attempts to 'femministizzare' their political organizations. In this attempt they were unique. 'Femministizzazione' (i.e., to make feminist) is a word coined by feminists of the New Left. It means to pick up feminist topics, to analyse the contradiction of the sexes, to abandon sexist behaviour and structures within the organization and to dismiss exclusively 'male politics' in favour of a political analysis that encompasses the day-to-day experiences of the oppressed. After their initial exposure to ridicule and defamation as being 'petty bourgeois' and as 'causing a split in the struggle of the working class for revolution', the feminists seem to have had some success. The men of these groups soon had to admit — at least formally — the importance of the women's struggle.

However, these groups were far from being 'femministizzato'. As a result, the feminists of the New Left felt a deep crisis in their double militancy. The third step was the withdrawal from their respective parties, once they saw that their organizations had no intention of changing substantially the manner of 'political action'. The feminists did this one by one and silently, or else in groups and with a kind of public 'trial'. Here, once again, they demonstrated a unique consistency in acting according to their beliefs. Leaving their political parties, however, did not mean that their political consciousness changed with respect to the capitalist system; they simply became an integral part of the autonomous feminist movement, affirming that the struggle for women's liberation had to be carried on by *women*. The women who remained in the parties of the New Left ultimately gave more importance to political party goals than to feminism. Shortly afterwards, however, these groups increasingly lost influence on the political scene in general, in part because of the rise of red terrorism.

Of course, there were also the 'revolutionary women' of the 'revolutionary' parties of Stalinist, Trotzkyist, Maoist or Marxist—Leninist orientation; these, however, were only splinter parties and were not represented in parliament. Women in these organizations often took up women's issues as a 'tab', especially after the feminist movement had become a real mass movement. In Italy, these women had neither a qualitative nor a quantitative role in the new women's movement or in politics in general.

The Movimento di Liberazione della Donna (MLD)
The MLD was founded in 1970 at the end of a seminar about the 'Liberation of Woman', sponsored by the Partito Radicale (PR), with which the MLD was federated until 1978. The MLD was a movement/organization consisting of groups and collectives from various cities. Officially they were autonomous, and their connection was established through national congresses, through the 'Federative Council' of the MLD, in which there were delegates from the different cities, and through a commitment to the statutes and

political guidelines voted at the congresses.

With this sketch, two essential differences between the autonomous feminist movement and the MLD are already obvious:

1. its existence as an organization with fixed structures and political roles (secretary, treasurer, council, etc.);
2. its federation and collaboration with a political party.

In fact, the MLD used the same strategies as did the PR: collecting signatures for a referendum for the abrogation of the anti-abortion law; hunger strikes for the same goal; 'civil disobedience', such as the practice of self-help abortions. For this reason, the women of the MLD have often been called disdainfully 'women of the Radical Party' by the autonomous feminists.

Nevertheless, the MLD women, who at first did not want to call themselves either 'feminists' or 'emancipationists', became 'more feminist' with the passing of the years. This can be seen clearly in their positions towards separatism. Until 1975 men who supported the platform of MLD could become members of the movement; after 1975 they could become only 'sympathizers' and from the beginning of 1977 they were excluded from most of the movement's activities. The final break-away from the PR was initiated when the MLD for the first time brought in a project that was not identical with the projects of the PR: the draft on popular initiative of a law for '50 per cent of all working places to women'.

The tool of proposing a draft on popular initiative was one of the preferred political actions of the MLD. The Italian constitution permits the possibility of such a *popular initiative*; that is, the voters may propose, with a minimum of 50,000 signatures collected within three months, a draft of a law, on which parliament then has to act in one way or the other. The MLD had already proposed a draft on popular initiative of a new abortion law in 1971 (which was unsuccessful), and a law on sexual and domestic violence against women in 1978. The latter draft caused the political parties to come up with their own bills, of which a unified text was put to parliamentary discussion. The issue still has not been decided on in parliament.

After the loosening of the links with the PR, the MLD made increasing use of feminist tools, such as the practice of consciousness-raising, separatism and a real autonomy from the party in its analyses. It also started to collaborate with autonomous feminist groups, especially on the issue of violence. After 1978, with the definite break-away from the PR, the MLD defined itself as a clearly autonomous feminist organization. When it became part of the autonomous movement, its organizational form vanished. Today the MLD does not exist under that label, but some of the women from the movement have formed collectives around single issues, first and foremost around issues of sexual and domestic violence. Many of the members are professionals who engage in legal and health counselling services for abused women.

The Unione Donne Italiane (UDI)

The description of the new Italian women's movement could, in the strict sense of the word, end here. However, the UDI needs to be included, not only because it was the biggest women's organization that has fought for an improvement of the social conditions of women, but also, as I mentioned at the beginning, because it changed as a result of the autonomous feminist movement.

The UDI was founded on a national level right after the second world war and oriented its politics mainly towards the improvement of the conditions of women workers (child care, protection of maternity, equity, etc.) and towards democratic reforms (family law reform, access of women to all careers, etc.). With this orientation and its self-assessment as a *democratic mass movement of women*, it accepted the rules of the parliamentary game and initially disdained the rising feminist movement as 'elitist' in its search for 'new ways of political action'. However, with the growth of feminism and the interests of feminist women who joined the UDI in the 1970s, the UDI opened itself to feminist issues.

The first step in this direction was a new analysis of society, adding to the division of the classes that of the sexes. Subsequently, it added the term 'liberation' to 'emancipation' in its goals for women. It started to get involved in 'typically' feminist issues, such as sexuality, women's health and the search for and association of their own identity. With a rising feminist consciousness, the UDI became also more critical of the traditional left. Its most decisive step of positive collaboration with other women's groups was definitely its adherence to the popular initiative of the MLD on sexual and domestic violence.

The UDI thus became an essential part of the new women's movement. It found a synthesis between a more traditional struggle for women's rights and feminist innovations of patterns of thought and action. The final step towards feminism was taken during the last national congress of the UDI in 1982, when it decided to eliminate its hierarchical structures, renouncing the idea of an 'elite' at the top of the organization. By dissolving the directorship, the UDI wanted to emphasize once more that it had become an organization *of* women and not only *for* women, giving each woman in the organization the same rights and responsibilities.

However, in depriving itself of its organizational structure and network, it also lost its force in mobilization. In a certain sense the UDI has withered away. In 1984 its journal, *Noi Donne*, the last of the women's movement's journals, also died.

In the 1980s it is no longer valid to distinguish four different branches of the women's movement. However, the movement is not dead. The women's sections of the political parties have absorbed many of the issues of the movement, at least their reformist aspects, and are quite active. They became much more independent of their parties, owing to the impact of the women's movements on them in the 1970s. New 'Housewives' groups have developed in many cities. Many women of the intelligentsia have attained positions of relative importance, where they continue to fight for women's causes. Projects and exhibitions continue and new ones are started.

However, the women's movement has lost its most important journals. It now has only very specialized journals on sale, directed to women of the intelligentsia. Unlike in other European countries, efforts to raise funds in Italy for a project that is not already institutionalized remain in most cases futile. While other countries have houses for battered women, well organized 'hot lines' for emergencies and paid jobs for research projects, these are all lacking in Italy.

The abortion case
The issue is raised
Until the 1970s, nobody in Italy had raised the issue of abortion, even though, according to estimates of participants of the Congress of Obstetrics and Gynaecology in 1968, between 1 and 3 million Italian women had abortions each year in spite of the then existing anti-abortion law, inherited from the fascist regime (Jourdan, 1976: 146). This is somewhat surprising, first because in other Western European countries the issue had already long been considered a social and political problem, and second because in 1970 80 per cent of the Italians had expressed their desire for 'reforms' (*Eurobarometer*, 1983:40). Obviously, the reform of the abortion law was not among these desired reforms. This is also demonstrated by the failure of an action of self-denunciation in 1971 initiated by the MLD, and following the French model of 1970. The MLD was also the first to move publicly against the existing anti-abortion law.

Within the first autonomous feminist groups, the problem of abortion was not an immediate concern. However, in 1971 some groups started to state their positions on abortion publicly, after several months of discussion of the topic in consciousness-raising groups. The UDI also took a stand. We can clearly see the differences here between the various branches of the women's movement: the feminist groups stressed the fact that they were interested not in the issue of abortion as such, but in women's right to choose, and that for this reason they refused any form of regulation brought about through legislation: they demanded the simple abolition of the anti-abortion law, stressing, however, the fact that they were not 'for abortion'. The UDI, on the other hand, although criticizing strongly the old law, attacked the MLD and the feminist groups for their demand for complete liberalization of abortions, and pressed for a new law legalizing abortions.

The increasing discussion of abortion within the movement and its actions in 1971 and 1972 caught the public attention. Newspapers and women's journals became interested. The Catholic Church also made itself heard: in 1972 Pope Paul VI spoke six times in favour of severe punishment for abortions. The battle of the 'pros' and 'cons' had begun. Congresses and seminars of Catholic lawyers, physicians, theologians and the like became frequent. Parts of the left-wing parties also began to take up the issue. In early 1973 the socialist deputy Fortuna presented the first bill; although it was extremely restrictive, parliament nevertheless reacted with indignation.

The state responded to women's mounting protest against the anti-abortion law first of all with repression. In early 1974, 263 women were arrested in Trento for having had abortions. These massive arrests were, as the newspaper *Il Giorno* put it, 'the most shocking of all the initiatives on the issue of abortion'. It resulted in a mobilization of the entire women's movement. From this moment on, we can say that the campaign heated up. Women's demonstrations attracted increasingly more women: from 10,000 at the beginning of 1975 to 30,000 at the end of the same year, to 50,000 in 1977.

During these years, the new women's movement experienced its most rapid increase and became a mass phenomenon, involving women everywhere and from all social strata. The abortion issue had by this time become the most discussed issue in the country. A large majority, among them especially women, put pressure on parliament to take action. An inquiry carried out in the second half of 1974 for one of the most prominent Italian political and cultural journals, *Panorama*, showed that 72 per cent of the 1,000 interviewed women between the ages of 16 and 64 were against the anti-abortion law and in favour of legislation that would allow abortion on choice (Teodori, 1975: 24).

The impact of the divorce law referendum
Alongside the activity of the women's movement, a major political event strengthened the abortion case and the movement itself: the outcome of the referendum of 12 May 1974 on the abrogation of the 1970 divorce law, which for the first time permitted civil divorce in Italy. Its result of 59.26 per cent in favour of retaining the law surprised both its supporters and its opponents, particularly because it was much higher than the opinion poll taken only a week earlier had predicted. Five years before, 68 per cent of women and 53 per

cent of men had expressed themselves against the institutionalization of a divorce law (see Tables 1 and 2). When the law was passed in December 1970 it had then been seen much more as a 'democratic issue' than a 'women's issue'. In fact, the impact of the new women's movement on the passing of the law had been non-existent (except for the UDI, which had fought together with the left for a family reform). Most of the population had not even taken notice of the existence of the law.

However, even though the divorce law was still quite restricted, especially in comparison with northern European countries, before it was passed the Christian Democratic Party (DC), which feared the 'dissolution of the Christian family model', had insisted on the passing of a law that made the holding of referendums possible in Italy. This had been provided for by the constitution, but for 23 years it had not been formulated into a law. The new law that provides for a referendum is restricted to the abrogation of *existing* laws only and requires a minimum of 500,000 signatures to be collected within three months. In fact, it was used for the first time for the repeal of the divorce law. The profound split within Italian culture and politics between Catholic dogmatism, the traditional family model and deep conservatism on the one hand, and the hunger for more democracy and independence from the doctrine of the Church on the other

TABLE 1
Divorce and referendum: opinion according to sex
(in per cent)

Question: If you had to vote for a law that institutionalized divorce, would you vote in favour or against it?

Year	In favour		Against		Don't know; no answer	
	M	F	M	F	M	F
1947	36	19	59	79	5	2
1953	45	25	45	66	10	9
1955	42	27	49	63	9	10
1959	41	22	50	70	9	8
1962	29	16	60	77	11	7
1969	37	23	53	68	10	9
1971	59	49	29	44	12	7
5 May 1974	57.5	43.7	29	41.9	13.5	14.4

Sources: 1947–62, results of DOXA, in Luzzato Fegiz, *Il volto sconosciuto dell'Italia*, Vol. II, Giuffré, Milan, 1966:349; 1969, results of DOXA, in *Bollettino Doxa,* 27 (4–5), April 1969; 1971, results of DEMOSCOPEA, in *Ricerche Demoscopiche*, 4(2), March 1972; 5 May 1974, results of DOXA, in Celso Ghini, *Il voto degli italiani*, ed. Riuniti, Rome, 1975: 444.

became very clear in this referendum. The women's movement had, in fact, joined the campaign for the maintenance of the divorce law as a campaign for civil rights and democracy, not as a specific problem of women.

The referendum on divorce was very important for the women's movement, because its outcome strengthened the possibilities for the movement to push for changes in the interest of women. This was especially true with regard to the abortion issue, because the referendum result had an enormous impact on political culture in Italy. In the first place, it showed that women were politically no longer to be defined as conservative voters upon whom the DC could count. It showed that the Catholic Church had very much lost its grip on women. Because of this, the parties of the left started to pay more attention to women and to 'women's issues'. Second, the growing strength of the women's movement had to be taken into account if these political parties wanted to strengthen themselves. Third, for the first time the conservative and reactionary forces had proved vincible, and this gave a new impetus to all forces wanting reforms. For those wanting revolution, the victory over the DC and the Catholic Church meant Utopia was that much closer, since it seemed that now *anything* was possible.

TABLE 2

Results of the referendum on the abrogation of the divorce law, 12 May 1974 (in per cent)

Regions				Selected cities and their obstetric clinics	
	No	Yes		No	Yes
North	62.81	37.19	Bologna	73.22	26.78
Centre	65.17	34.83	obst. clinic	80.73	19.27
South	47.94	52.06	Turin	79.84	20.16
Islands	51.70	48.30	matern. hosp.	85.00	15.00
Nat. medium	59.26	40.74	Florence	71.23	28.77
			obst. clinic	70.22	29.78

Source: Ghini (1975: 454)   *Source:* Weber (1977: 72)

Notes:

To vote 'no' to the abrogation of the new divorce law meant to support this law, which made divorce possible.

For lack of surveys, the votes cast by women in maternity hospitals is the only available information of how women voted in the referendum.

Parliament takes action — and fails

After the success in the referendum, the MLD together with the PR and the weekly *L'Espresso* each started to collect signatures for a new referendum, this time for the abrogation of the anti-abortion law. Now, parliament could no longer postpone taking up the issue. First the Social Democrats (PSDI) presented their bill. This was followed by Fortuna of the PSI, who affirmed that his former, more restrictive, bill had been made irrelevant by events, especially by the demands of the women as expressed by the women's movement. Subsequently Fortuna supported the women's right to choose. The PCI also presented a (very restrictive) bill, followed by bills presented by the Republicans (PRI) and Liberals (PLI). The last bill was presented by the Christian Democrats (DC).

When the collection of signatures for a referendum for the abrogation of the existing anti-abortion law had been successfully concluded, the six bills were unified by a parliamentary commission and presented in one proposal as a compromise. The result of this work was a text that the entire women's movement defined as insufficient, in particular because of the determining role of the doctor, and hence the denial of women's right to choose.

Even at this stage, the antagonism between the ideas of the movement and the 'attempts for a solution' by parliament had become obvious. Two different worlds seemed to exist: the 'inner' world of parliament, a male world, and the 'outside' world of the streets, in this period a 'women's world'. Notwithstanding the mass demonstrations of women all over the country on 8 March 1976, on 2 April the DC attempted a coup, and won: the DC deputy, Piccoli, one of the most prominent DC politicians, put forward a motion once again treating abortion as a crime. He called for a secret vote, and his motion was accepted by 298 votes to 286. The rapporteurs resigned, and the meeting was dissolved. The compromise between the parties, reached after so much effort, was definitively destroyed.

The indignation of the women's movement was at its greatest, especially in the UDI which had set its hopes on a new legal regulation. In most of the feminist groups a process of evaluation of public demonstrations and traditional politics was once again activated. They felt supported in their beliefs that nothing good could be achieved by a male-dominated parliament in a male-dominated culture, and therefore felt that the movement was only losing time and energy by engaging in demonstrations. More than ever before, they concentrated on self-managed activities, in particular on the self-help groups, including self-help abortions.

The broken compromise between the political parties and the mass protests of women did not keep the Moro government on its feet. The governmental crisis was officially announced, parliament was dissolved and new elections were held.

The election of 1976

In the electoral campaign of 1976 the forces of the left employed the lesson they had learned from the referendum on divorce and the steady growth of feminism. They gave women's issues top priority, and promised to legalize abortions on demand. The three major groups of the New Left, which came together to draw up a common list of candidates, adopted the demands of the feminist movement for women's right to choose and to have free abortions on demand, and promised to accept no compromise. They also offered well-known feminists candidatures in the first ranks, which were, however, refused by the feminists owing to their rejection of delegation and traditional politics. The PR presented a 55 per cent women's list, with the repeal of the anti-abortion law as its declared primary aim. The Communist Party (PCI), which up to this point had been reluctant to endorse the women's right to abortions on demand, out of fear of turning away the 'Catholic masses' it was trying to conquer, had to change its attitude. Its women's section and the UDI put pressure on the PCI to support women's self-determination. The UDI even threatened not to support the PCI in the elections if it were not to respect this right. The pressure was so strong that the PCI was forced to change its own abortion bill to one that would include women's right to choose. The PCI even doubled the number of women candidates. This was certainly the moment when the women's movement on the whole was making its greatest impact on the political forces.

The line adopted by the left to give so much importance to women and the abortion issue proved successful: for the first time, the New Left and the PR entered parliament, and the PCI got its biggest ever victory: it gained 50 seats in parliament and 22 in the senate, making a total of 229 and 116 seats respectively. The number of PCI women deputies went up from 21 in 1972 to 45 in 1976, which was twice as many women deputies as all the other parties had together (61 in total). Numerically, the left and lay forces had for the first time surpassed the conservative and reactionary forces: they had 30 seats more in parliament and 9 more in the senate.

The result of this election clearly expressed the people's desire for reform and for the rapid passing of a progressive solution of the abortion problem. It certainly also represented a victory for the feminist movement, which had given the general exhortation to 'vote left', without expressing any specific party preference, because of its general distrust of party structures and the traditional form of political action. In any case, with this new parliament and the feminist movement at its zenith, nothing 'should' have prevented a progressive law permitting abortions from being passed rapidly.

The 'black vote'
In December 1976 the unified bill, covering a list of grounds for abortion but giving decisive powers to the physician, again reached parliament. In January 1977 this bill was accepted by 330 against 296 votes (opposed by the DC, the neo-fascist MSI and the PR, which wanted a referendum). Seeing the limitations of the law, even the 'winners' of the vote expressed themselves rather reservedly. While the UDI welcomed it, notwithstanding its limits, the major part of the women's movement judged it once again to be completely insufficient. They felt it was a 'fraud' and out of touch with the anxieties and problems of women who had to remain pregnant against their will.

The 'total scorn for the drama that thousands of women live' (EFFE, 1977:35) was demonstrated when a group of DC senators called unexpectedly for a secret vote on the non-passage of the bill on the basis of its presumed 'unconstitutionality'. Owing to seven 'franchi tiratori' (senators who belonged to parties in favour of the bill, but who voted against it in the secret poll), the proposal of non-passage of the law was accepted by a majority of two votes. This meant that the bill was blocked for the next six months and could not be discussed in the senate.

Notwithstanding their negative evaluation of the content of the bill, the women's movement was furious about this vote, termed the 'black vote'. Their rage united a great part of the feminists with the UDI. In all major cities there were immediate protests and demonstrations. Three days later, on 10 June 1977, a national demonstration was organized by the UDI and feminist groups combined and brought 50,000 women back on to the streets, but only for a short time. In general, the events underlined the feeling of powerlessness that women of the movement felt with regard to the political system. Moreover, they felt no desire to struggle for a bill that they had judged a 'fraud'.

The 'black vote' had given new impetus to the 'anti-abortionists', who had meanwhile organized the 'Movimento per la Vita' (Pro-Life Movement'). It mainly consisted of the most conservative DC members and sympathizers and 'good Catholics'. It had a perfectly functioning network, since the churches opened their doors to it. In the churches the signatures for a 'Pro-Life' draft of a severe anti-abortion law on popular initiative were collected before and after mass. In small villages the priest went from door to door, collecting signatures and denouncing those who did not sign 'for life' in his Sunday mass. Little children were induced to declare from the altar how happy they were that their mothers had not aborted them. The amount of money the Pro-Life Movement had at its disposal was considerable. It distributed multi-coloured booklets in the worst possible taste to all Italian households. Senators were flooded with the movement's material and letters. Such a rich and well organized movement Italy had not seen before. In November 1977 the Pro-Life Movement presented its bill, which surpassed even the fascist law in the degree of punishment of a woman who had had an abortion. This bill did not even permit therapeutical abortion, which had been introduced by the Constitutional Court in 1975. Although the bill had no chance of being passed, it is an indication of the political atmosphere that characterized this period in Italy.

In general, the political climate had changed considerably by early 1977, making the reactionary and conservative forces strong again. Red terrorism had pulled off its biggest coup with the kidnapping and killing of the DC President Moro. At the same time, Italy witnessed a short-lived but rather violent new student revolt. This brought the autonomous feminist movement and the New Left into increasing political difficulties. Furthermore, it was difficult to take a stand on this new student movement, which did not want the help or recognition of the autonomous feminist movement and did not want to establish a rapport with the 'old' New Left. The new movement was a symbol of the fact that the new generation had completely lost confidence in existing political and social movements.

In this political climate the abortion issue became a second priority also for the women's movement. It took one year from the 'black vote' until the new abortion law was finally passed (no. 194/78), six months during which it was blocked by the 'black vote' and six months of ordinary administrative procedure. The DC tried once again to water down women's rights in the final reading by introducing 'the right of the father', but this was voted down. The UDI still engaged in activities in favour of the bill, but the MLD was not at all interested in it. The autonomous feminist movement had also abandoned active campaigning and no longer appeared in public.

The final law

When the law finally took effect, on 5 June 1978, nobody showed any great enthusiasm. The law is a compromise between the political parties, between the stand of the women's movement for women's right to choose and the strong position of the Catholic Church against abortion. On the one hand, it allows women the right to make the *final* decision on abortion and to have the abortion performed free in public hospitals. On the other hand, it limits this right to women over the age of 18 and sets certain preconditions: only on medical, social or economic grounds can a woman have an abortion. Moreover, an abortion cannot be performed after a period of 90 days after conception; the woman must have a seven-day 'reflection time' after her obligatory visit to a gynaecologist whose task it is to persuade her to keep the foetus; and, most important, the doctors have an unlimited right to 'conscientious objection'. They can object without giving any reasons, and nurses and other paramedical personnel are excluded from performing an abortion.

Since Italy is predominantly Roman Catholic, the rate of 'conscientious objectors' climbed immediately to 72 per cent, with some regions (DC-governed) registering more than 90 per cent (data of the Coordinamento Nazionale per l'applicazione della legge 194/78, 1979). Lack of hospitals and personnel, the high rate of 'conscientious objectors', the various delays along the way before a pregnant women can present herself at a hospital, long waiting lists, the obligation of minors to have their parents' permission or that of a judge of the Court of Minors — all this keeps the number of clandestine abortions still high, an estimated 80 per cent of all abortions in 1979 (Coordinamento Nazionale, 1979). The rate of legal abortions performed on minors is still lower, although it is slowly increasing: from 3 per cent of all the interventions in 1979 to 6 per cent in 1981. Still, it is extremely low compared with countries that have a more permissive legislation (CENSIS, 1982:422). This is also due to the double standard of morality in Italy, the country of the 'mamma' where a pregnant woman who is not married is seen as the 'dishonoured' one, who brings 'shame' over her entire family.

The right to legal abortion is therefore to a great extent a privilege of women over 18, residents of PCI-governed regions or women with time and money to travel to these regions. This becomes very clear when we look at the percentage of abortions performed in the different regions with reference to 1,000 women between 15 and 49: in Piedmont, Tuscany and Umbria the rate is around 20 a year; in Campagnia, Basilicata, Calabria and Sicily (all in southern Italy and DC-governed) the rate is under 10 (CENSIS, 1982: 420). The highest number of abortions was in Emilia Romagna, with 27, or 823.8 abortions for 1,000 new-born. However, this high number is also due to women coming from other regions to Emilia Romagna for an abortion, since in this traditionally communist region conscientious objection had been relatively low and hospitals function and are well equipped. The perennial problem of Italy, the gap between the north and the south, shows once again the bitter reality of the southern population cut off from national reforms, which in this case forces women to have clandestine abortions.

Although clandestine abortions still seem to be in the majority in Italy, there is no doubt that, except for a minority, women are glad to have this legal possibility to decide whether they want to continue with a pregnancy or not. This is shown in the constant increase in the number of *legal* abortions, from 187,752 in 1979, the first year after the law had been passed, to 234,593 in 1982, the last data available (Eurostat, 1984a:107).

Evidence for support of the law can also be found in the outcome of the referendum on the abrogation of the new abortion law, called for by the Pro-Life Movement: the percentage of those voting for the maintenance of the existing abortion law was even higher than in the divorce referendum: 67.9 per cent (Bardi, 1981:283). This also indicates the trend not to bow to the dictates of the Church, even though the Church engaged in a vehement campaign for the repeal of the law in the worst possible taste. This trend continues and grows stronger with the years. And, unlike the divorce referendum, this time the votes in favour of the law were distributed almost evenly among the regions, so that we have, for instance, 67.1 per cent of voters in Sicily voting against the abrogation (that is, for the abortion law).

That Italians want to keep the law the way it is was also demonstrated by the outcome of a second referendum on that issue, called for by the PR and put to the voters on the same day as the Pro-Life referendum. The PR wanted the law repealed in favour of a complete liberalization. But this time the women's movement also opposed this proposal, because it meant placing abortions in the hands of private clinics, thus excluding the poor from having access to abortion. The vote against this referendum was even more conclusive: 88.5 per cent voted for the maintenance of the actual law (Bardi, 1981:283). With these two referendums the abortion issue was definitely put aside.

The impact of the women's movement
In order to evaluate the impact of the new women's movement in Italy, one has to consider the cultural context of the country. When the autonomous feminist movement started, which proved to be the engine for the other groups and organizations of the women's movement, divorce still did not exist in Italy. The role of women was very much defined as that of a wife, housekeeper and mother, and this was generally accepted as women's destiny. Until 1971 and 1973 respectively, two laws inherited from the fascist regime prohibited the public discussion and advertising of contraceptive methods and the distribution of contraceptives. When they finally were allowed in 1973, only 2.9 per cent of Italian women used oral contraceptives, as against 28.4 per cent of German and 36.5 per cent of Dutch women; even in Portugal and Spain the percentage was higher (Dal Pozzo and Rava, 1977:54). To talk about sexuality in public was unthinkable. Motherhood and clandestine abortions were seen as a woman's lot. Sex education in schools did not exist, and even at the universities the

future gynaecologists learned nothing about contraceptive methods. In this context of ignorance and taboo, to have brought up the issue first of sexuality, then of abortion as a social problem was a big accomplishment of the women's movement.

To make women speak up, to make the issue of sexuality public, to bring into the open the enormous number of clandestine abortions being performed in Italy, without doubt constituted a cultural revolution; a revolution also in so far as the questioning of motherhood as destiny went not only against the Catholic tradition of Italy, but also against sexual customs. There was a widespread belief that sexuality was a pleasure for men, and was permitted only for procreative reasons to women. In the country of the 'Latin lover' who *has to* try to 'lay' women in order to prove his masculinity, and of the 'mamma' who *has to* accept sacrifice to prove her femininity, a change in these attitudes meant breaking up a whole system of values. This in fact was the case, and it also explains the aggressiveness on the part of the conservative forces and the Catholic Church in fighting against even small reforms.

The women's movement succeeded in a few years in doing what reformist forces had tried to bring about for decades: to gain widespread acceptance that the women's situation in general needed reform. This is also the finding of the first inquiry that the European Commission made on this topic in 1975, where Italy came second only to France in the importance given to the problem of women's situation (Commission of the European Communities, 1984:7). The perception that women's status was changing was in 1975 highest in Italy in comparison with the other EC countries, held by a total of 93 per cent: 81 per cent of those questioned perceived this change as an improvement of women's situation (Commission of European Communities, 1975:14). That the impact of the movement in this respect had a lasting effect is demonstrated by the fact that in 1983 Italy ranked first in giving importance to women's situation, although the percentage had dropped since the women's movement was at its peak (Commission of the European Communities, 1984:7).

It is interesting to note that, although the movement had a big influence on the entire Italian population, it had its major impact on women who were thought of as being the most conservative forces and, in fact, had been so up to the 1970s. The opinions expressed about the movements for women's liberation, and about the feminist movements in particular, were more favourable in Italy than the EC medium, both by men and women; but there was a considerable difference in men's and women's judgement. Moreover, the favourable judgement of both sexes, but especially that of women, has increased in the years between 1977 and 1983 (Commission of European Communities, 1983a:42,44). The first evidence of the change in women's attitudes was found in the outcome of the divorce referendum. A study of the votes in maternity hospitals — the only way of knowing how *women* voted — showed that they were always far above the national medium (see Table 2).

That women no longer accepted their traditionally ascribed roles as housekeeper, wife and mother is also emphasized by their desire to have gainful employment. Italian women's preference for work, at 76 per cent in 1975 and 78 per cent in 1983, is by far the highest of the EC countries and has changed little from 1975 to 1983 (Commission of the European Communities, 1984:25). During the 1970s there was also a considerable increase in women's access to higher education, so that in 1981 they represented 43.2 per cent of the university population (Eurostat, 1984b:116).

All this is evidence that the women's movement has had a huge impact on social change in Italy, and more so for women than for men. In fact, the differences in judgement on women's roles, especially concerning work, are quite marked between men and women, much more so than in other EC countries (Commission of the European Communities, 1984:27). The abortion issue has opened up the doors for these changes: first, by demonstrating women's right to self-determination, which cannot be confined to one area or the other but has to be a right in all fields, from one's own body to the choices of one's role in society; second, because it attacked the most backward conditions and customs, and by destroying the taboos in this field made it possible to discuss every-thing concerning women's conditions; third, because abortion touched on a situation that most women had experienced or were afraid of experiencing, a specific problem that could be understood easily by all women. The abortion issue therefore had a centrifugal force, and the power of the movement consisted in bringing it up at the right moment, namely, when Italy had expressed its desire for change.

The women's movement was not equally successful in the political arena. Its political impact, however, has to be seen in two phases. First, it had the power to raise the abortion issue to the political level and to get all the political parties involved in the issue. Its impact on the left was considerable. Never before, and not afterwards, had the left paid so much attention to women and their conditions and offered so much to women with respect to active participation and promises in reforms. Never before was the left so willing to accept the demands of the women's movement, at least in their reformist aspects. Never before had the left felt the necessity to put 'cultural items' such as sexuality on its political agenda. And never before had the left also brought its own sexist behaviour up for discussion. All this was due to the impact of the women's movement.

But the movement also demonstrated its ultimate powerlessness in having the abortion issue handled in a way that reflected adequately the dramatic conditions under which thousands of women each year had to have abortions. For the political system it was a question of its own legitimacy as a democratic and representative system, once public opinion pressed for a change. It handled the abortion issue as a legal and moral question only. In this respect the women's movement had no influence at all, and, as the feminist scholars, Ergas/Sassaroli state rightly, 'it suffered the dramatic wearing down which derives from the fact that the confrontation with the institutions takes place by definition on the most anti-feminine, most compromised and most dangerous terrain' (Ergas and Sassaroli, 1977:35).

The abortion issue was therefore also proof that the movement was not able to change the traditional way 'of making politics'. Moreover, the abortion campaign showed that, the moment the issue became political, the movement was divided. It was neither 'the' movement that wanted the law, nor 'the' movement that refused the law. The decision to take up the campaign against the old anti-abortion law was from the very beginning not supported by the whole movement. The crucial point consisted in the judgement of the political system, that is, whether an interaction was looked for or refused.

Part of the feminist movement had refused from the start to participate in the campaign, because it would have meant a confrontation with the traditional political arena from which they felt alienated. Another part of the feminist movement 'discovered', in connection with the issue of abortion, not only a central aspect of women's oppression, but also a concrete goal that directly concerned the masses of women. The 'entry into the public world' subsequently caused changes for this part of the movement. 'The sisters found themselves at a certain point squeezed between two walls . . ., on the one side the risk of the separation from the type of research done by the movement, on the other side the risk of an absorption from a strong institution which imposes on you its methods and contents' (Ergas and Sassaroli, 1977:35).

The movement was not absorbed by parliament. However, it felt defeated by the political system that had stripped the abortion issue of its feminist content and had converted it into a law. Although the abortion law is by no means the worst law possible, many women of the feminist movement withdrew from the public sphere and refused to fight for the application of the law. Renouncing this possibility, the movement weakened its impact in the field of public awareness. It also lost its impact on the left. Today, other problems occupy public attention, although the general recognition remains that women by definition have equal rights, but are still far from having them in practice.

Italy 47

List of abbreviations
CIF   Centro Italiano Femminile (Italian Feminine Centre)
DC   Democrazia Cristiana (Christian Democratic Party)
EC   European Communities
MLD   Movimento di Liberazione della Donna (Woman's Liberation Movement)
PCI   Partito Comunista Italiano (Communist Party)
PLI   Partito Liberale Italiano (Liberal Party)
PR   Partito Radicale (Radical Party)
PRI   Partito Repubblicano Italiano (Republican Party)
PSDI   Partito Socialdemocratico Italiano (Social Democratic Party)
PSI   Partito Socialista Italiano (Socialist Party)
UDI   Unione Donne Italiane (Italian Women's Union)

References
Bardi, Luciano (1981) 'Italy says "No": The Referendums of May 1981', *West European Politics*, 4(3): 282–5.
CENSIS (1982) *Rapporto sulla situazione sociale del paese*. Rome: CENSIS.
Commission of the European Communities (1975) *European Men and Women. A Comparison of Their Attitudes to Some of the Problems Facing Society*. Brussels: CEC.
Commission of the European Communities (1983a) *European Women and Men*. Brussels: CEC.
Commission of the European Communities (1983b) *Women in Statistics*. Supplement no. 14 to *Women of Europe*. Brussels: CEC.
Commission of the European Communities (1984) *Women and Men of Europe in 1983*. Supplement no. 16 to *Women of Europe*. Brussels: CEC.
Coordinamento Nazionale per l'applicazione della legge 194/78 (1979) Data supplied at its First National Congress in Rome.
Dal Pozzo, G. and E. Rava (1977) *Donna '70*. Milan: Teti ed.
Dambrosio, Badaracco and Buscaglia (eds) (1976) *Maternità cosciente*. Milan: Mazzotta.
EFFE (1977) nos. 7–8 (July–August).
Eurobarometer (1983) no. 20.
Eurostat (1984a) *Demographic Statistics*. Luxembourg: Eurostat.
Eurostat (1984b) *Review 1973–1982*. Luxembourg: Eurostat.
Ergas, Y. and S. Sassaroli (1977) 'Istituzioni: scontro o confronto', *Effe*, 5: 49–50.
Frabotta, Biancamaria (ed.) (1975) *Femminismo e lotta di classe in Italia (1970–73)*. Rome: Savelli.
Frabotta, Biancamaria (1976) *La politica del femminismo*. Rome: Savelli.
Ghini, Celso (1975) *Il voto degli italiani*. Rome: Ed. Riunite.
Jourdan, Clara (1976) *Insieme contro. Esperienze dei consultori femministi*. Milan: La Salamandra.
L'almanaco (1978) 'Luoghi, nomi, incontri, fatti, lavori in corso del movimento femminista italiano dal 1972'. Rome: Ed. Delle Donne.
La nuova luna (1977). Journal of the MLD, no 1.
MLD-PR (1975) *Contro l'aborto di classe*. Rome: Savelli.
Teodori, Maria Adele (1975) 'Cinque anni di lotta'. Introduction to MLD-PR (1975).
Weber, Maria (1977) *Il voto delle donne*. Turin: Einaudi.
Women of Europe, a journal issued by the Commission of the European Communities.

2
Women's movement and abortion: the criminalization of Irish women

Pauline Conroy Jackson

Introduction

'One step forwards and two steps back.' — Such has been the apparent fate of women's struggle to gain control over their reproduction in the Republic of Ireland in the 1980s. Women's groups in the 26 counties of Ireland entered the 1980s to confront not the approaching twenty-first century, but a nineteenth-century outlawing of abortion. Abortion has been illegal since the time of British rule in 1861, but the mobilization of an Irish-style majority led to a referendum in 1983, which wrote the right to life of the foetus into the Irish constitution.

Because of the many unresolved national political issues, the Irish women's movement has not developed the separatist and autonomous character prominent in so many other Western countries. The abortion issue became a catalyst for new feminist mobilization. In the course of the referendum, the whole issue of women's control over their reproductive functions got its first public airing on a national scale — an unforeseen consequence on the part of those seeking to curtail such thinking. In its aftermath, issues such as infanticide, new reproductive technology and female sterilization were taken up by various women's groups more articulately and forcefully than ever before. Yet power eludes the organizations of radical, militant or otherwise active women, and in the profound economic and ideological crisis that racks the country, the danger of further retrogressive mobilization remains.

The women's movement in Ireland

The history of Irish women remains unwritten. Only in the latter half of the twentieth century have women succeeded in recovering a hidden heritage of the nineteenth century and earlier periods. As a small partitioned island on the periphery of Europe, still part occupied, militarily, by the British army in 6 of its 32 counties, Ireland is an exception to many historical, economic, social and political tendencies.

At the turn of this century, Ireland had not yet recovered from decades of land agitation over colonial control of its rich pasture-lands. Since the great famine of 1845–8, emigration and disease had reduced the population by half. The two big cities of Belfast and Dublin were crowded with hungry and rebellious former peasants. This was the environment that generated a Women Workers' Union in 1916, nationalist women's groups among the intelligentsia and the formation of women's auxiliaries to support Europe's first Red Army: the Irish Citizens' Army. The outbreak of the first world war and suffrage agitation for the women's vote were to be overshadowed first by the Great Lockout or general strike of 1913 and then by a nationalist uprising in 1916. This was followed by guerilla war against irregular British forces until the country was partitioned by the treaty of 1922. Six north-eastern counties were retained by the British and 26 were to become the Irish Free State, an arrangement that prompted a civil war between pro- and anti-treaty forces. In all these turbulent and history-making events, women of all classes played an active but politically subordinate role (Ward, 1983).

Rebellion against this role is manifest in women's opposition to the 1937 constitution of what was to become an Irish Republic (of 26 counties). The Women's Social and Progressive League of 1937 was an alliance of women to oppose clauses in the draft constitution that could be interpreted as relegating women to the exclusive role of mother and homemaker. During the same (1930s) period, laws were passed to restrict the type of industrial work that women might undertake; censorship of publications was introduced and the sale of contraceptives was prohibited in a law dealing with the 'suppression of brothels'.

This repressive battery of sexual and social legislation remained for fifty years until the 1970s, when its undoing became a focus of much women's activity in the 26 counties. The partition of the country, the war in the 6 counties and the different material and legislative conditions that this has generated since 1922 has given rise to divergent political and social tendencies in the 6 and 26 counties of the country, producing the same tensions between nationalism and feminist thinking as confronted the Irish suffragettes and women nationalists of the turn of the century.

With so many unresolved national political issues, the Irish women's movement has not produced the same separatist and autonomous character that is prominent in women's organizations in the USA, Britain and other industrial countries. In the late 1960s women's groups formed in the major cities of the 26 counties. Among the middle- and upper-class women, a Committee on the Status of Women in 1968 became the focus of professional and business-women's resentment at their exclusion from public life. Among women with backgrounds as housewives, students and young journalists, a Women's Liberation Organization was formed which engaged in spectacular actions such as the mass importation of contraceptives illegally and publicly into the 26 counties, to flaunt a law that prohibited control of women's fertility. The rise of the civil rights movement in the north and the re-formation of republican and left-wing groups prompted many of the 'founding' women of this embryonic movement to join left-wing and republican organizations.

In a predominantly agricultural country such as Ireland, it is not surprising that feminist organizations were late in development. The close relationship between the Catholic Church and the state that was established in 1922 has led to a conservative interpretation of all social issues by all political parties and in public policy-making. In the 26 counties of Ireland, divorce remains prohibited, male homosexuality is a criminal offence and the age of criminal responsibility for children is seven years. Reforms to permit the development of public health services for mothers and their young children were all vigorously resisted by the Catholic Church. Consistent with the conservatism of a rural society dominated by big landowners, a centreground in public life, occupied in other countries by social democratic or liberal thinking, has not emerged in Ireland.

The appearance of women's groups in the late 1960s and early 1970s was greeted with horror and outrage by male-dominated trade unions, political parties, the Catholic Church, publicly owned mass media and the liberal professions. This reaction did not diminish with the formation in the early 1970s of new women's organizations such as the Dublin-based Irish Women United (IWU) and its newspaper, *Banshee*. 'Banshee' is a word in the Irish language meaning a woman spirit or fairy person who moves at night warning of imminent death or tragedy. The IWU organization was composed of radicals, feminists, left-wing women, students, housewives and office workers, and their programme of action included demands for equal pay for working women and contraceptive services for all women (Gaudin, 1983). This short-lived but stimulating organization dissolved in 1976, giving birth to a spate of single-issue-based women's groups and services such as the Rape Crisis Centre, the Campaign for a Women's Centre and the Contraception Action Programme.

Lacking, with notable exceptions, the support of female intellectuals, the women's movement failed to explore in depth many cultural, political and ideological issues during these early years. The void was filled by influences from British and US feminism. This can be perceived in the names chosen for new groups: 'Right to Choose', 'Irish Pregnancy Counselling Centre' and 'Wellwoman' all had their parallel counterparts in Britain.

With the passage of the 1970s, the hoped-for reforms never came. Abortion and contraception remained illegal. A weak Equal Pay Act came into force from which many employers immediately exempted themselves. The Anti-Discrimination (Equal Pay) Act provided for equal pay between men and women performing the same work or work of equal value in the same place of work for the same employer. Where a woman claims equal pay from her employer under the Act, the determination of 'equal value' is made by Equality Officers employed by the state. The armed forces and residential institutions, such as church-run children's homes, hospitals and special schools, were among the employers exempted from the operation of the equality law.

The new centres and support groups of unmarried mothers (Cherish) and battered wives (Women's Aid) remained without state recognition or funding. The underestimated rigidity of the state and party system of the 26 counties quickly separated the radical younger middle- and working-class women from their sisters in more affluent and powerful milieus. The latter formed a Women's Political Association to get women into the party system (i.e., any party) or fostered hopes that Ireland's accession to the European Economic Community would impose and force equality on to the Irish state from without.

The repressive legislation and women's reproduction

Among its early legislative acts, the new state of the 26 counties of Ireland was to outlaw the importation into the country or the advertising of, or the offering of services for, control of reproduction. Strict penalties were introduced for anyone breaking these laws, and police prosecutions have taken and continue to take place. The origins of this state of affairs lie not so much in pro-natality policies as in a desire to restrict any control that women might exercise over their bodies and to restrict sexual mores. These extraordinary prohibitions reflect the close interlocking of the state with Catholic teaching on the immorality of contraception.

Since the late 1960s, women's groups have attempted by every means to change this situation. Pickets were placed on church and party buildings. Contraceptives were imported illegally. Illegal clinics were set up. Contraception Action Campaigns have been run and are still being organized. Meetings attended by government leaders have been disrupted and test cases taken through the courts. Since the mid-1970s, tens of thousands of women have attended and are still attending illegal family planning clinics or using the pill prescribed by their doctor in breach of the law. The outcome of all this activity has been discouraging. In 1979 a Family Planning Law was passed which legalized contraception for married couples. It failed to provide a framework for any public family planning service. The Catholic Church now 'authorizes' the use of family planning for married couples but restricts this to the use of so-called 'natural methods'. Failure of methods such as abstinence, Billings and temperature charts are among the reasons women cite today for seeking abortion in Britain. In part to counteract women's and liberal medical services, the Catholic Church opened its own parallel services: phone-in advice for pregnant unmarried mothers and courses in 'natural methods' in church buildings. The reaction of the Church to reproductive control may account for the fall in church-going not only among young and working-class people but also among formerly devout Catholic couples.

In September 1985, a reform to the 1979 law on family planning was finally implemented permitting single persons of 18 years of age or older legally to buy contraceptives. This ameliorates the legal situation but in no way fills the void in health services in this area. Colleges and universities who wish to make contraceptives available to students are still prohibited from doing so. No advertising of family planning services is available on television, radio or in the national press. The problem of granting licences to the existing family planning clinics has not been resolved. For women outside the principal urban centres, access to contraception still poses real difficulties.

The consequences of the legal situation in the 26 counties have been not only social and political, but practical and medical. There is no post-abortion counselling service, no public advertising of hazardous forms of contraception, no health education on the mass media in this area, no public advertising of the handful of clinics that treat sexually transmitted diseases. Many women and young girls are condemned to a frightening ignorance and have no means of informing themselves. Popular women's magazine editors in Britain are astonished by the thousands of letters they receive from Irish women seeking help with sexual and reproductive problems.

It is interesting that in an agricultural country based on cattle rearing, control of reproduction in cattle herds has been scientifically studied and practised for decades. Indeed, prior to the 1983 Amendment, the only debates on abortion that I could locate in the parliamentary records were on the problem of spontaneous abortion in cattle!

Until the opening of the debate on abortion in 1981, abortion and contraception have tended to be treated as entirely separate issues. With the exception of the Women's Right to Choose lobbyists, few other women's groups dealt with it. Illegal since 1861, under a law passed during the British colonial regime of Queen Victoria, abortion had remained a taboo subject. Veiled in a curtain of secrecy, shame and fear, the old British abortion law passed into the legislature of the Irish state in 1922 and remained in operation in the north as well. Rose (1977), in his study of the subject, argues persuasively that, historically in Ireland, infanticide has been the preferred option of women with an unwanted pregnancy.

In the post-famine period of the late nineteenth and early twentieth centuries, female married fertility has carried high approbation in providing heirs to private agricultural landholdings and security for ageing parents (Jackson, 1984). The official views of the Catholic Church on abortion were unlikely to have been assimilated by farmers, tenants, labourers and their local priests. Of greater interest is the Catholic belief that unbaptised infants cannot enter Heaven, mingled with deeply held and pre-capitalist beliefs in the power of spirits of the dead, spirits residing in nature and magic.

In the twentieth century the practice of abortion and infanticide has followed closely the liberalization of British legislation and ease of travel between Ireland and Britain. During the second world war, when travel restrictions between the two countries were introduced, a flourishing trade in back-street abortion was plied in Dublin; this tapered off between the end of the war and the introduction of the 1967 Abortion Act in England (Rose, 1977).

Since then, British clinics and Irish counselling services have provided the outlet for the increasing number of women seeking to terminate their pregnancies. Until the early 1970s, British cities provided the anonymity sought by exiled unmarried mothers. The price of remaining pregnant and unmarried can be high. In July 1984 Eileen Flynn lost her court case when she appealed against the decision of an all-male Labour Tribunal to uphold her dismissal as a secondary schoolteacher from a state-funded convent. She had been fired when she gave birth to a baby as an unmarried mother; the father of the baby, her companion, was a separated married man. Her legal struggle has become a focus of interest for unmarried mothers, separated persons and women trade unionists. This highly repressive environment provides the backdrop to the thousands of Irish women from the 26 counties who seek abortion in Britain every year.

Women and the campaign to amend the constitution
In 1981 a Conference on Abortion, Contraception and Sterilization was organized by women at the University of Dublin. The mounting discontent among many women with their subordinated and oppressive reproductive status and their determination to change it provoked, in reaction, the formation of an unholy alliance of right-wing forces calling itself the Pro-Life Amendment Campaign (PLAC). PLAC was pledged to use abortion as the issue around which to rally conservative and patriarchal forces opposed to all changes in the status of women.

The alliance known as PLAC quickly lobbied the three main

political parties into agreeing to hold a referendum on the abortion issue. In a moment of weakness, all three parties (including the Labour Party) agreed to this proposal, imagining it would be uncontroversial. The wording of the proposed referendum eventually put before the population was:

> The State acknowledges the right to life of the unborn and, with due regard to the equal right to life of the mother, guarantees in its laws to respect and, as far as practicable by its laws, to defend and vindicate that right.

Voters could vote simply 'Yes' or 'No' to the amendment. Commenting on the wording of the amendment, Parliamentary Deputy Monica Barnes of the governing party, Fine Gael, remarked:

> We are now into the third Act of a lunatic farce, where politicians have voted to present to the people of this country the wording of an Amendment to the Constitution that is deliberately vague, ambiguous and downright dangerous. What has divided doctors, lawyers, churches and politicians will now be put for the people to vote 'yes' or 'no' on and an attempt will be made to claim that this is democracy. (Barnes, 1983)

The small lobby for the decriminalization of abortion was extremely new and weak, and was taken aback at the proposal of a referendum and a national debate on the issue. The PLAC forces were aware that abortion was illegal under the 1861 Offences Against the Person Act and that they could not propose an additional law since one was already in existence. The only path open to them was via an addition to the constitution. All changes to the constitution require a referendum, and this was the precise proposal put to the politicians, to which they readily agreed. Previous referendums had been held on such issues as the adoption of children and Ireland's accession to the European Community. The turnout was often extremely low and the abortion issue was, as it emerged, no exception to this pattern.

Right to Choose groups, prominent women journalists, family planning clinic workers and other women tentatively formed an Anti-Amendment Campaign. It was an extremely difficult task. Most women had never discussed abortion in public — indeed, not outside an intimate circle of friends! None knew how to make a speech on the subject. None of the left-wing political parties would agree at first to join the campaign. It seemed for a time that every official legitimate political faction was going to support an amendment to the constitution to 'give an absolute right to life to the foetus'.

Condemned to marginality, women's groups found themselves on the defensive, confronting a *national* referendum that they were ill-equipped, ill-financed and ill-prepared to oppose. Many women experienced a sickening fear that, if they opposed this referendum publicly, they would be ostracized in their own homes. Between 1981 and September 1983 the gap between the two sides widened until no political group, party or faction could avoid taking a side. Compelled by weakness to form alliances with other centrist, liberal and minority church forces, the voice of women in the campaign was swamped by persistent and successful efforts to project the issue as 'gender-neutral', as purely legalistic, constitutional or technical–medical.

Opposing the referendum, that is, seeking a 'No' vote, were the Methodist and Protestant churches as well as the Jewish community. Members of the teaching, legal and medical professions were divided on the issue. Students' unions generally opposed the referendum along with many women's organizations. The Irish Congress of Trade Unions, after much delay and procrastination, succumbed to pressure from women trade unionists and issued a weak statement of opposition. The Women's Committee of the Labour Party as well as the Communist Party, the Workers' Party and some branches of the Labour Party, belatedly took up the issue. Other left-wing groups such as People's Democracy, Revolutionary Struggle, Socialist Workers' Movement and the Democratic Socialist Party joined the anti-amendment campaign.

In favour of holding a referendum and of a 'Yes' vote were the majority of the opposition Fianna Fail party, the majority of senior maternity hospital consultant obstetricians and the bishops of the Catholic Church. The Irish Nurses Organization and most lay Catholic organizations such as Opus Dei and the Knights of Columbanus canvassed actively for a 'Yes' vote. The issue divided men and women on both sides. In favour of the referendum were women across the political spectrum. Many were probably influenced by the official condemnations of abortion issued by the Church regularly as the referendum approached. Pamphlets and leaflets were issued to Catholic churchgoers on Sundays. Church-run hospitals and schools were used as organizing centres in favour of the amendment.

Women who were not regular church-goers would nevertheless be influenced by Catholic religious belief that the foetus contains a spiritual soul which is destroyed in abortion. On the 'Yes' side were also women who were straightforwardly anti-feminist and regarded changes in contraception and abortion laws as threats to the status of motherhood.

As left-wing parties joined the myriad of local organizing committees to oppose the holding of a referendum and later to get a 'No' vote on polling day, the politics of the campaign tended to suppress women's autonomy and even to suppress women's reproductive control as an issue of the amendment. While this might seem incredible, it occurred. The youth branch of the conservative Fine Gael Party published tens of thousands of leaflets saying: 'No to the

Amendment! No to Abortion'. The supposedly left-wing Workers' Party published similar quantities of leaflets giving reasons why the amendment should be opposed: women's right to control their bodies was not among them; women were excluded from mention at all.

The Women's Right to Choose Campaign tried to organize a public statement from prominent women who would admit to having had an abortion. Extraordinary pressure was brought to bear on the women to discourage them from taking such an action. Indeed, the campaign elicited an atmosphere of violence that paralysed individual women from opposing the amendment other than in the context of a large group. A picket on the port terminals where boats carry women to Britain for abortions was physically attacked by a male on-looker in the presence of the police. On the rare occasions when women were invited to discuss the issue of abortion on national media, they had to be ready to be accused of being 'baby-murderers'. A woman senator who spoke in opposition to the amendment received hate mail and obscene phone calls. Women in employment in religious-run schools, hospitals and social services feared for their jobs if they wore badges opposing the amendment. One woman put opposition stickers on her car and had the windows smashed in.

In this intimidatory atmosphere, women's groups formed alliances in which women's autonomy suffered, as the abortion issue was medicalized into the pros and cons of whether cancer of the womb justifies a termination, whether ectopic pregnancies can survive and whether twins have two souls or one!

Voting at the referendum
No polls were taken that would enable an analysis of the results of the referendum by social class, age, gender or other characteristics. Only geographical constituency results give an indication of the social class composition of the voting patterns. On the day of the referendum half the electorate failed to turn up at the polls, and of those who did, a third opposed the amendment. The results are shown in Table 1.

The voting patterns in the referendum seemed to confirm an urban–rural divide. Only five electoral constituencies rejected the amendment to the constitution on abortion — all of these were in the Dublin area. The highest 'No' vote was in the Dun Laoghaire constituency where the anti-amendment campaign had been active for a year prior to the vote and eventually attracted some 100 campaigners to its activities. Areas with no anti-amendment group or committee tended, like Roscommon, to have very high 'Yes' voting. Where anti-amendment committees were formed outside Dublin, as in Galway, Cork and Waterford, the 'No' vote appeared to rise accordingly. This was certainly the explanation in the case of the anti-amendment campaign in the western constituency of Galway, whose activities

TABLE 1
The result of the 1983 referendum, selected constituencies
(in per cent)

Constituency	% voting	
	Yes	No
All constituencies	67	33
Dublin (all areas)	51.6	48.3
Dun Laoghaire (Dublin)	42.1	57.9
Roscommon (rural)	83.8	16.2

Note: 'Yes' means supporting the amendment.

Source: Irish Press, Dublin, 9 September 1983: 4.

stretched out into sparsely populated rural areas and where the proportion voting 'No' was noticeably higher than in comparable areas where no anti-amendment committee was active.

For women seeking control of their bodies, the amendment was a defeat. On the day after the referendum, the body of a dead foetus was washed up in the sewers of Dublin. As voting on abortion took place, somewhere in the city a mother had struggled in desperation and despair . . .

The amendment arose from a campaign to suppress even further women's control over their fertility. By projecting the issue on to the public arena, a taboo on abortion was lifted for the first time ever. Indeed, the whole campaign may have encouraged women to seek abortions who otherwise might not have dared.

The referendum attracted into political activity hundreds of younger women who had never before been connected to any women's group or who had never thought of themselves as feminists or as concerned with feminist issues. In this sense it gave a new impetus to the formation of a more coherent women's movement. On the negative side, it clearly places women of the 26 counties of Ireland in an exceptional situation vis-à-vis their sisters in European countries where some minimal reforms have been achieved by the women's movement. While the amendment represented an ideological crisis for the 26-county state, it clarified many ideological problems for feminists, demonstrating clearly that control over our bodies is considered in Ireland, in 1985, to be a subversive activity. Before discussing some of the consequences of the 1983 amendment for women's movement activity, it is worth describing the practical situation of women seeking abortion.

Irish women seeking abortion
In the two months prior to the referendum, 200 women sought the

advice of a Dublin pregnancy counselling service on the termination of their pregnancies (Burke, 1983). The majority were young and unmarried, and were students, unemployed, housewives or office workers. The majority cited social and economic pressures as their reasons for needing an abortion. However, health reasons are the principal grounds for actually obtaining an abortion under the British Abortion Act, and it is on these grounds that Irish women obtain their abortions. They are not only criminalized, but have to hide their real reasons for seeking an abortion in order to obtain one.

It is possible to make estimates of the numbers of Irish women having abortions in Britain using data furnished by the British Office of Population Censuses and Surveys (OPCS). Their abortion statistics give a breakdown of terminations carried out on women under the 1967 British Abortion Act according to their place of residence. Women giving addresses in the 26 counties of Ireland appear as Irish; Irish women giving temporary addresses in Britain are included in data on British women. Using an alternative method, Dean (1984:3) estimates that in 1983 some 3,700 Irish women had their pregnancies terminated in Britain, based on data derived from British clinics. If one examines estimates as to the numbers of Irish women who give Irish addresses and adds these to projections for the numbers who do not, the number of women seeking abortions in Britain would be close to 5,000 a year.

Irish women obtain abortions in Britain in the same way as their British counterparts. The vast majority use licensed private clinics, where the opinions of two doctors are required before permission can be granted for an abortion. The total cost in 1984 would be equivalent to $250 or more. For an unemployed single woman, this sum is equivalent to eight weeks' welfare payments.

Rape, repeated caesarian sections, exposure to rubella or radioactive substances, incest, difficulties with previous pregnancies, allergies to contraception, severe psychological disturbances, multiple miscarriage or stillbirth, the presence of one or more handicapped children in the family — none of these situations is a ground for abortion in the 26 counties of Ireland. It is possible to get an abortion in Northern Ireland under a 1945 amendment to the Infant Life Preservation Act, but the British Abortion Act of 1967 has never been implemented in this British-occupied territory of Ireland. The grounds for permitting an abortion are so narrowly interpreted that in 1983 over 1,000 women from Northern Ireland went to Britain to have their pregnancies terminated. So the total number of women from Ireland, north and south, seeking abortions in Britain is about 6,000 a year using official estimates. Women from the North tend to be younger than their southern sisters and more are married, but about the same proportion are not using contraception:

one third of all women seeking an abortion.

The presence of a total ban on abortion in the 26 counties of Ireland has led to definite gaps in the health services in other gynaecological and maternity areas. Family planning advice is not available to women in all maternity hospitals. Only one hospital in the country is equipped to respond to women victims of rape, and abortion referral is not offered. For fertile women there is no genetic counselling service. One of the consequences of this under-development is greater difficulties for many women in dealing with miscarriage and spontaneous abortion. Women who have had terminations try to hide this fact from gynaecologists when they later become happily pregnant for fear it will be written on their medical record. Fear and ignorance compound each other.

The two pregnancy counselling services that operate in Dublin have had intimidating pickets placed at their doors by right-wing groups to prevent women from entering their premises. In 1985 the two services were summoned to the High Court in Dublin to answer allegations that their activities were contrary to the 1983 amendment to the constitution. This prosecution was initiated by the same right-wing groups who had sought to outlaw abortion for posterity with their anti-abortion referendum. Once again, the criminalization process of women taking control, or helping others to take control, of their reproduction is used relentlessly to undermine and erode women's emancipation. Given present trends, there is every reason to believe that, despite this criminalization, the numbers of women seeking abortion from the 26 counties of Ireland will continue to rise.

The post-amendment situation
The amendment was a severe setback to women's emancipation in Ireland. Never before had Irish people been so divided on a single issue since the treaty that partitioned the country in 1922. However, the debate generated by the referendum prevented right-wing forces from claiming the victory they had hoped for.

Within months of its passage into the Irish constitution, a rebirth of women's activity could be witnessed. In contrast to the earlier periods of the 1960s and 1970s, this rebirth has been marked by political, ideological and theological debates, groups and publications. Absent are programmes of reform, new single-issue groups or parallel women's services: in their place, a mushrooming of women's study groups leading to the formation of a Women's Studies Federation of Ireland. A large North–South Women's Conference has taken place, a Dublin Women's Centre has been revitalized with younger women and a Women for Disarmament Group has played an active part in opposing the visit of US President Reagan to Ireland. This latter led to the detention under emergency legislation of thirty women for setting up a peace camp at the gate of the residence of the US Ambassador to Ireland. There has been a proliferation of women's pamphlets, publications and book plans. Gender has been chosen as the theme of sociological and history conferences. Radical nuns have formed a 'Sisters for Justice' group in solidarity with the oppressed of Ireland and the Third World. Women who have attended courses in feminist theology organized a visit by US feminist Mary Daly (author of *Gyn/Ecology*) who addressed over 600 women in a North–South tour of Ireland. A new women's network of organizations has been formed.

On the theme of reproduction the Dublin Wellwoman Centre, which runs contraception and health services for women, organized, in conjunction with University College Dublin Women's Studies Forum, a workshop and radio discussion on the theme of new reproductive technology during 1984. The ensuing discussion brought to the surface themes that had been neglected during the campaign preceding the abortion referendum: the pressures for motherhood, the feelings of distress among infertile mothers and the medicalized and commercialized responses of the medical profession who intervene with infertile couples.

There is no evidence that back-street abortion has been operating since the passage of the amendment; indeed, it has all but disappeared since the passing of the 1967 Abortion Act in Britain (Rose, 1977; Jackson, 1983). The last court case would appear to have been prior to the passing of the 1967 Abortion Act in Britain. There have been no instances of prosecutions being entered against Irish women residents who, having had legal terminations in Britain, return to Ireland.

There has been an increase in the media reporting of infanticide-related cases. Five cases have been reported from rural areas. In one instance a fifteen-year-old schoolgirl died giving birth alone in an open field. Her newborn baby died with her of exposure. She was yet another victim of Ireland's repressive policies on reproduction. Such is the fear and atmosphere of criminalization of women that this young mother preferred the risk of death in isolation to communicating her unmarried and pregnant condition to any authority. In a second instance, a newly born baby was washed up on the remote shores of County Kerry in south-east Ireland. It had been stabbed to death. In a third instance, which has come to be known as the 'Kerry Babies Case' a young mother was accused of murder and her mother, aunt, two brothers and sister were accused with her. She and her family confessed to a crime they did not commit. Indeed, she had given birth to a baby, not in hospital but near the family cottage in a rural village. The baby was apparently dead on birth and she buried it in a pond near her home (McCafferty, 1985). These instances of contemporary rural birth concealment, maternal death and infant death among young unmarried mothers suggest that Rose's hypothesis (Rose, 1977) that infanticide in nineteenth-century Ireland was the preferred option to abortion may still hold true. However, it would be speculative to impose his hypothesis on late-twentieth-century conditions. What these tragic cases illustrate is the strong and persistent taboo on unmarried motherhood — so strong that some young mothers risk their own and their infants' lives rather than reveal their secret.

It would be premature to define the upsurge in political consciousness and activity as a coherent 'women's movement'. It is undoubtedly a new stage in the development of a women's movement in Ireland, which more clearly than ever polarizes into two political camps those who believe that reforms in women's position and status can be developed from within the present political state and party system and those who, after the abortion debate, hear the death knell on any reform of women's position, in work, reproduction or social status.

In the 6 counties, 'womens issues' are beginning to be redefined among politically active women in the urban nationalist districts where republican political resistance to British occupation forms the dominant context of all political debate on any issue. A separate women's centre has been opened by republican-minded women which functions as an advice and organizing focus for part of West Belfast. The existence of the Falls Women's Centre responds to the real desire of nationalist women for greater recognition of the leading role they play in founding and coordinating campaigns of political opposition. Its existence in no way resolves the historical tension between struggles for national liberation and women's liberation. The cautious optimism of some feminist writers like Ward (1983) can be counterposed to those who have experienced women's 'return to the home' from national liberation battlefields elsewhere (Minces, 1982). The dilemma cannot be facilely slotted into a nationalism-versus-feminism formula. Separate women's groups, organizations and services have now long existed in the 6 counties, and have led an uneasy coexistence with the continual appearance/disappearance of separatist tendencies among active women in the republican and nationalist organizations. Among some Irish emigrant women in Britain there is evidence of a new nationalist militancy. They have formed Irish women's study and action groups in London, at times getting greater financial and moral support from the Labour-run Greater London Council (now abolished) than women in Ireland have ever got from the 26 counties.

The amendment on abortion in Ireland has been a turning point in the development of a women's movement. If it has been a defeat in practical terms, it has been a victory in lessons learnt. It has thrown to the forefront the apartheid conditions of life for women in so far as their reproductive capacities are concerned. It has demonstrated the gynocidal consequences of bans on women's control of their reproductive capacities. It has demonstrated the crucial and pivotal character of fertility, sexual and body control in women's struggle for emancipation. It has laid the basis for clarifying the patriarchal character of political control over women in Irish society.

By the end of the decade of the 1980s, just ten years short of the year 2000, women in the 26 counties of Ireland are likely still to be without legal right or control over their fertility. There is no sign whatsoever of any loosening of present controls over sterilization, abortion or contraception. Like water rising at the edge of a dam, resentment, disillusion and anger are growing. New organizational forms of study and action are being experimented with. An increase in obscurantist thinking is also to be expected, rationalizing and obscurely justifying, in a more subjectivist mode, the barriers encountered by Irish women on their road to emancipation.

Between the new political clarity and the hazards of obscurantism lies an uncharted zone which we are now entering. A symbol of the uncharted path ahead of us is a new postcard being sold by the Women's Community Press. It reads:

DANGER — YOU ARE NOW ENTERING POST-REFERENDUM IRELAND

References

Baker, S. and G. McDonnell (1984) 'Women and the Roman Catholic Church in Ireland', *Good News* (journal of the Women's Group of the European University Institute, Florence), Spring.

Barnes, Monica (1983) Address to Dun Laoghaire Anti-Amendment meeting, 16 June, Dublin (extract from a supplied script).

Barry, Ursula (1984) 'Ideology in Crisis: the Anti-Abortion Amendment'. Paper read to the Sociological Association of Ireland Conference, February, Co. Louth.

Burke, Sandra (1983) 'A Profile of the First 202 Women to Attend Open Door Counselling'. Dublin: Open Door Counselling Ltd.

Council for the Status of Women (1981) *Irish Women Speak Out*. Dublin: Co-Op Books.

Dean, G. (1984) 'Termination of Pregnancies, England, 1983. Women from the Republic of Ireland'. Dublin: Medico-Social Research Board.

Gaudin, Elizabeth (1983) 'Femmes dans l'Evolution de la Société Contemporaine en Republique d'Irlande'. PhD dissertation, University of Lille, France.

'No' (1983) *In Dublin*, 25 August, 186: 6–17.

Jackson, Pauline (1983) *The Deadly Solution to an Irish Problem — Backstreet Abortion*. Dublin: Women's Right to Choose Campaign.

Jackson, Pauline (1984) 'Women in Nineteenth-Century Irish Emigration', *International Migration Review*, 68(4): 1004–20

Jackson, Pauline (1986) 'Outside the Jurisdiction — Irish Women Seeking Abortion',

In C. Curtin, P. Jackson and B. O'Connor (eds), *Gender in Irish Society*. Galway: Galway University Press.

MacCurtain, Margaret and D. O'Corrain (eds) (1978) *Women in Irish Society — the Historical Dimension*. Dublin: Arlen House.

McCafferty, Nell (1985) *A Woman to Blame*. Dublin: Attic Press.

Minces, Juliette (1982) *House of Obedience — Women in Arab Society*. London: Zed Press.

Office of Population Censuses and Surveys (OPSC) (1984) *Abortion Statistics*. London: HMSO

Rose, R. (1977) 'An Outline of Fertility Control — Focusing on the Element of Abortion in the Republic of Ireland'. PhD dissertation, University of Stockholm.

Smyth, Ailbhe (1983) *Women's Rights in Ireland. Irish Council for Civil Liberties*. Dublin: Ward River Press.

Steiner-Scott, Liz (ed.) (1985) *Personally Speaking — Women's Thoughts on Women's Issues*. Dublin: Attic Press.

Ward, Margaret (1983) *The Unmanageable Revolutionaries — Women in Irish Nationalism*. Kerry: Brandon Press.

3
The feminist movement and abortion policy in the Netherlands

Joyce Outshoorn

Introduction

Without doubt, the abortion controversy has been the most prominent issue of the feminist movement that arose in Western Europe and the USA in the course of the 1960s. It was a central issue for the movement, as it was defined not only as a woman's right to choose, but also as a necessary condition for the reproductive freedom of women. As an issue, it also raises the question of the impact of the new movement, since few nations up to now have incorporated the feminist demand in law although many of them have reformed their existing laws over the past two decades. Also, very few nations have an on-going policy that even begins to approach the feminist ideal. In the Netherlands, women have had the right to choose an abortion since the 1970s, and abortion has also been widely available for women coming from abroad.

In this chapter I shall examine the impact of the Dutch feminist movement on this one issue: abortion. I shall first make some comments on the Dutch feminist movement; then I shall explain why abortion has not been perceived by government as part of the more general issue concerning the position of women. After that I shall develop my theoretical approach and consider the abortion controversy itself. My contentions are:

1. That the feminist movement played a major role in redefining the abortion issue, which has now achieved agenda-status (see below for a discussion of this concept) as a women's issue, whereas prior to the rise of the movement the issue was defined as a medical or psychiatric problem;

2. that the feminist movement has been quite successful in the course of the abortion struggle in speeding up political and parliamentary proceedings and in countering the usual Dutch political-style reaction to a contentious 'moral' issue.

The feminist movement in the Netherlands

Prior to 1968, which is the starting point for the renewed feminist movement, there were the so-called 'traditional' women's organizations such as the Nederlandse Bond voor Plattelandsvrouwen (Dutch

Federation of Countrywomen) and the Nederlandse Vereniging voor
Huisvrouwen (Dutch Federation of Housewives), with their Catholic
and Protestant affiliations and with very large memberships (in 1975,
about 300,0000 altogether). By statute politically neutral, they
concerned themselves with traditional women's activities such as
childcare, handicrafts, health and hygiene problems. Although since
1975 the feminist movement has influenced them, their reluctance to
get involved in politics has meant that they have played no role in the
abortion controversy, though they have organized discussions on it
(Dogro, 1976: 143–57).

Then there was the Vereniging voor Vrouwenbelangen (Union for
Women's Interests), a 'left-over' from the first wave of feminism, and
one of the very few feminist organizations that had kept up the fight
for equal rights during the 1950s and early 1960s. Attracting mainly
professional women as members, they had some contacts among the
Liberal and Socialist Parties. They were one of the first interest
groups to decide that abortion was a women's issue in which women
should have the final say. In addition to these organizations, there are
the women's groups in each of the political parties, the most
important of which is the Vrouwencontact in de Partij van de Arbeid
(Women's contact group within the Labour Party), which later
changed its name to the 'Red Women' (1972). Another important
group is the Vrouwenbond NVV (League of Women affiliated to the
socialist Dutch Confederation of Trade Unions), which traditionally
organized the wives of the trade-unionists. (See list of abbreviations
at end of chapter.)

The starting point of the new feminist movement is in 1968 (De
Vries, 1981; de Vries et al., 1984), when Man–Vrouw–Maatschappij
(Men–Women–Society) (MVM) started its career. This well
organized group of men and women, mainly well educated and many
of them with careers, can be compared to the American NOW,
although it never became so large. It set out to be a women's lobby
participating in the pressure group system, and up to 1975 it was a
major source of expertise on women's issues, of which the Labour–
Christian Democrat coalition made generous use. In fact, by that
time most of the top members had been coopted into government
committees on the status of women, and the ensuing loss of
leadership was at least one of the reasons for its decline in the later
1970s; more important probably is the arrival of other feminist
groups, as well as the changing ideological atmosphere, which
favoured less traditional forms of organization and politics.

But the feminist movement really 'took off' with the rise of Dolle
Mina (DM) in 1970, who attracted much publicity and whose name
almost became a generic term for 'liberated women'. An offshoot of
the various student and left-wing radical groups of the 1960s, it

attracted a wide following, but its success also proved a disadvantage as the group could not permanently organize itself through lack of leadership resources. It proved expert in using the media, having learned from the Dutch Provo movement, which was one of the forerunners of the youth protest in the 1960s, the tactics of imaginative confrontation. Men played a large part in the beginning of this organization, especially in the theoretical debates imported from the student movement. After its clearly anarchist start, Dolle Mina soon developed a rather orthodox Marxism. When consciousness-raising sprang up as one of the most important feminist activities a year later, men were excluded from DM activities and began to disappear. From 1972 onwards there was a proliferation of consciousness-raising groups, which started the process of rediscovering women's issues in new terms, no longer along the lines of liberal or socialist ideology.

There was no national platform, however. An attempt to link the many groups was made by the various Women's Congresses, and in 1974 by the platform of socialist–feminist groups; but neither led to any permanent form of organization. There was a radical-feminist tendency in the movement which stressed organizing women's centres and cafes, and a series of groups of changing political colour organized around single-issue campaigns such as day care, health issues, rape, women's aid projects, battered women, etc. Up to 1982 there was never at any time one major organization in which all groups were represented — except for the coalition formed for the abortion campaign in 1974, Wij Vrouwen Eisen (WVE) (We Women Demand), which is another factor making the abortion issue unique. In 1982 the Breed Platform (Broad Platform) was founded, uniting non-aligned women with party women covering all political parties, except the far right, on issues concerning economic independence.

The lack of a central organization has not meant that the Dutch feminist movement has not been effective. On the contrary: apart from the real changes that have taken place in the daily lives of thousands of women, the movement has also led to an enormous revival of feminism in all sorts of women's organizations, and especially in political parties and trade unions. Feminists are by now firmly entrenched not only in these, but also in many other sectors of society, such as education, social welfare and the like. At the moment the movement is still fragmented in many groups. The major division in it has become the question of whether to work through existing institutions, the famous 'long march through the institutions', or through women at the grass-roots level. Although this variance has always been in evidence, it has deepened during the last three years under the influence of the large extra-parliamentary activities of the anti-nuclear energy and anti-nuclear weapons movement and the squatters' movement. I will return to this point below when I discuss this division as it showed up in the abortion campaign coalition of WVE.

Abortion and public policy on women
Anticipating the UN's International Women's Year, the Netherlands government set up an official committee on the status of women in 1974. From 1977 onwards a public policy on the position of women emerged; since then, an under-secretary for 'Emancipation' has been responsible for this area of policy. Abortion, however, was not included in this domain of government policy. There are two major reasons for this.

First of all, abortion was the older issue; it had what I will call, following Van der Eijk and Kok (1975:286), *agenda-status* (the agenda is 'the set of issues, that is, problems recognized by decision-makers to be acted upon') before there was a policy on women by the national government. Abortion in the Netherlands emerged as a political problem in the mid-1960s, and by the end of that decade the government had implicitly acknowledged that something should be done about it as the nineteenth-century statutes prohibiting abortion in most instances were no longer feasible. As an issue, abortion had its network of interest groups; most political parties had taken a stand on it by 1972, and it was highly politicized by 1974 when the government acknowledged that the 'emancipation of women' also fell under its competence — in other words, the issue had reached agenda-status. This is not to say that the government did not previously have a policy on women, but that its policy, implicit in numerous provisions of the welfare state and in incomes and tax policy, pinned women down to the position of housewives and mothers. The emancipation policy was outlined in such a way that it was confined to 'making role change possible, helping women to make up for their second-rate position and re-appreciating feminine values', as official government reports phrase it. This meant that abortion was *excluded*, along with other reproductive issues such as contraception and women's health care. What was positive about this exclusion was that the controversial abortion issue could not 'contaminate' the newer issue of the emancipation of women. It must be said that this advantage has disappeared in the long run as the abortion issue was redefined as a women's issue, and women's emancipation became politicized as a result of debates around the anti-sex-discrimination legislation and the debate on a feminist incomes and social policy.

Second, the abortion issue was not perceived in terms of a women's issue by the various governments, whether the Liberal–Christian

Democrat coalition that was in power from 1973 to 1977. The former coalition produced a bill in 1972, which never made it to the vote, in which abortion was defined as a medical problem to be handled by a team of experts who could grant a woman an abortion if there were, it its opinion, sufficient medical or psychiatric grounds. The latter coalition tried to get rid of the abortion problem by not taking any legislative initiative and leaving it to parliament, because government members could not come to a unanimous view of the problem. However, by this time a woman's right to choose had become one of the two issues on which public discussion had centred, with a majority already in favour of it.

In this chapter I will concentrate on this redefinition of the abortion issue. I will try to answer the question of what part the feminist movement played in redefining the issue in such a way that all legislative efforts that were brought into parliament after 1972 were judged, by all actors concerned, in terms of who had the power to decide over an abortion; in other words, in terms of how much room it left for women to choose. Prior to 1972, abortion had been seen as a medical or ethical problem to be judged by experts; later, it became a woman's issue on which most people felt they were competent to judge. As I shall show, this transition was due in large part to the efforts of the feminist movement. Abortion is one of the issues through which the movement confronted the state and on which it had to fight the state through the regular channels of politics, whether it liked it or not. Given the ideals held by a large part of the movement, with its emphasis on direct democracy, the importance of small-scale organization and face-to-face contacts and its egalitarian ideology, dealing with parliamentary strategy, government committees and political parties brought along some specific problems.

Abortion politics
The Netherlands had a strict prohibition of abortion laid down in statutes dating from 1886 and 1911. In practice, there was some leeway for therapeutic abortion, but very few were carried out on these grounds. As in other Western European countries and the USA, the 1960s became the decade in which abortion resurfaced as a problem and became part of public debate, after which pressure was mounted on the national governments to revise or repeal the restrictive legislation. I will not go into the causes of this change (on the Netherlands, see Ketting, 1978; Veenhoven, 1975). While the Dutch national government looked on from a distance, various medical practitioners, aided by a more liberal interpretation of the old statute by an eminent legal authority, Prof. Enschedé (Enschedé,

1966), started experimentally to validate psychological and social grounds for abortion, working with so-called teams of 'experts' who considered all cases applying for an abortion. However, these doctors could in no way meet the huge demand for abortion that was surfacing by the end of the 1960s. Initiatives by Stimezo (Foundation for Responsible Medical Abortion) and the NVSH (Dutch Society for Sexual Reform), backed by women's groups, resulted in their setting up their own clinics in which abortion on demand became the regular practice.

By 1973 it had become possible for most women in the Netherlands to get an abortion, not in the state-subsidized hospitals but in private clinics, which also catered for many women from abroad who could not get abortions in their own countries. It is notable that the government refrained from prosecuting these initiatives: there was a sort of gentlemen's agreement not to interfere until there was a new bill, so long as there were no 'excesses'. The government lagged behind in its reaction. It took until 1972 for it to come up with a bill (which had been preceded by a private member's bill in 1970, on which no vote had been taken), and only in 1981 was a repeal bill passed. This led to the paradoxical situation that the Netherlands had a most restrictive statute until 1981, but probably had the most liberal and easily available abortion situation except for perhaps Sweden and Denmark.

Why, then, did it take until 1981 to reach a repeal? Referring to the controversial character of the abortion issue is not a sufficient explanation, because controversial questions can always be settled by a parliamentary majority (Van de Eijk and Outshoorn, 1980). Of course, abortion *is* a controversial issue, and one not easily solved, as it is about conflicting values. (For other countries see Neef, 1979; Tatalovich and Daynes, 1981; Greenwood and Young, 1976; Marsh and Chambers, 1981; Yisai, 1978; Swärd, 1982; Ketting, 1978; Outshoorn and van Soest, 1977 and De Bruin, 1979.) Following Stokes (1966: 170–1), one can say that abortion is a *position issue* rather than a *valence issue*. Valence issues refer to a general good on which everybody is agreed; differences in opinion occur in the method of strategy to be adopted to reach the goal, not about the goal itself. Position issues are issues in which there is no agreement on *ends*, which means there are always two or more conflicting positions. They are more difficult to solve, as compromises are often not feasible. The role of the state in the abortion issue strengthens its position-issue character: in the view of the pro-choice movement, the state should refrain from interference in what is defined as a private matter; while in the view of the anti-repeal movement, the state should uphold the sanctity of life. Abortion is a position issue; compromises have proved hard to reach and new creative 'in-between' solutions are unlikely (Van der Eijk and Outshoorn, 1980: 222; Outshoorn, 1984).

But abortion was not always a position issue. It became one through the process of issue definition. A study of the issue's life-cycle shows us that other alternative definitions and solutions were whittled away in this process. In the Netherlands this happened in such a way that abortion became a one-dimensional issue, judged in terms of who decides whether or not a woman will have an abortion. Parliament and the government had held off for so long that by the time the issue had become polarized around the two 'extremes' they had lost almost all leeway in which to manoeuvre. Public opinion and the interest groups watched over their shoulders and followed their steps very closely. They had placed themselves in an 'off-side' position, but they had good reasons for doing so.

Trying to avoid the issue

If its position-issue character is not a sufficient explanation, one should look at the peculiarities of the Dutch party system and political culture. The Netherlands is always governed by a coalition government of various parties, of which the Christian Democrats (CDA) always are a partner, as they are usually the largest party. Before 1977 there were three Christian parties; then they fused. They are in power alternately with the Liberals (VVD) or the Dutch Labour Party (PvdA), as no party can form a majority government on its own. The Christian Democrat position on abortion is influenced by Christian morality, which made the party unwilling to bring any change in the existing statutes. However, as the dominant dimension in Dutch politics is formed by socio-economic issues, which also decide who forms the coalition governments, the tendency in Dutch politics is to avoid issues such as abortion that cut across this dimension: not only will parties be internally divided on such issues, but the old religious–secular dimension in Dutch politics is reactivated. So the political parties will avoid having to confront potentially disruptive issues. Lijphart (1968) has delineated the 'rules of the game' in the Netherlands when such issues occur. Several tactics will be adopted by party elites and the government. They will try to delay taking any sort of action, by denying for instance that the government has any responsibility for the matter, or by installing a research committee. Or they will try to depoliticize issues by defining them as technical matters or matters requiring expert knowledge, and leaving the solution to the experts. Or they may adopt a combination of these tactics. Both strategies have been tried by the successive coalition governments in various stages of the life-cycle of the abortion issue. However, the changes in public opinion about abortion in the 1970s left the government little room to reach a compromise. There was a growing majority in favour of women's right to choose; this was unacceptable for the Christian Democrats and a constant minority of around 15 per cent who were opposed to abortion on any grounds and who censured even the Christian Democrat politicians sharply (Outshoorn, 1981).

1981 — finally a new bill
In 1981 a new bill was finally enacted by parliament; it received a majority of only one in the Second Chamber and a small majority in the First Chamber. This was a government bill of the Liberal–Christian Democrat coalition. Both parties were eager to get rid of the issue, which meant that (1) the Christian Democrats watered down their principles by implicitly accepting a woman's right to choose (the bill uses more mystifying language) and (2) the Liberals watered down their principle (the freedom of conscience) by making the vote in parliament a party-line matter. Abortion had been a 'free' issue in parliament from 1973 onwards; now individual conscience was subordinated to party discipline. This time the Liberals voted en bloc for the bill. Compared with countries in which the abortion vote was a free issue, this is a major exception (Marsh and Chambers, 1981; Yisai, 1978; Swärd, 1982; Neef, 1979; Tatalovich and Daynes, 1981). The danger was the risk of having to start all over again right from the beginning, which could lead to a split in the coalition and the fall of the cabinet: this is a risk nobody wants to take in a political system in which government coalition formation is an extremely tortuous affair.

The agenda-building approach
The agenda-building, or agenda-setting, approach studies the policy process from the point of view of the life-cycle of an issue. Various authors have by now contributed to this approach (see Bachrach and Baratz, 1970; Cobb and Elder, 1972; van der Eijk and Kok, 1975; Cobb, Ross and Ross, 1976; Nelson, 1978; Kok, 1981; Dahlerup, 1984; and, as applied to the abortion issue, Dogro, 1976; Yisai, 1978; Tatalovich and Daynes, 1981; Swärd, 1982). Agenda-building conceives of the political process as a series of consecutive stages; the political agenda is the sum of political issues up for consideration for some set of authorities (Kok, 1981:9) This approach tries to answer the question of why some issues, and not the multitude of many other issues and alternatives, make it to the decision-making stage — in other words, to agenda-status.

Here I will use van der Eijk and Kok's (1975) idea of the *political agenda* and refine it following Swärd (1982:3), so that I will speak of agenda-status as 'the moment that decision-makers recognize an issue as to be acted upon, either by: forming an official government committee to investigate the issue, or by taking the initiative themselves by having a measure drafted in the cabinet bureaucracy, or leaving it to parliament, which takes the ultimate decision in a parliamentary system'. Swärd does not mention the case in which parliament itself takes the initiative because the government has not taken any steps itself (which happened in the Netherlands during the abortion struggle, and also occurred in Britain).

On how issues attain agenda-status there is an abundant literature. For my discussion of the stages following the attainment of agenda-status, I will begin with three observations gleaned from the relevant literature:

1. There is the importance of issue-maintenance for groups striving for change. Interest groups should keep the issue alive until the point of substantive decision-making (Nelson, 1978:21). I will divide this into two targets: keeping the issues fresh in the mind of the public, and keeping them fresh in the minds of government and other legislative bodies. Put more formally, attention-holding is necessary, as it tends to become marginalized in a party system based on socio-economic cleavages. Of course, it is not always necessary to keep an issue in the mind of the public: some issues don't need public support; in other cases it may even be counter-productive. For abortion, however, it was necessary.
2. The issue may become 'perverted'. Van der Eijk and Kok (1975) point out, following Bachrach and Baratz (1970), that the decision-makers may take up only a part of the original demand for serious consideration or may modify the issue through the process of demand aggregation. At stake for interest groups, then, is the need to maintain their definition of the issue through lobbying parliament and bureaucrats. This is also a form of issue-maintenance, but in the sense of maintaining the definition.
3. If an issue tends to become politicized for a longer period of time, the authorities will tend to withdraw it (Hall et al., 1975:30).

All these aspects may be discerned in Dutch abortion politics in the decision-making stages. I will follow Van der Eijk and Kok's model, adapted from Bachrach and Baratz, as it has the strength of precise concepts and is tied to the idea of Cobb and Elder (1972) about the political agenda. Following the major concepts of Van der Eijk and Kok, which they adapt from Easton (1965), there are

1. *Wants*: 'opinions, interests, ideologies and similar ideas and attitudes which are cognised in a non-political way, i.e. which are not perceived as ultimately dependent for their fulfilment upon the political process';
2. *Demands*: politicized wants. In the words of Easton, 'a person or

group must be brought to the point of giving voice to the idea that the members charged with the responsibility for making binding decisions ought to enact as to fulfill this demand' (Easton, 1965:80);

3. *Issues*: these are not clearly differentiated by Easton, but Van der Eijk and Kok define them as 'demands which are recognized by the decision-makers as problems to be decided upon: they are demands which become part of the agenda for decision-making' (1975:283). The idea of the political agenda is tied to this concept of issue and to the crossing of the barrier, 'demand–issue conversion'.

Van der Eijk and Kok then divide the policy process into five stages, with a barrier between each:

Wants	Demands	Issues	Decisions	Outputs
1	2	3	4	

— *Barrier 1*: prevention of want–demand conversion;
— *Barrier 2*: prevention of issue formation and demand perversion: once this hurdle is taken, a demand becomes an issue; it has achieved agenda-status;
— *Barrier 3*: decision-making (in which issue-perversion can take place) or postponement;
— *Barrier 4*: implementation: here, perversion is again a possibility, as is non-implementation.

In their model it is not quite clear when an issue reaches the political agenda: here I consider it to be attained when the third barrier is passed.

Abortion politics: crossing the barriers
Wants: want–demand conversion
In discussing the life-cycle of issues, one major problem has always been to prove that there are objective needs whose conversion to demands is prevented by a 'non-decision' — for instance, by prevailing norms and values and ideology — without falling into the trap that the researcher (or political group, for that matter) knows better than the people involved what is good for them. Lukes (1974: 41, 45) has pointed to the necessity of the search for 'the relevant counterfactual', to show that there is a non-decision operating to prevent want–demand conversion. Various routes out of this dilemma have been explored (Crenson, 1971; Bachrach and Baratz, 1970:49 (who deny that one can prove a non-decision at this stage empirically); Van der Eijk and Kok, 1975; Dahlerup, 1984; Offe, 1972).

For abortion, the problem of finding the relevant counterfactual is not so difficult. It lies in the fact of illegal abortions and the well-documented history of the lengths that women will go to in their attempt to get rid of an unwanted foetus. It is not unreasonable to suppose that women will prefer clean and safe abortions if these can be provided, a supposition that is borne out by the rise in the demand for abortions once doctors started to perform them openly, and by the accompanying decline of illegal abortion. Estimates of illegal abortion vary; Treffers and De Winter (1965, 1966) put the figure anywhere between 14,000 and 60,000 a year in the Netherlands. That the number of women coming to doctors for abortions in the mid-1960s increased is also testified in various sources (Ketting, 1978).

At this stage it was the doctors who started to break the taboo covering up the subject, but they were aided by the publicity surrounding the thalidomide scare in the early 1960s, when a drug sometimes prescribed to pregnant women caused deformities in foetuses. The first dissertations on abortion were published around 1965, giving careful opinions about permitting abortion. But even then non-medical people were beginning to make more outright demands for a woman's right to choose. Not a few of these non-medical people were women, which is significant because in public debate in the Netherlands women had tended to take the backstage. By 1967 public debate on the abortion issue was well under way: articles had begun to appear in the popular press and there was an important television documentary of one of the major networks that year. From then on, two steps can be described in the process of converting want into demand.

First, there was the matter of the doctors. Their primary concern was to be able to perform abortions on a modest scale without risking prosecution. Armed with the authoritative interpretation of Enschedé, which advocated the performance of therapeutic abortions, they started carrying out abortions after a team of 'experts' had interviewed the woman making the request. This liberalized practice, however, actually *prevented* the formation of a demand, for it made it seem unnecessary to change the law. Ketting and De Bruin (1979) have stressed the role of the medical profession at this stage in making abortion possible; but the political demand for changing the law came from other quarters, and in this issue therefore the medical profession was no pioneer.

Second, there were the emerging interest groups who came forward with the first demands. The demand for changing the law was voiced by the small Pacifist Socialist Party in their election programme of 1967; they were the only party to have any sort of demand on abortion. In 1968 the leadership of the Vrouwencontact declared that the law should be changed and that abortion be permitted for any woman demanding it. In 1967 the NVSH came up with the same demand, and MVM, Dolle Mina and the Federatie van Instellingen voor Ongehuwde Moeders (Federation of Institutes for Unwed Mothers, FIOM) followed soon after. By then the barrier of want–demand conversion had definitely been crossed.

Demand–issue conversion

Most of the professional groups concerned with abortions had by now come up with reports on abortion, none of which, except for the Vereniging voor Psychiatrie en Neurologie (Association for Psychiatry and Neurology), advocated much more than the recognition of medical and psychological grounds for an abortion. The big change in medical circles came after the demand to change the law in favour of a woman's right to choose had firmly caught the public's attention. Basic to the change in medical opinion was the bankruptcy of the team approach. Ketting (1978) has described this well: teams could no longer cope with the huge demand for abortions; there were great differences in the criteria for granting an abortion, which led to more lenient and less lenient teams; and the doctors themselves became convinced that any sort of approach based on 'medical, social or psychological' grounds was becoming untenable.

Three developments speeded up the demand–issue conversion:

1. A group of doctors in Stimezo decided in 1971–2 to open abortion clinics which started to perform abortions on demand. This is not how they publicized it, probably wisely, but it was the way they worked in practice.

2. Dolle Mina made abortion on demand a central issue from the very beginning. It was its spectacular action at a gynaecologists' congress in 1970 that made its abortion slogan, 'Baas in eigen Buik' ('Boss of one's own Body'), almost a household word in the Netherlands and the Dutch form of the demand for a woman's right to choose. Women gate-crashed the conference with the slogan written across their bare stomachs. Dolle Mina gave financial support to Stimezo by collecting money in the streets.

3. Two Labour politicians, Lamberts (a doctor) and Roethof (a legal expert), introduced a private member's bill in 1971 in the Second Chamber of parliament. In this draft the woman and her doctor jointly were to decide about an abortion (Roethof, 1982). Lamberts and Roethof responded to demands in the Labour Party, especially the Vrouwencontact, and entered the bill despite the opposition of some of their fellow Labour MPs.

After 1971 the differences between 'Baas in eigen Buik' as a demand and 'The woman decides with her doctor' were lost in the political controversy. There remained an ideological difference, but in everyday politics this meant little. This merging was due to the solid opposition to both demands by most 'moderates' and the anti-abortion lobby, so that one pro-choice front originated (composed of the feminist movement, Stimezo, the NVSH, the Labour Party, two of the small left-wing parties and the neo-liberal Democraten '66 (D'66)). Also, concerning the day-to-day routine of abortion practice, there was no difference either. On the one hand, abortions by medical professionals were unavoidable, as the public prosecution was ignoring them but clamping down on 'quack' abortions. On the other hand, the doctors' power was not absolute; a woman requesting an abortion had already made up her mind by the time she came with her request, which proved irreversible in most cases, so that a doctor could either give her an abortion or see her go off to a colleague who would do so. At this stage, the importance of the activities of the feminist movement in redefining the abortion issue can best be summed up in the words of Ketting (1978:8; my translation):

> The role the emancipation movement plays from now on in the further developments is first and foremost this: it impedes individualization of the problem. Abortion is regarded as a principle directly connected with the oppressed position and rights of women. And that means that the justification of the medical intervention (the abortion-job) becomes divorced from the arbitrary situation of just any individual woman.

For the conversion of demand to issue to take place, in other words for an issue to attain agenda-status, the government has to acknowledge that it is part of its task to do something about the problem under consideration. The Liberal–Christian Democrat coalition in power from 1967 to 1971 had maintained silence in spite of the public debate, and the Minister of Justice had said explicitly, in answer to questions by MPs, that he wanted to let the matter rest so that opinion among the medical professionals could be formed and they could come up with a solution. By 1968 it became clear that the medical professionals, despite the wish of most of them not to change the law, could not reach a consensus, so after increasing pressure from the Labour opposition (who in their turn were pressed by their women's organization), the government in 1969 installed the inevitable study committee (the Committee Kloosterman, named after its chairman, a professor who performed abortions at the renowned University of Amsterdam hospital). The government responded to the demand from women's organizations to have women on the committee; this turned out to be on a fifty–fifty basis because, as the Under-Minister of Health said, 'there are a lot of emotions attached [to abortion], which differ for women and men' (De Bruin, 1979:179). Thus, although it was admitted that abortion was in some way a women's issue, this slender recognition disappeared later. Agenda-status had been achieved by the route of a government committee, but the problem reached the agenda defined as a social problem, not as a women's issue.

The decision-making stage

The issue had reached agenda-status, but what next? The Committee Kloosterman, staffed according to the best tradition of 'the politics of accommodation' (Lijphart, 1968), which meant that all views were represented, came up with a divided report in 1971, so that a stalemate threatened. It became important for the pro-choice front to keep the issue on the agenda and to prevent its perversion. At first it was Dolle Mina with its spectacular actions which succeeded in keeping abortion in the public eye. Individual members also resorted to traditional lobbying of MPs. The formation of the coalition Wij Vrouwen Eisen (WVE) in 1974 was the next important step. Initiators were ex-Dolle Minas; they managed to organize a broad front of women from political parties (mainly the left-wing ones), the Women's League of the NVV, MVM and Dolle Mina.

The WVE followed a double strategy. First, they carried on lobbying and keeping up contacts with other pro-choice groups. This was important when the government and its parties tried to withdraw the issue. But they also aimed at keeping the issue in the public's attention by staging demonstrations, holding grass-roots actions such as public meetings and handing out leaflets. In addition, many articles appeared in newspapers and weeklies, and there was regular television coverage. The polls indicated a growing majority supporting a woman's right to choose; other research showed that, of many political issues, abortion was the issue on which most people felt most competent to have an opinion and it scored the lowest number of 'Don't knows'. This indicates its politicization but also its redefinition as a non-expert matter (Van der Eijk and Outshoorn, 1980).

In public opinion research it also is interesting to examine the alternatives that were being asked: they themselves are an indication of the alternatives being debated on in society at large. By 1976, all sorts of 'grounds' on which abortion should be/not be possible had disappeared from public questionnaires (Outshoorn, 1981). Another contribution to issue-maintenance (in the sense of holding the public's attention) was the private member's bill of Lamberts and Roethof, still languishing in parliament, which forced the government to come up with its own bill in 1972, and forced other parties at a later stage to draw up new bills.

The *anti*-abortion groups were also important in keeping the issue in the public eye. In response to the rise of the pro-choice front, they demanded that the government enforce the old statutes, and they were quick to point out, when government and various parties came up with their own proposals, that these were a digression from the old statutes. In 1976 they presented 600,000 signatures to parliament demanding maintenance of the 'right to life'. Their support remained confined to religious minority groups and traditional Catholics, and their demand received little support from parliament, although it contributed to the delay of the reform.

Issue-modification (or perversion — depending on one's point of view) is another 'danger' in this stage of the life-cycle of an issue. As we have seen, by 1972 abortion practice was firmly grounded in a woman's right to choose and there was a growing number of people speaking out in support of this alternative. When the Liberal–Christian Democrat government finally produced a bill, it was at least three steps backward, and a clear case of issue-perversion. The bill proposed a 'team' solution, and included a rule that abortions could be performed only in hospitals; as the majority of them were taking place in clinics on an out-patient basis, this would have curtailed most abortions. It also introduced a twelve-week barrier beyond which abortion would not be allowed, another new definition of the issue. The bill met widespread opposition, this time also from the organized medical profession, which had learned to live with the fact of the clinics. It was shelved through the fall of the coalition government that year (on a totally different issue), and the succeeding government withdrew it. This coalition, a Socialist–Christian Democrat one, tried to get rid of the problem by leaving the legislative initiative to parliament, where it was to be a 'free' question. This was a feasible proposal, leaving the old statute on the books and the abortion activities untouched. But the Catholic Minister of Justice did not stick to this gentlemen's agreement and in 1974 tried to shut down one of the clinics, the only one performing abortions after thirteen weeks of pregnancy. When he tried to do so for a second time in 1976, feminists prevented it by occupying the clinic, 'Bloemenhove', and keeping the police out. This provided a great opportunity for issue-maintenance: it made headlines for two weeks running — an act of civil disobedience that received widespread support from the public at large, and also from some in the cabinet!

This action forced an abandonment of the postponement strategy, for now all three major parties in parliament and most of the pro-choice activists were convinced of the need for a new bill. A Liberal–Socialist proposal encompassing a woman's right to choose was passed by the Second Chamber in 1976, but failed in the First Chamber at the end of that year. The Liberals split and several of them voted down their colleagues' private member's bill.

It took until 1981 for a new bill to reach the voting stage. The Liberal–Christian Democrat coalition government came up with a proposal that received a majority of one in the Second Chamber and a very narrow majority in the First Chamber. It was passed because all major parties wanted to be rid of the issue; it was causing too much internal turmoil and kept interfering with the coalition-formation of governments.

At first glance the new bill looks like a redefinition of the abortion issue. It has a woolly clause about the woman and her doctor who take the decision between them; the woman has to think it over for five days before her request is granted. The private clinics that perform the bulk of all abortions will have to apply for a licence. The effects of this bill are hard to foresee, but many women in the movement regard it as a failure because of the paternalistic five-day clause (which is meant to stop women from abroad from having abortions in the Netherlands).

Summing up this stage, the most important breakthrough was that Dolle Mina and WVE managed to break two Dutch 'rules of the game': the postponement strategy and the depoliticization-of-issues strategy. Their definition of the situation won through: all bills proposed after 1972 were judged by all actors in the light of how much freedom was given to the woman to decide. Dolle Mina and the WVE also managed to keep the major parties from 'backsliding', especially the Labour Party, which, although it was 'pro-choice', found the issue too much of a nuisance in its dealings with the Christian Democrats. The three slogans of the WVE campaign —

— Abortion is not a criminal matter and should not be included in the penal code;
— Abortion should be refunded to all women by national insurance;
— The woman decides —

have become the slogans for the whole pro-choice movement. And they are widely known among the Dutch public.

Implementation
The 1981 bill did not go into effect immediately. Several crucial parts had been left open to be worked out by further government regulation. The decision-making procedure between a woman and her doctor had to be clarified; and there was also the matter of licensing the clinics. It has taken three years to work these out; in May 1984 the regulations were finally passed by cabinet and the law went into effect on 1 December 1984. It took so long because none of the major parties had much interest in bringing up the divisive issue again; also, the feminist movement now had little interest in speeding up matters, as the bill was seen to lead to less satisfactory abortion procedures than the one in practice, which in fact works according to a woman's

right to choose. It is too early to say in what respects this right will be circumscribed; but the five-day clause will hinder women seeking abortions from abroad; several clinics in the Catholic south may not be licensed, which means poor access for women living there; and doctors may become more reluctant to perform abortions as the new regulations demand written medical evidence that the abortion was inevitable on 'objective grounds'.

Effects of the abortion campaign on the feminist movement, in particular WVE
Because the abortion issue had achieved agenda status by the time the feminist movement emerged, its groups were more or less forced to occupy themselves with parliamentary politics. This had not been a problem for MVM, which saw itself as a pressure group the aim of which was to lobby. Nor was it a problem for the women's groups within the political parties; their problems lay in the domain of a divided loyalty between their party and the autonomous groups of the movement. Both MVM and the women's party organizations had a traditional structure of regional groups with a national, representative council; the continuity that this ensured helped them to cope with a long-term parliamentary struggle. This was far more difficult for the autonomous or non-aligned groups.

The coalition of WVE encountered a series of problems when faced with the long-term campaign. WVE can be seen as a part of the autonomous movement, although it had partywomen among its activists. It is a loosely organized umbrella organization on the national level; there is also a network of local committees in most of the major cities. To be able to sustain the long struggle, aimed at keeping the abortion issue on the agenda and maintaining public interest in it, it had to organize more formally than the spontaneous action group that started with a demonstration in 1974. Ideological currents in the movement at the time were becoming very distrustful of formal organization; the small group was the most common and popular form. It took about two years before WVE had established a more formal structure and procedures for taking democratic decisions.

Another problem lay in its coalition character. Apart from the predictable differences on strategy (on the slogans of the campaign there was unanimity after 1975), a procedure had to be developed on how to represent large organizations such as the Red Women on the one hand and individual, non-organized women on the other. A compromise was reached after some years: representatives of large organizations had three votes; individual women, one vote. To keep up a good lobby campaign it is necessary to have regular contacts with relevant MPs and with other pro-choice groups such as Stimezo and

NVSH; also, the mass media prefer dealing with the same women. The ideology in the feminist movement of equality — the idea that one woman's opinion is as good as another's, with its accompanying distrust of leaders and 'stars', and also of expertise and knowledge — was a handicap from this point of view. Spokeswomen, contacts and tasks kept changing.

Less of a problem than might be expected were the political resources that women in WVE brought along. Several feminists had acquired political experience in the student movement and the know-how of the mass media of Dolle Mina. Women from the political parties had their networks of influence and their organizational skills. The cooperation worked well till 1977; then the near sell-out of the socialists on the issue during the negotiations for a coalition government (when the leadership of the Red Women followed the party but their local chapters backed the views of WVE) caused permanent tension.

After several years of campaigning, with this continual dilemma at grass-roots level, there emerged a definitive dislike of parliament, political parties and the 'rules of the game'. Women's traditional distrust of politics combined with the heritage of the 1960s and its radical politics and with a feminist ideology that politics was all male anyway. In addition, given the experience of the campaign, in which the politicians were so eager to get rid of the issue that issue-perversion was for them the solution and not the problem, it can hardly be surprising that during 1981 an anti-parliamentary line won out in WVE. The movement lost its coalition character, and the party-political women left.

The division was sharpened by a 'generation gap' which has emerged in the whole feminist movement: the younger generation does not share the more optimistic view of social and political change held by women socialized into politics in the 1960s and early 1970s. Illustrative of this is the shift in the meaning of the word 'autonomous'; for the generation of the 1960s, this had meant autonomy from male political parties and groups and the right to organize one's own group or caucus. For the younger women, 'autonomous' has come to mean 'outside of the existing institutions and society'. This internal division is exacerbated by the dilemma WVE faced in 1981 of whether to press for a new law in the hope of blocking implementation of the 1981 bill, or to forget about parliament altogether and start to think about performing self-help abortions.

Conclusions

As I have already noted, Dolle Mina and WVE managed to break the rules of the game, which is an achievement in Dutch politics. Their definition of the issue won out; after 1972, all bills were judged in terms of how much freedom was given to women to choose an abortion. They managed to keep the Labour Party from selling out too soon, and their slogans for the campaign were the ones that became the slogans for the whole pro-choice campaign.

Another conclusion is that the feminist movement did indeed play a major role in the redefinition of this issue. It should be said, though, that this was not only through their skilful campaigning, but also because the existing abortion aid had proved that other definitions of the issue were not feasible. And the whole pro-choice front could only operate under the gentlemen's agreement of the legal and political elite that the old statute would not be enforced as long as abortions were done by competent medical professionals. But it took all the pressure of the pro-choice groups to keep a new bill on the agenda and to maintain their issue-definition. Parties would have preferred to keep the matter non-politicized and quiet, but this was not acceptable to either the pro-choice or the anti-choice group. This makes the question of whether it would have been better to keep the issue non-politicized and low-key and to have depended on the gentlemen's agreement — as has been suggested by the medical profession and some leading commentators — rather academic. Undoubtedly, that would have saved a lot of energy; but it did not work. A gentlemen's agreement works only if all those concerned are gentlemen, that is, are willing to keep it up. And the Minister of Justice proved that he was not willing to keep it by trying to shut down an important clinic on an insufficient pretext.

A third conclusion is that the abortion issue gave the feminist movement a tremendous opportunity to mobilize and to achieve high visibility. But this is not the reason why the movement chose to organize on the issue: one can say the issue chose us a long time before.

List of abbreviations

CDA   Christen Democratisch Appel (Christian Democrat Appeal)
D'66   Democraten '66 (Liberal Party)
DM   Dolle Mina
FIOM   Federatie van Instellingen voor Ongehuwde Moeders (Federation of Insti-
       tutes for Unwed Mothers)
MVM   Man–Vrouw–Maatschappij (Men–Women–Society)
NOW   National Organization of Women (USA)
NVSH   Nederlandse Vereniging voor Sexuele Hervorming (Dutch Society for Sexual
       Reform)
NVV   Nederlands Verbond van Vakverenigingen (Dutch Confederation of Trade
       Unions)
PvdA   Partij van de Arbeid (Dutch Labour Party)
Stimezo Stichting voor Medisch Verantwoorde Zwangerschapsonderbreking (Found-
       ation for Responsible Medical Abortion)

VVD   Volkspartij voor Vrijheid en Democratie (People's Party for Liberty and
        Democracy)
WVE   Wij Vrouwen Eisen (We Women Demand)

With thanks to Cees van der Eijk, Jan van Putten, Selma Sevenhuijsen and Petra de
Vries for their comments.

References

Bachrach, P., and M. S. Baratz (1970) *Power and Poverty. Theory and Practice.* New
    York: Oxford University Press.
Bruin, J. de (1979) *Geschiedenis van de abortus in Nederland.* Amsterdam: Van
    Gennep.
Cobb, R. W. and C. D. Elder (1972) *Participation in American Politics. The Dynamics
    of Agenda-building.* Boston: Allyn and Bacon.
Cobb, R. W., J. Keith Ross, and M. H. Ross (1976) 'Agenda-building as a Com-
    parative Approach', *American Political Science Review,* 70(1):126–38.
Crenson, M. A. (1971) *The Un-politics of Air Polution: A study of Non-decision-
    making in the Cities.* Baltimore-London: Johns Hopkins Press.
Dahlerup, D. (1984) 'Overcoming the Barriers: An Approach to How Women's Issues
    Are Kept from the Political Agenda', pp. 31–66 in Judith H. Stiehm, *Women's
    View of the Political World of Men.* New York: Transnational.
Dogro, (1976) *Abortus in Nederland, 1965–1975. Een onderzoek naar abortus als
    politiek strijdpunt.* Report, Department of Political Science, Section on Collective
    Political Behaviour, University of Amsterdam.
Easton, D. (1965) *A Systems Analysis of Political Life.* New York: John Wiley.
Eijk, C. van der and W. J. P. Kok (1975) 'Non-decisions Reconsidered', *Acta Politica,*
    10 (3): 277–301.
Eijk, C. van der and J. Outshoorn (1980) 'Too Hot to Handle: Abortus als politiek
    strijdpunt', pp. 220–42 in G. A. Banck et al. (eds), *Gestalten van de dood.* Baarn:
    Ambo.
Enschede, C. J. (1966) 'Abortus op medische indicatie en strafrecht', *Nederlands
    Tijdschrift voor Geneeskunde,* 110: 1349–53; reprinted in *Nederlands Juristenblad,*
    41: 1109–18.
Francome, C. (1984) *Abortion Freedom. A Worldwide Movement.* London: Allen &
    Unwin.
Greenwood, V. and J. Young (1976) *Abortion on Demand.* London: Pluto Press.
Hall, P., H. Land, R. Parker and A. Webb (1975). *Change, Choice and Conflict in
    Social Policy.* London: Heinemann.
Ketting, E. (1978) *Van misdrijf tot hulpverlening. Een analyse van de maatschappelijke
    betekenis van abortus provocatus in Nederland.* Alphen a.d. Rijn: Samson.
Kok, W. J. P. (1981) *Signalering en selectie. Rapport over een onderzoek naar de
    agendavorming van de rijksdienst.* The Hague: Staatsuitgeverij. Achter-
    grondstudie no. 3, Cie. Hoofdstructuur Rijksdienst, Ministerie van Binnenlandse
    Zaken.
Lowi, T. (1964) 'American Business, Public Policy, Case Studies and Political
    Science', *World Politics,* 16: 677–715.
Lijphart, A. (1968) *Verzuiling, pacificatie en kentering in de Nederlandse politiek.*
    Amsterdam: De Bussy. (Dutch version of *The Politics of Accommodation:
    Pluralism and Democracy in the Netherlands,* Berkeley: University of California
    Press, 1968.)

Lukes, S. (1974) *Power: A Radical View*. London: Macmillan.

Marsh, D. and J. Chambers (1981) *Abortion Politics*. London: Junction Books.

Neef, M. Huss (1979) *Policy-formation and Implementation in the Abortion Field*. Ann Arbor, Michigan: University Microfilms International.

Nelson, B. J. (1978) 'Setting the Public Agenda: The Case of Child Abuse', in J. V. May and A. Wildavsky (eds), *The Policy Cycle*. Beverley Hills/London: Sage.

Offe, C. (1972) 'Klassenherrschaft und politisches System, Die Selektivität politischen Institutionen', in C. Offe, *Strukturprobleme des kapitalistischen Staates. Aufsätze zur politischen Soziologie*. Frankfurt a.M.: Suhrkamp.

Outshoorn, J. (1981) 'Bent U van mening dat dit wetsvoorstel niet deugt?' pp. 143–7 in *Meningen over abortus in Nederland*. Amsterdam: Kongresbundel Zomeruniversiteit Vrouwenstudies.

Outshoorn, J. (1984) 'What's in a Name? Abortion as a Political Issue'. ECPR paper, Salzburg, Joint Sessions and Workshops.

Outshoorn, J. and M. van Soest (1977) *Lijfsbehoud. Tien jaar abortusstrijd in Nederland (1967–1977)*. The Hague: Dolle Mina.

Roethof, H. (1982) *De abortuskwestie en meer dan dat*. The Hague: Stimezo Nederland.

Stokes, D. (1966) 'Spatial Models of Party Competition', pp. 161–79 in A. Campbell et al. (eds), *Elections and the Political Order*. New York: John Wiley; reprinted in *American Political Science Review*, 57: 368–78.

Swärd, S. (1982) 'How Sweden Changed its Abortion Policy'. ECPR paper, Aarhus, Joint Sessions and Workshops.

Tatalovich, R. and B. W. Daynes (1981) *The Politics of Abortion. A Study of Community Conflict in Public Policymaking*. New York: Praeger.

Treffers, P. (1965) *Abortus provocatus en anticonceptie*. Haarlem, Erven Bohn.

Veenhoven, R. (1975) 'Vier jaar abortus in Nederland. De kernproblemen van liberalisering in stilte opgelost', *Medisch Contact*, 30: 37–42.

Vries, P. de (1981) 'Feminism in the Netherlands', *International Women's Studies Quarterly*, 4(4): 389–409.

Vries, P. de, S. Sevenhuysen, J. Outshoorn and A. Meulenbelt (eds) (1984) *A Creative Tension. Essays in Socialist Feminism*. London: Pluto Press.

Walker, J. L. (1977) 'Setting the Agenda in the US Senate: A Theory of Problem Selection', *British Journal of Political Science*, 7: 423–45.

Winter, R. E. de (1966) *Abortus provocatus*. Deventer: Kluwer.

Yisai, Y. (1978) 'Abortion in Israel: Social Demand and Political Response', *Policy Studies Journal*, 7: 270–90.

4

Radical democracy and feminist discourse: the case of France

Anne Batiot

Introduction

Confusion still persists as to the relationship existing between women as social agents and political subjects on the one hand, and feminism as a political force on the other. In an attempt to clarify this confusion, the concept of political mobilization (of women, and men, against social relations specific to sexism), as held by different political theories/ideologies, is here evaluated.

The grafting of the notion of 'women as a social group' on to that of 'women as a political force' is rejected, and a distinction is introduced between feminist and anti-sexist struggles to explain men's potential mobilization to change, or women's to defend, existing relations specific to sexism. Mobilization around the liberalization of abortion in France in the first half of the 1970s is then analysed in this context.

Radical democracy and feminist discourse

Following the French Revolution, and continuing in France until 1944, only men were *formally* equal in front of all other men. In spite of their contribution and later autonomous organizing, French women were left out of this first phase of what Laclau and Mouffe have recently called 'radical democracy' (Laclau and Mouffe, 1985: 152ff.). French women became *formally* equal to men in France only in 1944, when they won the right to vote and participate in French political life. Soon they were to join in another phase of radical democracy.

Although women have resisted male domination for centuries in the various ways open to them, it is only under certain conditions that a political force — feminism and anti-sexism — anchored in claims to rights formally legitimated but hitherto denied by a dominant democratic discourse, has emerged to change women's social relations and conditions of existence.

Until the advent of these conditions, women were subordinated (in all relations of sexism) to decisions legitimately made by others. However, once women became *formally* as equal and free as any other democratic subject, the relations of subordination characteristic of the sexism in which women had been entrapped were displaced by the illegitimate relations of domination. Formal democratic rights were met by a denial of *real* conditions of equality and free choice. Women's repeated demands for real equality and liberty — a struggle to reconstruct a new democratic femininity — now became externally legitimated by a democratic system defended by all sides of the French political tradition but denying women these rights. Hence arose, on the political terrain, the social antagonism existing between the relations of sexism imposed on women and Western democratic principles.

Political theories and women
Political theories have varied as to the form of political organization that women — as a 'social group' — represent when mobilized to change their conditions of existence. Liberalism limits women's political participation to formal liberal representation mechanisms: voting, party membership, candidate nomination and election, interest groups. Acknowledging as a given that the sexual division of labour makes it difficult for women fully to participate politically, liberalism totally ignores the private sphere of power relations, offers little analysis of sexism as a surviving social order, and fails to explain why women have been discriminated against within political systems that 'defend equality and liberty respectless of race, sex or religion'.

The pluralist approach differs in that it sees the political terrain as one of free political bargaining, a sort of power free-market where private interests, pressure groups and state institutions are in competition to secure for themselves the most profitable political position. Again, it is often assumed that women are a coherent 'social group' and as such represent one of the interest groups competing for the best political gains. Both liberalism and pluralism operate at the level of representative rather than participatory democracy.

The struggle for real participatory democracy, however, must extend far beyond the narrow confines of parliamentary politics. It needs to involve the radical reorganization of those social relations that contradict the ideals of participatory democracy. This reorganization in part implies the abolition of existing sexual, racial and class divisions of labour.

Classical Marxism emphasizes class contradictions and antagonisms as points of rupture and political struggles fixed in a unified (capitalist) political space. Other social antagonisms — for example, democratic struggles against sexism, racism and national domination — are attributed a secondary political significance determined by class struggles.

Since the 1970s, feminist, anti-racist and other democratic discourses have taken an autonomous stance vis-à-vis both liberal democracy and orthodox Marxism and have developed forms of political or cultural expression and struggles directly attacking the

specificity of their respective social relations. In their specificity and differences, all share the fact that they are articulated in demands for rights legitimated by formal democratic discourse and are aimed against existing relations of domination.

Recent feminist theories have contributed to identifying sexist social relations specific to women in capitalist and non-capitalist societies and therefore to locating sites of antagonisms directly affecting women. Confusion has arisen, however, as to the identity of feminist and anti-sexist political subjectivities and as to the form of political organization and mobilization that women and men can and do take to change sexist social relations.

Feminism and anti-sexism
If, according to radical feminist critiques, women are a specific 'social group' characterized by specific social relations, then, given the pluralist notion of 'defending one's interests' or even the classical Marxist concept of 'consciousness', women as 'a group' should form a specific political force.

Claiming to best defend women's interests, feminism would be a women-only pressure group (men could not be mobilized 'against their interests'). Or, raising women's consciousness as a 'class', feminism would remain a women-only caucus inside the proletarian party. In any case, men would not be mobilized on issues that directly and specifically affect women only: it would not be in men's 'interests' to do so, nor could they be 'feminist-conscious'. If they were, there would be no need for women to organize in the first place.

Recent political experience has demonstrated that feminist mobilization is far more complex than pressure group or internal caucus activities (Marsh, 1983:8). That is why I choose to draw a distinction between feminist and anti-sexist struggles, feminism being *women's* struggles to establish new social relations constructing non-sexist (democratic) femininity, and anti-sexism being *women's and men's* struggles to change *women's and men's* social relations, constructing democratic femininity and masculinity. Obviously, anti-sexism has drawn on feminism, but it differs in acknowledging the possibility of the mobilization of all men in changing social and sexual relations.

It is argued, therefore, that no *political* specificity is linked in a necessary way to any one given *social* group: women may be sexist or become feminist; men may be chauvinist or become anti-sexist. Anti-sexism is not women's privileged point of rupture in democratic practice, although, as they are most directly affected by sexist relations of domination, women are most likely first to initiate political struggles against sexist relations. (But, as we shall see below, this is not always the case.) Political specificity (feminism, anti-sexism, sexism) is related not to sex (female, male) but to gender (femininity, masculinity), and as such is not reducible to an empirically recognizable 'social group'. If this is so, then not all women will necessarily defend the (full) liberalization of abortion and men may be mobilized in anti-sexist struggles such as the Right to Choose. Similarly, not all men will necessarily oppose the liberalization of abortion.

Second, it is argued that anti-sexist struggles are led autonomously from, but possibly in conjunction with, other social struggles, of which class is one but is not determinant.

Third, ideologies that aim to change existing gender or sexual relations (feminism, anti-sexism, 'gayism', etc.) are not necessarily socialist or 'capitalist' in themselves. To be so, they must necessarily be articulated with a socialist or 'capitalist' discourse. A social antagonism around either gender, race, ethnic or national relations, for example, is not progressive or regressive *in itself*. It may give rise to different political analyses anchored in other progressive or regressive discourses. For example, in feminist discourse, biological essentialism, which reduces women's physiological traits and capacities to social functions, is definitely regressive whereas radical and socialist feminisms, which refuse to reduce femininity to physiology and attempt to change women's *social* relations of domination, are definitely progressive. Progressive (anti-capitalist, democratic) or regressive (capitalist, conservative, moralist) meaning is necessarily given *externally* by one or more discourses (socialist, radical democratic, sometimes religious, national self-determination, etc.).

Whereas all those women and men who mobilized in France to liberalize abortion aimed at further deconstructing private (in sexuality, personal and domestic life) and public (state, medical) relations of sexist domination, not all were necessarily struggling against capitalist, racist or other relations of exploitation and domination. Therefore we can expect to witness factionary antagonisms within the new French feminist movement itself as well as in the pro-abortion front regarding their political alliances with other organizations and movements on the issue.

Women as democratic subjects

To identify the possibilities of political strategy open to women engaged in feminist/anti-sexist struggles, we need to situate women as political subjects in three interrelated systems of social relations found in Western countries: relations of sexist domination, relations of exploitation characteristic of advanced capitalism and relations inherent in other relations of (bureaucratic) domination (as in state domination).

Referring to women as a 'social group' fails to account for women's *political* specificity and to distinguish between those women who want to change sexist relations and those who go as far as defending them. That is why, in order to situate women politically in all three interrelated systems mentioned above, I adopt Laclau and Mouffe's concept of *democratic subject position*. This refers to a specific political space: that of a clearly delimited antagonism that does not divide society into two fields — the oppressed and the oppressor, the 'people' against the 'rulers', women against men.

Democratic antagonism occupies a precise location in a system of relations with other social elements. Its political space does not coincide with the empirically given social formation. It is *relatively* sutured, formed by a multiplicity of practices that do not exhaust the referential and empirical reality of the agents forming part of them (Laclau and Mouffe, 1985:131–3). Each woman therefore has several democratic subject positionalities — gender, racial, ethnic, national, religious, etc. — and women as such do not share *all* positionalities by the mere fact they are women.

Social relations are constituted and organized by a discursive structure which is more than a cognitive entity; it is an articulatory practice. In social discourse, social elements are established into a relation and their identity is modified as a result of their being articulated with other elements. For example, sexuality articulated in conservative discourse as reproductive and functional differs from sexuality articulated in feminist discourse as freedom of choice and the right to pleasure.

A given discourse derives its coherence from the regularity of a system of structural positions. Social practices do not simply make up discourse in a cumulative fashion but are subtly structured into a system of meaning. The articulation of social elements into a relation is not constituted prior to, or outside, the dispersion of articulated elements. It consists of the construction of nodal points (privileged discursive points) which partially fix meaning. Free choice in reproduction is a nodal point in feminist discourse: it partially fixes the meaning of sexual relations as well as social relations between women and men (contraception, abortion, celibacy, parenthood, marriage). The denial of free reproduction is, in a symmetrically opposed direction, a nodal point in sexist discourse.

Every subject position is a discursive position and therefore cannot be totally fixed in a closed system of differences. It is not unified, nor does it have a unifying essence. A social agent has several subject positionalities. It cannot be reduced to a single identification with a single position, nor is it equivalent to the simple accumulation of various positions. The subject is discretely structured. It does not represent the immediate existence of an agent in terms of an existing person, nor is it an ideal Other (e.g., the Feminine Mystique, or Man), externally establishing a norm to be complied with (Laclau and Mouffe, 1985:115–22).

Feminist/anti-sexist hegemony then emerges in the general field of articulatory practices where the social retains an incomplete and open character. Non-sexist hegemony can be achieved by changing existing meaning, and to do so by changing the meaning of nodal points such as reproduction, sexuality or parenthood, among others. A new meaning is then constituted to dominate the field of discursivity.

It is argued here that the struggle for non-sexist hegemony has not always been initiated by women, nor has it always been women's privileged point of rupture in democratic practice, but that, within the overflow of social discourses on gender and other relations of domination, and here in particular on the issue of abortion, feminist discourse through the women's movement has imposed a radical discourse drawn from women's specific experience and relations of domination on to this general field of discursivity and has found enough political space to further radicalize some of the competing discourses.

French feminism
The suffragettes
It was not until the right of free association was gained in France in 1868 that French feminists opened their own clubs and published their own newspapers. Many participated in the Paris Commune of 1870. But the press remained their most overt form of political expression. The *Gazette des femmes* (1836–48) had already published a Women's Rights Charter asking for women's access to public functions such as teaching, post office work, etc. In 1869 the Ligue du droit des femmes (League of Women's Rights), with its journal *Le Droit des femmes*, was created; both have survived to this day. Equal rights in work, marriage and the family were demanded. The right to vote was not mentioned until 1904. The newspaper *La Citoyenne*, created by Hubertine Auclert in 1881, was the first to ask for women's political rights and was the suffragettes' first mouthpiece. In 1897 Marguerite Durand created the very feminist newspaper *La Fronde* (Sullerot, 1963: 97).

The Conseil national des femmes françaises (CNFF) was created in 1901. It grouped together about forty women's voluntary associations and organizations working on the demands of equal political, economic and family rights. They obtained several reforms: in 1907 married women workers gained the right to use their wages freely; in 1912 a series of laws was passed to protect women against men not recognizing paternity; later women gained entry to employment in the civil service. The CNFF also fought for a minimum wage for women working at home in various kinds of cottage industries and for equal pay for men and women teachers (Michel, 1979:81). The CNFF has continued to press for women's formal equality. Whereas the demands of the suffragettes concerned mainly *formal* rights and women's *public* participation, modern feminists' demands have been of a more everyday kind (housework, child care, violence) and have turned *personal* aspects of women's oppression into a political struggle.

Changes in French society
After the second world war, a new generation of technocrats set out, under the Plan Monet, to modernize France. It was not until the 1960s that France generally witnessed the results hoped for. By 1962 women's full-time employment marked a sharp increase. This economic renewal had far-reaching social implications. Many traditional social relations were deeply altered by state-encouraged new relations of consumption, home-ownership, management, family and education. The transition from an extensive to an intensive regime of capitalist accumulation characterized by intensified individual consumption created new antagonisms or at least accentuated already-existing ones. By the late 1960s social relations had still not adapted to the new demands created by this capitalist impetus, and the events of May 1968 were a reaction to this gap. The institutionalization by the welfare state of new penetrations of capitalist relations (commodity and cultural consumption) into social relations further accentuated existing antagonisms.

Women were affected by these changes. Some were uprooted because of the general rural exodus towards urban employment, while others enjoyed the greater geographical (and social) mobility facilitated by improved transport and communications. Working mothers became increasingly antagonized by the double work/ housework shift, while greater access to education and employment provided young women with the means to achieve economic independence and gain autonomy from parental authority. French women had been straightjacketed into traditional social relations, and now suddenly they were expected by French 'progressives' to participate fully in national progress.

Closely linked to advances made in research on birth control, a general wave of 'sexual liberation' spread throughout the Western world in the 1960s. Although on the one hand not particularly liberating for women, who still remained the sexual objects of sexist fantasies, it nevertheless triggered off the desire of many women to free themselves from sexual constraints. In that respect, and regarding a general feminist radical denunciation of 'women's position in society', French feminism benefited greatly from similar movements in the USA and Britain.

The Mouvement de liberation des femmes (MLF)

As early as the second world war, a generation of French women had been politicized in fighting for the Resistance against Nazi occupation. A later generation was radicalized in anti-imperialist struggles (Cambodia, Algeria, Vietnam) and the growing left-wing radicalization of the 1960s. During the events of May 1968, a mixed group (Feminin–Masculin–Avenir — FMA) was formed following a well attended spontaneous meeting at the Sorbonne. When, a few months later, the few remaining men were asked to leave the group, FMA changed to Feminisme–Marxisme–Action. Sexuality, very much debated in 1968 by the various political groups increasingly taking their distance from orthodox Marxism, was also at first the spearhead of feminist debates. Marriage, child care, psychoanalysis and the family were the main themes of controversy in this early phase of the new French feminism.

By 1969, several groups were started in the Paris area (Les Oreilles vertes, Les Petites Marguerites, Les Féministes révolutionnaires), and these were joined within a year by a multitude of *groupes-femmes de quartiers*, or local women's groups. Generally these groups witnessed an effervescence of women talking, behaving freely in front of one another and no longer being so aware of or worried about the feminine image constantly demanded of them in public. Meetings were usually held informally in a woman's flat and, whether among radical or socialist feminists, were as much social gatherings as political occasions.

Local women's groups had little to do with more traditional revolutionary cells or leftist groups. They were more like a kind of political door-to-door network, allowing women to live closely together and communicate easily. Meals were often shared, cooked by the women in turns or jointly, and evenings were spent in discussion, preparing the next event or simply being together. A local group's dynamics depended entirely on the women who were in it. Some groups flourished in creativity, affection and initiative while others struggled to survive amidst tension or personal conflicts. Because the private aspects of militants' life were so important in analysing their oppression, attempts were made from early on to remedy those problems thus far identified, for example the need for crêches (Bernheim, 1983:57).

The first open feminist action was on 26 August 1970 when nine feminists attempted to lay a wreath to the wife of the Unknown Soldier whose tomb, a symbol of French nationalism, lies underneath the Arc de Triomphe in Paris. The wreath bore large bands saying

'One man out of two is a woman' and 'There is one about whom even less is known than the Unknown Soldier: his wife'. By the following September, the first women's General Assembly was called by the FMA and other groups in Paris. The first non-tendential newspaper of the new French feminist movement, *Le Torchon brûle*, was born out of that assembly.

It was also following this first General Assembly that a debate arose as to the form of political action feminists should adopt. Existing tendencies now took firmer positions. One was around a more classical Marxist analysis (Cercle Dimitriev, Les Pétroleuses); another one very much radicalized orthodox Marxism into a feminist critique (Les Féministes révolutionnaires — FR — later to create *Questions féministes*). A third attempted to combine psychoanalysis and Marxism (Psychanalyse et politique), while a fourth regrouped all those feminists, usually more pragmatically oriented, who felt out of step with the other three factions and the endless debates taking place between them. This fourth faction later founded the Ligue du droit des femmes.

Very quickly, some women either took on or had imposed on them by more passive feminist followers a distinct position of power. What became known as 'Psych. et po.' (Psychanalyse et politique) soon crystallized around Antoinette, while Christine certainly played a charismatic role in Les Féministes révolutionnaires; Anne, Annie and Cathy, among others, were faced with similar responsibilities in their factions. This falling back on self- or group-imposed leaders is quite characteristic of and peculiar to French feminism.

The French feminist movement decidedly took shape between late 1970 and 1972. Public meetings open to women only were regularly held in the Beaux Arts, information bulletins were circulated, addresses were exchanged — a network was rapidly being established. Writings and interventions were directed at all abuses committed against women. Marriage, housework, sexual harassment, but also sisterhood, organizing the movement, poems and letters on 'being a woman': these were themes and means most often repeated in the new feminist press.

It was also at the end of 1970 that abortion became an important feminist rallying point. Posters and graffiti soon covered Parisian and provincial walls alike:

ONE MILLION TAKE THE RISK EACH YEAR.
WHEN WILL ABORTION BE FREE AND LEGAL?

By November 1970 the MLF struck with its second big action: a national demonstration in Paris in favour of the liberalization of abortion laws. But this time the specificity of the new women's movement lay not so much in initiating this action but in contributing

an analysis that went far beyond those presented by various other
political bodies in favour of liberalization.

After 1974 the Ligue broke with the Féministes révolutionnaires.
However, the split was never as definite as it was with Psych. et po.
Whereas the Ligue had long ceased to recognize common grounds
with Psych. et po., it continued to coordinate with FR on general
feminist actions. Yet differences of analyses, methods of work and
areas of intervention, coupled with conflicting personalities, were
sufficient to justify each taking its distance from the other. Generally,
it can be said that both groups shared a radical approach, although
only FR was committed to a Marxist analysis. The Ligue was perhaps
more pragmatic; although reluctantly it agreed to set up an organization to follow up initial denunciatory actions such as the campaigns
on abortion, rape, pornography and the bill against sexism. The FR
was more theoretically than organizationally oriented.

Abortion as a political issue
Women's specific conditions of existence differ from men's in that,
owing to their reproductive capacity, they are assigned a con-
tradictory highly-valuable-but-subordinate social status, defined, in
the last instance, in terms of a 'natural and necessary' reproductive
'function'. Among all discourses on the liberalization of contraception and abortion, feminist discourse is the most radical in
refuting this notion of 'natural function' and replacing it with that of
'free and unconditional choice'. The dilemma remains, however, in
creating possibilities of 'free and equal choice in parenthood', as
women's 'free choice' is not always compatible with men's 'equal
choice'. This dilemma is inherited directly from the tension existing
between the democratic rights of freedom and equality.

Feminism and abortion
There are several reasons why abortion proved a great mobilizing
issue for feminist movements. First, it concerns the choice that all
women, potentially at least, may have to be faced with one or more
times in their lives: whether or not to remain pregnant. With
contraception, the choice to become pregnant or not is rational and
usually planned in advance. And it is reversible. But with abortion
the immediacy of the choice is most felt. It intervenes between a
sexual experience and an acceptance or refusal of a pregnancy. It is
reducible to neither, yet links the two. And the choice is permanent:
either you do remain pregnant or you don't.

Second, as an experience, it is exclusive to women. No man has
ever had an abortion. Yet not all women have favoured, nor all men
opposed, the liberalization of abortion. Third, the immediacy in
personal decision-making is the woman's 'natural' privilege: she is

the first one (and *can* be the only one) to know of her pregnancy, and therefore, whether legitimately or not, she can be the only one to decide to want an abortion, even at the risk of her life. This immediacy and personal aspect in decision-making made it all the more difficult for different sectors of political opinion to accept legislation.

Fourth, by posing the problem in terms of choice, feminists forced the state and political and public opinions to acknowledge for the first time in history not only the specificity of women's conditions of existence, hitherto ghettoized into 'the family', but also the fact that women are not objects. By posing abortion in terms of responsibility, a concept that is attributable only to subjects free to decide, feminists displaced femininity from a position of 'subordinated object' to one of 'responsible subject'. (The concept of subject used here is not that used above by Laclau and Mouffe: here it stands as opposite to 'object'.)

Abortion in France

The reasons why abortion became a political issue in France at the time it did differ from the reasons why abortion became a catalyst in mobilizing the feminist movement. First, several countries had already liberalized their own abortion legislations (the Soviet Union, Britain, Switzerland, the Netherlands, etc.), and there was a general concern among progressives and technocrats that France was 'behind the times'. Also, the Soviet experience between 1920 and 1936 had proved to specialists that abortion need not be a dangerous operation. Second, during the 1960s many French women who could afford it travelled to Britain, Holland or Switzerland to have abortions. It was increasingly felt by progressive French medical, legal and social workers that this situation resulted in a double standard, whereby women of means could easily have an abortion while poorer women could not or had to resort to unsafe back-street abortions. Third, since French women had gained the vote in 1944, French political parties had begun in the early 1960s to seek ways of mobilizing women's votes. The fact that women over that period had begun to vote more in favour of the Left perhaps explains why it was a party of the Left (Fédération de la Gauche démocratique et socialiste — FGDS — soon to become the Socialist Party) which first raised the question of abortion on a political platform (in Mitterrand's election campaign of 1965).

Fourth, by the 1950s neo-Malthusian ideas had gained renewed support in France among several progressive professional groups. The French Family Planning Association (MFPF) was created in 1956. From 6,000 members in 1961, the MFPF expanded to 15,000 in 1962, 33,000 in 1963, 40,000 in 1964 and 60,000 in 1966 (*Bulletin du*

MFPF, 1971). At first supported by the Liberals, the progressive wing of the Union pour la défense de la république (UDR), some socialists, the Freemasons and part of the Reformed Protestant Church, as well as by members of the medical profession and/or parents concerned to eradicate the haunting experience of an unwanted child, the MFPF set out to inform and educate French public opinion on questions relating to birth control and to secure the repeal of the contraception and abortion bills of 1920 and 1923 respectively (Wolton, 1974:80). Its work was made difficult by the 1920 bill making illegal any activities related to distributing information on contraception and birth control.

Contraception
Until 1964 several proposals to change the 1920 bill on contraception had been put forward by various parties. Some intended to liberalize it, while others proposed to make it even more repressive. None of these proposals ever reached even debating point at the National Assembly. However, Mitterrand's electoral mention of abortion put pressure on the Gaullist government; threatened with the issue of abortion, the government agreed to settle on the relatively lesser problem of contraception. Whereas the Liberal Party and the progressive faction of the UDR advocated a reform, the Catholic wing of the UDR opposed it. The government majority, led by de Gaulle's government, was bitterly divided between the progressives (led by MM. Neuwirth, Peyret, Poniatowski and Taittinger) and the traditionalists (led by M. Foyer). The Left was also divided. The socialists were in favour while the communists opposed liberalization, partly for tactical reasons (the socialists helped the Majority to pass the bill) and partly because it condemned contraception as a weapon used by the bourgeoisie to control the growing numbers of the working class (Wolton, 1974:81).
   The bill legalizing contraception was passed in 1967. This helped to open the way for the possible later legalizing of abortion. Simultaneously, during and after the events of May 1968, the notion of individual choice and control in matters of sexuality appeared in the political vocabulary of an increasing number of libertarian groups and specialist organizations. Finally, the Karman method of vacuum-abortion had already crossed the Atlantic to Britain.

Events
Again, it was an association issued from medical specialists at first working closely with the MFPF, the Association nationale pour l'étude sur l'avortement (ANEA), who first put forward a draft bill on abortion (known as the Peyret text) in June 1970. This initiative was due to a male member of the progressive faction of the UDR.

The following November, the MLF and the Mouvement pour la liberalisation de l'avortement (MLA, later to become the MLAC) held their first major national demonstration demanding the full liberalization of abortion. The ball had been set rolling by progressives belonging to different political parties; the feminists unknowingly seized it as a political opportunity to mobilize women into the feminist movement and numerous men into anti-sexist discourse. That same month, M. Foyer of the UDR's traditionalist wing founded the anti-abortionist Laissez-les-vivre (Let Them Live).

In early 1971 journalists from *Le Nouvel Observateur* approached MLF militants to publish a manifesto on abortion. Signed by 343 women declaring they had had an abortion, the manifesto was published on 5 April 1971: it publicly opened the national debate on abortion. The Bobigny trial in October 1972, in which a seventeen-year-old girl was tried for having had an abortion, further mobilized support both in favour of liberalization and against it. In addition to the MFPF (1956) and the MLAC (1973) as militant specialist organizations, CHOISIR (1971) and the Groupe information santé (GIS, 1969) were also mobilized into the pro-abortion front. These were all mixed-sex groups and, after 1971, were influenced by feminist discourse. The MLAC involved militants from any and all of these organizations plus others from trade unions (CFDT, FEN, FO, MGEN) and political parties (PSU, LCR, OCI, PS).

The reform proposed by M. Taittinger (UDR) was given priority on the opening of parliament in the autumn of 1973. The government majority was increasingly divided while the left opposition hesitated to lend its support to a text it considered inadequate and weak. At first defeated on 29 November 1973, the Taittinger proposal was thoroughly revised under Simone Weil's supervision when she was entrusted by Giscard Valery d'Estaing, who was elected president following Pompidou's sudden death, with producing a text that more accurately reflected public opinion. Following heated parliamentary debates fed by a public debate taking place in the media, and numerous amendments, a bill legalizing abortion was passed in January 1975.

Discourses on abortion and party mobilization
In the election campaign of May 1974, appealing to organizations or individuals regrouped under Laissez-les-vivre's banner, the ultra-right candidates MM. Foyer and Le Pen had been definitely opposed to any liberalization of abortion while the ultra-left candidates, Ms. Laguiller and MM. Krivine and Dumont, had been categorically in favour of free abortion without any restriction. Their position was fully libertarian: it demanded the total repeal of the 1923 legislation, free access to contraception and abortion for all women (immigrants

and minors included), full reimbursement by the French national health system and the final choice to be the woman's only, without any interference from her general practitioner or social workers. This discourse was anti-sexist in that it sought to construct new non-sexist relations between women, their reproduction choices and the institutions or individuals directly concerned with that choice. It had been adopted by GIS, MLAC, CHOISIR and the radical faction of the MFPF, and had been largely inspired from the feminists' radical position adopted after 1971.

The three competing candidates adopted less forthright positions. Inclined towards therapeutic abortion only when pregnancy endangered the woman's life or when the woman found herself in 'a situation of real hardship', Chalban-Delmas (RPR) opted for individual choice according to one's conscience. Giscard d'Estaing's proposals centred on four key points: respecting human life, lending an open help to women physically threatened by a pregnancy, making it possible for women to keep their children in the best possible conditions, and letting women and members of the medical profession make up their own minds freely regarding the practice of abortion. This latter position was shared by the progressive centre–right (UDR and liberals), the Freemasons and the Reformed Protestant Church. It was defended by the ANEA.

Within this discourse, the Taittinger proposal of 1970 had provided for the practice of abortion up to the tenth week of pregnancy within rigidly defined conditions. The later Peyret text (1973) permitted it up to the twelfth week with limited possibilities for it past the twelfth week. It also authorized abortion for girls between the ages of 16 and 18 when permission was given by one of their parents.

As for M. Mitterrand, relying on the bill proposed by the PS, he insisted on total freedom of abortion up to the twelfth week of pregnancy, to be carried out within a state-approved medical establishment (although not necessarily a hospital) and fully reimbursed by the French national health system. This position was shared by the traditional Left generally.

The position adopted by the three candidates competing with ultra-left ones respected the legitimacy of the family and insisted on sexuality within marriage for reproductive purposes. It was oriented towards institutional pragmatism: the role of the legislator and of public institutions in determining women's reproductive rights, the medicalization of sexuality and reproduction, the improvement of 'women's position' and the social problem of back-street abortions. Abortion was to be legalized to ensure medical control over its practice and make it medically safe and legally restricted.

Feminist discourse

Feminist discourse on abortion shared with other discourses a concern about back-street abortions and the distress and many deaths they cause women. It also regarded contraception as a necessary means of birth control and abortion as temporarily necessary until contraception, fully integrated into social norms, made abortion redundant. Along with the traditional Left, it asked for the full repeal of the 1923 legislation repressing abortion and demanded that strict measures be taken by the government to avoid any kind of financial trafficking on abortion once a new legislation was adopted.

However, feminist discourse was far more radical than other discourses in several ways. First, in arguing that all women, potentially at least, were vulnerable to choices and conditions regarding abortion, feminists took women's direct interests as their discursive starting point. A woman's choice, therefore, had to be final and decisive, and could not be legally interfered with by medical or institutional veto.

The argument of women's choice rested on the democratic ideal of liberty: women should have the right to control their bodies, which are not reproductive machines, and to decide on whether or not they want children, and how many they want. They should have the right of freedom to live with their sexuality as they wish and to seek pleasure for themselves rather than to restrict themselves to a reproductive 'function'.

Using the democratic ideal of liberty itself rested on a distinction reintroduced by feminists: that between nature and culture, sexuality and reproduction. Whereas other discourses blurred women's sexuality into a 'natural reproductive function' legitimated by marriage and protected by the family structure, feminists rearticulated reproduction as a social element and a site of sexist subordination. Rejecting traditionalist norms, feminists put forward a radical concept of gender relations in sexuality, emotional and economic independence, formal and real equality in marriage, the family and other existing relations of sexist domination. Also, because feminists rejected a purely natural and functional concept of reproduction, they argued that priority must be given to a women's existence over the potential existence of a foetus.

Second, feminist discourse differed from other discourses in the forms of public expression it adopted. Following on from similar processes initiated .n May 1968, new forms of organization, mobilization and public participation were invented. Unlike traditional political organizations, the MLF developed unstructured networks where leadership and hierarchical power relations were discouraged, even though desired results were not always obtained. Decision-making was personalized, always relating to individual experience and needs. While still relying on traditional forms of alliance with supportive organizations (MFPF, MLAC, CHOISIR, GIS), the MLF also developed a more personalized press, added humour and fun to its provocative actions and made self-help groups — whether consciousness-raising or practical, as in the case of Karman abortion method — the cornerstone of its mobilization.

Within this process of rearticulating sexuality and reproduction into non-sexist gender relations, feminism radicalized other specialist organizations in demanding the freedom of abortion up to the twenty-fourth week of pregnancy for all women, including immigrants and minors; full reimbursement by the French national health system; and the setting up of efficient social, medical and educational means to make this freedom a real and practical possibility. Articulating the *desire* to have children, where passivity or submission had been the norm, feminists rejected both the traumatization and the banalization of abortion.

Conclusions

Women's resistance to sexism became a political force only when certain political (democratic participation) and socio-economic conditions were fulfilled. Overspilling the confines of a 'social group', a pressure group or a class contradiction, feminism has been identified as a democratic discourse aimed against relations of domination specific to gender. As political specificity is not reducible to sex or an empirically recognizable 'social group', feminism has been distinguished from anti-sexism inasmuch as the former is drawn from women's direct experience and expression whereas the latter involves both women's and men's attempts to articulate non-sexist social relations from their experiences.

As autonomous movements, feminism and anti-sexism are not necessarily socialist or 'capitalist' in themselves. Articulation with externally produced discourses defines their progressive or regressive nature. Finally, feminist discourse on sexuality, reproduction, contraception and abortion developed from women's specific experience of domination and resistance and radicalized the position in favour of abortion adopted by other political organizations. In this sense, it can be said that feminist discourse hegemonized the discursive terrain regarding abortion.

List of abbreviations

AMR	Alliance marxiste révolutionnaire
ANEA	Association nationale d'éducation pour l'avortement
APBG	Association des professeurs de biologie et géologie
CCA	Comité communiste d'autogestion
CFDT	Confédération française démocratique du travail

CGT	Confédération générale du travail
FCPE	Fédération des conseils de parents d'élèves
FEN	Fédération d'éducation nationale
FMA	Féminin-masculin-avenir
FO	Force ouvrière
FPPF	Fédération internationale pour la parenté responsable
GIS	Groupe-information-santé
GNIES	Groupe national d'information sur l'éducation sexuelle
GD	Gauche démocratique
IFOP	Institut français de l'opinion publique
INSERM	Institut national supérieur d'éducation sexuelle et de recherche sur la maternité
LC	Ligue communiste
LCR	Ligue communiste révolutionnaire
MDF	Mouvement démocratique féminin
MFPF	Mouvement français pour le planning familial
MGEN	Mutuelle générale de l'éducation nationale
MLA	Mouvement pour la liberté de l'avortement
MLAC	Mouvement pour la liberté de l'avortement et de la contraception
MLF	Mouvement de libération des femmes
MRG	Mouvement des radicaux de gauche
OCI	Organisation communiste internationale
PCF	Parti communiste français
PR	Parti radical
PS	Parti socialiste
PSU	Parti socialiste unifié
RCDS	Réformateurs centristes démocrates sociaux
RDS	Réformateurs démocrates sociaux
RI	Républicains indépendants
RIAS	Républicains indépendants d'action sociale
RPR	Rassemblement pour la défense de la république
Révo.	'Révolution'
SNAIASSU	Syndicat national des assistantes infirmières et adjointes de santé scolaires et universitaires
SNES	Syndicat national des enseignements de second degré
SNI	Syndicat national des instituteurs
SNISSEPE	Syndicat national des infirmières de santé scolaire de l'enseignement
SOFRES	(Statistics and public opinion institute)
SRG	Socialistes et radicaux de gauche
UC	Union centriste
UCDS	Union centriste démocratique et socialiste
UDF	Union démocratique française
UDR	Union des démocrates pour la république
UNAF	Union nationale des associations féminines

References

Bernheim, Cathy (1983) *Pertubation, ma soeur*. Paris: Seuil.
Brimo, Albert (1975) *Les Femmes françaises face au pouvoir politique*. Paris: Editions Montchrétien.
Bulletin du Comité du Travail (1979) 'Actualités de travail des femmes', no. 23, December.

Bulletin du Mouvement de libération des femmes (various issues). Can be consulted at the Bibliothèque Marguerite Durand, Mairie du Vème Arrondissement, Place du Panthéon, 75005 Paris.

CHOISIR (1973) *Avortement: une loi en procés, l'affaire Bobigny, collection Idées.* Paris: Gallimard.

de Pisan, Annie and Anne Tristan (1977) *Histoires du MLF.* Paris: Calman-Levy.

Editions des Femmes (1973) *L'Alternative: libérer nos corps ou libérer l'avortement.* Paris: Editions de Femmes.

Fougere, Danielle (1971) 'Avortement', *Antoinette*, April.

Fourth International (1979) *Le Droit de choisir: avortment–contraception, lutte internationale des femmes.* Paris: Editions La Brêche.

Garcia Guadilla, Natty (1981) *Libération des femmes: le MLF.* Paris: Presses Universitaires de France.

Isambert, Francois A. and Paul Ladriere (1979) *Contraception et Avortement — dix ans de débat dans la presse (1965–1974).* Paris: Actions Thématiques Programmées (ATP) no. 31.

Laclau, Ernesto and Chantal Mouffe (1985) *Hegemony and Socialist Strategy: Towards a Radical Democratic Politics.* London: Verso Press.

Marsh, David (1983) *Pressure Politics.* London: Junction Books.

Marsh, David and Joanna Chambers (1981) *Abortion Politics.* London: Junction Books.

MFPF (1975) *Qui vient au Planning Familial et pourquoi — Etude socio-démographique faite à partir du fichier national du MFPF (1973–74).* Paris: MFPF.

Michel, Andrée (1979) 'Que sais-je?', *Le Féminisme*, no. 1782. Paris: PUF.

MLAC (1973) *Libérons l'avortement.* Paris: Maspéro.

MLAC (1974) *Avortement d'accord, contraception d'abord.* Paris: MLAC.

MLAC (1975) *Vivre autrement dés maintenant.* Paris: Maspero.

MLF (1970a) *Partisans: Libération des femmes, Année Zéro*, nos 54–5, July–October.

MLF (1970b) 'Contraception et avortement libres et gratuits', *Le Torchon brûle*, no. 1.

MLF (1970c) 'Nous ne sommes pas des fanatiques de l'avortement', *Le Torchon Brûle*, no. 1.

MLF (1972) *Maternité esclave.* Paris: Maspéro.

MLF (1973) *De l'autre côté de la maternité.* Paris: Maspéro.

Mossuz-Lavau, Janine, and Mariette Sineau (1981) 'France', pp. 112–32 in Joni Lovenduski and Jill Hills (eds), *The Politics of the Second Electorate: Women and Public Participation.* London: Routledge & Kegan Paul.

Parti Communiste Français (1974) *Avortement et libre choix de la maternité.* Paris: Editions Sociales.

Sullerot, Evelyne (1963) *La Presse féminine.* Paris: Armand Colin.

Wolton, Dominique (1974) *Le Nouvel ordre sexuel.* Paris: Seuil.

II

MOVEMENT STRATEGIES: INSIDE OR OUTSIDE THE 'SYSTEM'

5

Feminism in Britain: politics without power?

Joyce Gelb

Introduction

The 1960s and 1970s saw the resurgence of feminism as a social movement in virtually every Western nation. However, in each nation the movement adapted to the history, culture and politics of its own society (Bouchier, 1984). This chapter will consider the ways in which British culture and political institutions have shaped the country's feminist movement, while attempting some comparisons, in terms of movement structure, resources and impact, with the feminist movement in the USA.

The chapter will focus on several aspects of British feminism. First, the structure and goals of the 'women's liberation movement', a movement distinguished by its emphasis on life-style change and personal expressiveness, will be considered. A second 'face' of British feminism — that of participation in political parties and trade unions, which plays a dominant role in the political process — will then be analysed. Finally, a recent development in British politics, the role of women's committees in local government, will be discussed.

In this study, movement development, effectiveness and impact are seen as being largely dependent on external factors such as political environment and resources available. Among the environmental variables that appear to be particularly significant are the current political complexion of government, the structure of the central administrative process and the state of the economy (Whitely and Winyard, 1983:10–11). Examination of the structure of British politics, economics and social life suggests a highly traditional society and values, a stagnant economy and a centralized, secretive and bureaucratically dominated system. These factors contribute to a political setting in which feminists tend to be isolated from the formal political system, from feminists with different perspectives and women in general, and from potential allies. Ideological divisions, rooted in class and other conflicts, inhibit the formation of coalitions dedicated to resolving women's political and economic needs.

The political and cultural setting

As suggested above, British society is distinguished by its traditional structure and values. This structure, with its low educational attainment for women, norms of 'good' motherhood and marriage, low wages and a stratified labour market and class structure, has greatly narrowed opportunities for political involvement (Hills, 1981:13). Over 10 million women were employed in Britain in 1981, constituting about 40 per cent of the labour force. The number of part-time women workers increased to almost 40 per cent of the female labour force in 1981 (EOC, 1983:76, 750).

The traditional family remains entrenched, to a degree unusual in Western society, with marriage rates high and divorce rates low (Hills, 1981:11). Equal pay and sex discrimination legislation have not altered patterns of relatively low educational attainment for women (EOC, 1982:56). In professions generally viewed as compatible with political involvement, such as law, women have made few gains: only 7 per cent of British barristers are women (Robarts, Coote and Ball, 1980). (In contrast, 14 per cent of lawyers and judges in the USA are women: Deckard, 1983.)

Of particular note is the limited nature of value change which has taken place in Britain. Inglehart (1977:34), in his cross-country survey, found that the smallest amount of generational change in any nation existed in Britain. Studies comparing attitudes towards feminism and women's social role in the USA and Britain offer some striking differences in attitudes. One study found British youth much less supportive of women's liberation than their European or US counterparts (and their parents, as well), suggesting that generational change has been far more limited in Britain (Jennings, Aurbuck and Rosenmeyer, 1979:497). Another report of intra-European opinion on feminism reveals that British women (and men) hold a higher proportion of negative views about it than citizens of any other European nation (matched only by Italy). While strictly comparable data are difficult to obtain, a 1979 poll showed 63 per cent of Americans (compared with 40 per cent of the British) agreeing that the part played by women in their nation had changed a lot (International Gallup Poll, 1981).

Eurobarometer 19 (1983) found more Britons 'disagreeing with the claim that there should be fewer differences between men's and women's roles in society' than in any other European nation surveyed (question 134); there were also more profound disagreements regarding female family roles (e.g., housework and child care) than elsewhere in Europe (q. 137). More British men preferred their wives not to be in paid employment (q. 164). In terms of social movement approval and value change, Britons had the poorest opinion of women's liberation of any Europeans interviewed (q. 179).

Norms of political efficacy are unusually low in Britain, no doubt owing to difficulties of access in a centralized bureaucratic state (to be discussed below), suggesting that political participation in general is likely to be limited (Kaase and Marsh, 1979). Participation and efficacy are related to high income and educational attainment, both of which are especially lacking for most British women.

Finally, the backwardness of the economy has further constrained opportunities and value change for women in the class-ridden, elitist British society (Bouchier, 1984).

Among the major assumptions that will be made regarding the distinctions between the US and British systems which affect feminist structure and strategy are the importance in Britain of centralized government and parliament and the primacy of the administrative process. The British administrative process emphasizes ministerial responsibility and neutrality and operates behind closed doors, in contrast to the USA, where there is greater emphasis on public scrutiny and intervention in bureaucratic politics. British courts play a more restricted role than their US counterparts; constitutional review and the use of law to aid social reform movements, especially through class action suits, are virtually unknown.

The British policy-making process is organized to make exclusion from access remarkably easy (Ashford, 1981:8). Grass-roots lobbying, common in the USA, has little impact in a system as centralized as that in Britain. A consequence of centralization and secrecy is to limit the role of 'promotional' or attitude groups seeking change: they tend to be poor in size, in finances and in the ability to obtain benefits (Christoph, 1974:144; Blondel, 1974:221). As we shall see, the British feminist movement is no exception to this general rule.

Although political parties are, by general consensus, declining in importance, they are major agents for the resolution of key political issues (Richardson and Jordan, 1979:12). British parties, more than those in the USA, tend to be parties of social integration rather than individual representation. Trade unions play a dominant political role, particularly in the Labour Party — 90 per cent of total Labour Party membership and 85 per cent of the funds are derived from the unions (Punnett, 1980:127). The tradition of class-based ideology, socialism and a strong organized left has often — but not always — involved British feminists in Labour Party or trade union politics.

While occasionally the relationship between feminism and the left has produced support for women's concerns, more frequently women's demands have been subordinated to larger social and economic interests while leaving the male-dominated structures of power intact.

Relationships with other reform/change-oriented groups may foster political consciousness and alliances that provide resources, access and legitimacy for new movements (Parkin, 1968). In Britain, movements such as the Campaign for Nuclear Disarmament (CND) helped to set the stage for change-oriented politics in the 1950s and 1960s. The CND was probably the first major group to aim its strategies at the public — not only decision-makers — and thus it provided a model for the feminists who followed (Rivers, 1974). However, it lacked a formal bureaucratic structure or formal membership, and while it was a major political presence and a force leading to the mobilization of political consciousness for women, it was unable to provide a continuing institutional base on which feminists could rely. In addition to the CND, the emergence in the 1960s of other social reform and environmental groups — including those campaigning for the legalization of abortion and homosexuality, and against capital punishment — helped to create a climate of reform in which feminism could flourish.

Like their US counterparts, traditional women's groups in Britain survived the doldrums of the 1940s and 1950s and continue to have a mass membership base (see Stott, 1980; Randall, 1982). While they do not identify with women's liberation, they do support some feminist demands and efforts to achieve them. But such British women's organizations as the Women's Institutes, Townswomen's Guilds and National Council of Women by and large eschew relationships with socialist and radical feminists. They have felt little in common with a women's liberation movement perceived by the media and general public as anti-male. Hence, the links to civil rights and other movements that provided resources and access for feminists in the USA have not existed in the same manner in Britain (Costain, 1982; Gelb and Palley, 1982), although there are ties to such groups as the National Council for Civil Liberties (NCCL) and the Child Poverty Action Group (CPAG), as well as historic links to the socialist left, to be explored further below.

Economic resources for promotional groups are also scarce in Britain. There is relatively little money available for charitable gifts, and little incentive to individual donors who derive no direct financial benefit from contributions (Phillips, 1982:2). The limited nature of charitable income available is evident from a study that reveals that 81 per cent of British charities have incomes of less than $500 per annum (NCVO, 1981). Of the relatively few charitable trusts that do exist in Britain, few contribute to 'radical' feminist groups; and those that do support women primarily sponsor research efforts. Only government agencies such as the Equal Opportunities Commission (EOC) and Manpower Services Commission (MSC) and local council governments have provided significant funds for feminist-related activity.

In sum, cause-oriented groups in Britain lack funds and expertise, as well as access to ministries and civil servants (Rivers, 1974). In a real sense, they are isolated from the centres of decision-making power. Finally, in Britain (as well as the USA), politics in recent years has been dominated by conservative interests which have sought to slash budgets and 're-privatize' numerous public sector functions, including those specifically related to women dependent on the state.

The structure of British feminism

As suggested in the introduction to this chapter, the feminist movement in Britain comprises two sets of groups, roughly comparable to those categorized as 'radical' and 'reformist' in the USA (Freeman, 1975). The first set embraces the women's liberation movement in Britain — decentralized, localized and anti-elitist — described as anarcho-libertarian (Stacey and Price, 1980). Such groups occasionally come together in national structures such as the National Abortion Campaign (NAC) for abortion rights or the National Women's Aid Federation (NWAF) for domestic violence. To the extent that they are involved in political action, they mainly engage local authorities in efforts to obtain funding and other assistance.

A second set of groups operates within existing political/economic institutions, primarily trade unions and political parties. Since the latter play a key political role, efforts to influence the political system naturally gravitate in their direction.

Women's liberation

The contemporary British feminist movement received its impetus from radical and new left politics, especially the CND, student politics, anti-Vietnam campaigns and Marxist and socialist parties (Randall, 1982; Wilson, 1980). In the 1960s, working-class women organized as well — at Hull in 1968 for better conditions for their fishermen husbands, and at the Ford motor company in Dagenham, where the demands for equal pay and equal work resulted in the creation of a short-lived Joint Action Committee for Women's Rights (Wandor, 1972). The revived feminist movement in the USA provided the immediate spark for much women's liberation activity, which early on developed strength among socialist and university women. A London-based women's liberation workshop coordinated over seventy local groups and published a journal, *Shrew* (Randall,

1982; Wandor, 1972). To a greater degree than in the USA, socialist and Marxist feminists were the virtual 'midwives' of the British women's liberation movement (Randall, 1982).

In 1970, the national women's liberation movement held its first national conference at Oxford. The demands that emerged from the conference — twenty-four-hour child care, equal pay and education, free contraception and abortion on demand — reflected a practical orientation, new to some movement activists. The British movement developed numerous factions; one chart listed at least fourteen different 'tendencies' within it (Sebestyen, 1979). Conflicts within the movement — largely between militant (or 'revolutionary') radicals and socialist feminists — have prevented national conferences from meeting since 1978. The conflicts have centred largely on the scrapping of the initial feminist demands in favour of a sole demand against male violence (Randall, 1982).

Like the so-called 'younger', more radical, branch of the US movement, the British movement lacks a coordinating structure other than national, regional or issue-oriented conferences. At the time of writing, *Spare Rib*, a monthly publication produced by a feminist collective, and the Women's Research and Resources Centre (WRRC) in London, provide the only comprehensive focus relating to different elements within the movement. (A Woman's Place, also in London, is similarly run by a collective of women and operates a bookshop and reference facility as well as publishing a weekly newsletter.) The once active Women's Information, Reference and Enquiry Service (WIRES) has been severely circumscribed.

Despite the absence of a focal point, feminist activities in Britain continue energetically. *Spare Rib* (with a circulation of 30,000) and other publications advertise a whole host of feminist activities, and there are numerous groups listed under 'Women's liberation' in the London and regional telephone directories.

Ambivalence about lobbying. The major locus of activity is the small local group, which, eschewing formal rules and leadership, prefers to arrive at decisions by consensus. The movement's character is also defined by the proliferation of small groups, each with a single-issue orientation. It should be noted that even non-'liberation' women's groups such as Women in Media and the National Housewives Register (founded in the early 1960s by liberal-minded housewives) operate on the basis of principles of participatory democracy and a minimization of hierarchy and rigid structure (Stott, 1981).

Feminists have developed a plethora of activities including legal groups such as Rights of Women (ROW), day nurseries, rape crisis centres, battered women's shelters and pro-abortion groups. Within specific issue areas such as abortion and domestic violence national coordinating structures have evolved (respectively, the National Abortion Campaign (NAC) and National Women's Aid Federation (NWAF), dealing with domestic violence), but their scope and breadth are limited. These groups lack coherent membership and leadership as well as means of resolving conflicts and insuring cooperation with conference resolutions (Bouchier, 1984).

In Britain, even groups with a national focus are ambivalent about campaigning (lobbying) and the legislative process, although in fact the NWAF and NAC have intervened effectively in the political process. Because NAC's members are socialist feminists, they have ties to the Labour Party and trade union movement. The potential of this alliance was evident in 1979, when a mass demonstration, with major participation by the Trades Union Congress (TUC), helped to stop the Corrie bill which threatened to reduce access to legal abortions.

However, the focus of most British feminist groups is interaction emphasizing value and life-style change. Consequently, the politics of personal experience has often eclipsed the avowedly political. While women's liberation politics may provide a model for other leftist groups in its emphasis on autonomy, flexibility and democracy, the lack of a coordinating mechanism presents continuing problems (Rowbotham, 1979).

The British feminist movement lacks an overall network in which different views may find expression and audience (Coote, 1981). If, as suggested here, it is a 'deliberately dispersed collection of groups, campaigns and political tendencies with no single ideology', the absence of coalitional structures prevents organization around multiple issues on a continuing basis (Bouchier, 1984).

There can be little doubt that such elements as networking, lobbying and emphasis on legal change are more evident in the US movement. Activists have mobilized around state legislation and legal change — and have often been less reluctant than their British counterparts to engage with political and bureaucratic forces and to seek legitimacy. Hence, questions relating to leadership and structure, engagement with political forces at all levels and the need for coalition have been treated differently in the USA than in Britain. An area of congruence lies in the fact that in both countries women's liberation groups have tended to focus around single issues, and do not necessarily join together with other movement activists in multiple-issue alignments. While in the USA a more radical women's movement still exists, primarily at the grass-roots level, it is less visible and to a greater degree has joined forces with the more 'middle-class establishment' sector of the original movement.

Women's Action Day. Several new developments in Britain represent steps towards coalition-building among different ideological groups in the women's community. In November 1980, a Women's Action Day was held in London which involved some sixty-seven organizations from a variety of women's perspectives and sought to discuss and develop common policies. A 'women's agenda' was distributed, dealing with issues of equal opportunity in law, education, work, politics, finances, the family, health and the media. Groups represented included unions, the NAC and ROW, traditional women's groups such as the National Council of Women and elements of the Liberal and Labour Parties. With a grant from the EOC, Women's Action Group (WAG) has got together a Lobby Pack with questions to be put to candidates for by-elections and parliamentary elections (interview, Pamela Robinson, 1982). A number of feminist groups, aided by funds from the Greater London Council (GLC), have purchased a new building to share cooperatively in London. The NCCL and EOC have provided forums for a diverse group of women activists.

A new political advocacy group — the 300 Group — has sought to increase the number of women in the House of Commons (now 25 out of 635, or about 4 per cent). Like its US counterpart, the National Women's Political Caucus (NWPC), it seeks to recruit and train women candidates for political office. Now under new leadership, the 300 Group has a central staff and offices, indicating its ability to endure and grow even while continuing to encounter hostility from traditional party groups which resent external intrusion, and from feminists who dislike its relatively centralized entrepreneurial style. None the less, it has trained over 1,500 women and helped them to gain interest and confidence in politics.

The future of WAG and the 300 Group is unclear, and, as suggested above, networking across ideological lines is still rare in Britain, although support for the concept is growing from many feminist activists. The close relationship that has developed in the USA in terms of resource-sharing, political access and even consensus on goals between the so-called traditional women's groups and their reformist and even radical feminist allies has no analogue in the political culture of Britain.

The role of women in political parties
As suggested in the introduction to this chapter, historically British feminists have also been organized and influential as pressure groups within existing institutions, namely, political parties and trade unions. Despite concern about cooptation and ideological dilution by male-dominated structures, feminists, especially those on the left, have sought to develop alliances with these institutions in order to

further their political goals. None the less, increased activism by feminists has not ended a pattern of women's participation in these institutions, which has been marked by 'marginalization' and isolation from power.

In general, although women comprise at least half of the membership of the Labour and Conservative Parties, their role within party structures is circumscribed (Hills, 1978). Women in political parties and trade unions are organized into separate advisory groups with few powers and have limited ability to gain acceptance for resolutions they have passed. In addition, they are limited to statutory or set-aside seats on decision-making bodies. In the main, the more significant a policy-making body is, the fewer women it has on it. It should be noted that the Labour Party, although closer to feminists on some policy issues and in ideological terms, has had no better a record on representation and power-sharing than its Conservative opposition; in fact, it is arguably worse. Because of union dominance in the Labour Party, and the fact that unions cast their votes in a bloc fashion, the so-called 'women's seats' (5 out of 29) on the powerful National Executive Committee are union-controlled and do not represent an independent feminist influence (Hills, 1981).

Still, the extent of feminist participation within the Labour Party is impressive and often channels socialist feminist energy into party activities. In recent years, women's labour groups have grown and proliferated — from the Women's Action Committee (WAC) associated with the far left Campaign for Labour Party Democracy (CLPD) to a Women's Rights Study Group established with MP Jo Richardson as chair. A group called Fightback for Women's Rights is active at the party's fringes. The latter has been especially vigorous in pressing for more channels to the Labour Party hierarchy — in the form of five resolutions to be automatically sent to the Labour Party Annual Conference by the Women's Section and the election of women members to the National Executive Committee by the Women's Conference. Fightback and WAC also advocate an end to all-male parliamentary short-lists. A Women's Charter has been developed and promoted by the Women's Action Committee of the CLPD. (A measure of increased interest in women's activities is to be found in the increased number of women's delegates, from 320 to 650, at the annual Labour Women's Conference from 1980 to 1981: (interview, Rachel Lever, Fightback, July 1982.) As yet, their repeated requests for greater influence within the party power structures have gone unheeded.

While women are better represented at the Conservative Party conferences, such bodies lack the policy-making authority of the Labour Party. Tory power is concentrated in the parliamentary leadership and the National Union. In the latter, women have comprised between 20 and 25 per cent of the total, although they are often not very vocal despite their greater numbers (Hills, 1978). The British section of the European Union of Women and Women's National Advisory Group has been active in pressing for greater representation for and responsiveness to women in the party.

In both parties, women have consistently been under-represented as candidates standing for election. The trade union 'A' lists in the Labour Party had 3 females out of 103 candidates in 1977 (Hills, 1978). The 'B' or constituency lists had 9 per cent women's names in 1976, with women commonly nominated for marginal or losing seats, as is often common in the USA (Hills, 1978). In 1982 Labour had 25 women on a list of 250 candidates, and 4 new female Labour MPs were elected. While the Conservative Party attracts more women candidates (largely as a result of economic status, available time and educational level — Hills, 1978:2), 1982's list had only 10 per cent women, down from 15 per cent in 1977 (*Guardian*, 16 April 1982). Only the new Social Democratic Party (SDP) has gone further than its better established colleagues in meeting feminist demands for better representation within the party hierarchy and on short-lists. It mandates women on every short-list (at least 2 out of 9) and representational equality for women on the party's National Steering Committee (interview, Polly Toynbee, July 1982).

Each party seems to be firmly committed to the continuation of separate women's committees; these are endorsed by feminists as an important forum through which demands may be articulated, and attention focused on women's issues. Women have used their separatist organizations to press demands for feminist concerns including equal pay, child care and positive action in employment and education. In each case, feminist party activists would like to see women's groups play a stronger consultative role.

None the less, political parties may provide less of a link to policy-making in a system such as the British one, increasingly controlled by bureaucratic functionaries. In addition, the hierarchical mass-based structure of party groups in Britain is antithetical to that of women's liberation — and the relationship between many women and party activism is at best ambivalent.

The role of women in trade unions
In contrast to the USA, where only 16 per cent of women are unionized, the comparable percentage in Britain is about 44 per cent, with a dramatic increase in the last decade (Hills, 1981; Randall, 1982). Of 12 million TUC members in 1980, about 4 million were women (TGWU, 1980). Female union membership increased between 1961 and 1980 by 110 per cent, while male membership

increased by only 17.6 per cent (Coote and Campbell, 1982). Perhaps
to a greater degree than in the USA, the concept of a 'family wage' —
for the breadwinning man — has been entrenched, and this has
limited equal job access for women in the labour market (Land,
1979). But once in the labour market, women in Britain are
unionized more commonly than women in the USA.

While many socialist and non-aligned feminists organized
autonomously in their local communities and sought to develop
specific feminist projects and activities for battered women, day care,
self-help clinics and the like, other socialist feminists have sought to
forge links with trade unions in order to reach out to working-class
women. While efforts to politicize newly organized women workers
(especially in white-collar unions, where their numbers have greatly
expanded) have met with some success, and socialist feminists have
gained support for some key issues from the trade unions, in the main
women have virtually no power in unions and have been unable to
alter existing patterns of low pay and job segregation. Women lack
representation in key union committees, among full-time officers and
at the local shop level as stewards and district committee members.
While a number of unions have a majority of women workers, men
remain in control of top positions in individual unions and the TUC.

A survey by Anna Coote and Peter Kellner in 1980 showed that,
while 38 per cent of union members surveyed were women, only 11
per cent of the executive members, fewer than 6 per cent of the full-
time officials and under 15 per cent of delegates to the TUC in these
unions were women. The 1981 TUC annual meeting had 116 women
among the 1,188 delegates present (TUC, 1982:1).

Feminists have sought greater influence in two ways. In political
parties, they have advocated 'positive action/discrimination', retaining or establishing 'set-aside' or 'statutory' seats on executive
committees and seeking other types of special representation,
through advisory committees, women's conferences and the like. In
some instances, such efforts do not represent a 'new approach';
in the TUC Women's Advisory Committee and annual women's
conference they date back to the 1920s and 1930s respectively
(Randall, 1982). As is the case for political parties, advisory
committees have a solely consultative role and depend on the (often
lacking) sympathy of general councils and other policy-making
bodies for acceptance. Like the Labour Party, the TUC, to which
most British unions are affiliated, responded to women's demands by
increasing the number of statutory delegate places reserved for
women in the TUC Executive Committee: from 2 to 5 out of 41.

Among the white-collar unions whose female membership is
growing especially rapidly, there have been particular efforts to
create special opportunities for women. These include the

appointment of national women's officers, statutory executive council seats for women, the establishment of women's advisory committees and the creation of equal opportunities or women's rights groups at the district level. Consciousness-raising and special training sessions for women have even been introduced into several unions — including GMWU, TASS and the TUC. Feminists have also sought union support for feminist-related issues.

A dramatic and impressive instance of union support for feminist issues came in a massive demonstration — a joint TUC–feminist march in 1979 — to protest against the possibility of restrictive anti-abortion legislation, then pending in the House of Commons in the Corrie bill. This marked a unique expression of union support which moved beyond the rhetorical level to practical action.

With regard to other key feminist demands (also endorsed by the TUC) — equal job opportunities for women and an end to pay discrimination — only limited progress has been made. As suggested above, male dominance still exists in the unions at all levels, from regional councils to the shop floor and in industry-wide negotiation teams. Hence, while the focus has been on 'social issues' of concern to working women, such as abortion, welfare, housing benefits, day care and the mobilization of women — impact has been minimal on economic and industrial matters such as pay and maternity leave. It is the latter over which men still retain firm control and discretion and limit possibilities for the implementation of the numerous resolutions passed in union conferences. To a large degree, women's concerns are viewed as part of a larger concern for social and economic issues, with a resulting subordination of feminist demands (Scott, 1982), leaving male bastions of power and sexism untouched. (See Bouchier, 1984, for a similar point.)

Government-based advocacy of women's issues in Britain

Not surprisingly, given the institutional setting described, women are poorly represented in British political life. Only 25 women serve in Parliament, although a record 210 stood for election in 1982 (European Union of Women, 1982). In addition to the female (though hardly feminist) prime minister, Margaret Thatcher, there are 3 other women ministers in the present Conservative government. Of 97 senior judges, only 2 are women. In the senior civil service in 1974, only 4 per cent of high administrative officers were women. Few women are nominated to, or serve on, government committees, councils or other public bodies. And at the local level, there were only 2 chief women's officers out of 500 (Hills, 1981:27). Women have increased the proportion they make up of local councillors — in 1982 they comprised 18.4 per cent (EOC, 1983:95). However, as suggested above, the structure of power in Britain is predominantly male.

Against this backdrop, during the 1960s and early 1970s pressure arose within parliament for the creation of a quasi-independent body to 'act as an amalgam of recipient and investigator complaints relating to sex discrimination, conciliator where possible and pro-secutor in the courts where this failed' (Byrne and Lovenduski, 1978:57). The result was the creation of the Equal Opportunities Commission (EOC) to enforce the Equal Pay and Sex Discrimination Acts. The EOC was given law enforcement powers, research and investigative capacity and jurisdiction over a number of policy areas related to women (education, housing and employment) (Meehan, 1983:70–1). It was hoped that the EOC would be a strong voice on behalf of women and would play a strong enforcement role. In practice, the Commission has not developed as the strong defender of equal rights that many hoped, although it does provide a forum and base for feminist-related issues, one of the few that exist in a system essentially closed to change-oriented groups.

In recent years the number of cases brought to the EOC under the Sex Discrimination Act has remained at a relatively low 250 annually, while equal pay cases have dropped from 1,742 in 1976 to 54 in 1981 (EOC *Annual Report*, 1981: App. 3:32). Those figures suggest that the Equal Pay Act (EPA) in particular has limited impact today (*Guardian*, 16 June 1982).

It is difficult to escape the conclusion that disillusionment with the EPA has resulted in the reluctance of women to press their cases under it, because the Act has failed to live up to expectations. The failure to address issues of equal pay may be responsible for at least part of the Act's diminishing impact. Additional factors limiting the effectiveness of the EOC are its location in Manchester (though it does maintain a small London office) and the absence of regional offices (interview, Lady Betty Lockwood, August 1982). As a result of Conservative government cuts, the Commission was forced to reduce its staff from 400 to 148 (*Guardian*, 10 July 1980).

A second potential institutional base for women's advocacy, the Women's National Commission, established and sponsored by government in 1969, has a strictly advisory role and lacks diverse membership as well as resources (Stott, 1978).

The policy process
Analysis of public policy reveals a number of legislative enactments related to women in Britain. In the area of equal rights, Britain has passed an Equal Pay Act (1970) and a Sex Discrimination Act (1975) — the latter establishing the Equal Opportunities Commission to enforce the new laws. The Employment Protection Act (1975) gave women a statutory right to paid maternity leave, protection from

unfair dismissal during pregnancy and the right to regain their jobs up to twenty-nine weeks after giving birth (Coote and Campbell, 1982). (This provision was, however, made more restrictive by the Thatcher government.) With regard to violence and victimization of women and the right to self-determination, the Domestic Violence and Matrimonial Proceedings Act (1976) strengthened procedures by which women could obtain injunctions to restrain violent males with whom they lived (although it provided no funding for victims), while the Sexual Offences (Amendment) Act provided better safeguards for a rape victim's privacy during trial (Coote and Campbell, 1982). The 1967 Abortion Act authorizes abortion up to twenty-eight weeks of pregnancy in cases where two doctors agree that the life of the mother or other children would be at risk or if the baby were likely to be handicapped (Randall, 1982). The law has been interpreted liberally, with the demand for abortions accommodated both by the National Health Service (NHS) and the private sector. Implementation has varied with physicians' attitudes in different areas in the country and the Conservative government's spending cuts.

Most women-oriented legislation in Britain did not come about as a result of pressure from feminists, but rather from political parties and trade unions, which have 'literally pre-empted feminist demands and have put their political clout behind numerous proposals to advance equality between women and men' (Scott, 1982:180). The European Economic Community (EEC), which Britain joined in 1972, served as a catalyst in the area of anti-discrimination legislation. As suggested above, it appears that in Britain the implementation of policies enacted regarding equal rights has often been more difficult than securing the legislation itself.

Analysis of legislative enactments related to feminist concerns leads to the conclusion that feminists have been able to influence public policy primarily as an auxiliary resource for parliamentary actors who are responsible for initiating and passing the legislation (see Randall, 1982; Pym, 1974; Marsh and Chambers, 1981). As suggested earlier, support for measures relating to women's equality and welfare has left political parties and trade unions free to pursue issues of equality in the work-place and in their own decision-making bodies at their own (snail's) pace and on their own terms, leaving basic structures of power and male dominance largely untouched. In addition, given the nature of the administrative process outlined earlier, there is virtually no mechanism for interested groups to ensure compliance with enacted policy, nor are feminists able to exert influence over processes of enforcement because of their fragmented, localized structure.

Thus, the impact of policy aimed at women's concerns in Britain has been less than impressive (with the exception of abortion rights), while at the same time legislation may have served as a convenient symbol muting further demands for political change.

Grass-roots activism revisited

This chapter has suggested that British feminists have, in the main, been concerned more with changing consciousness than with public policy (Bouchier, 1984). None the less, a recent development in numerous British urban areas has interfaced effectively with the decentralized structure of British feminism. Since 1969, a variety of multifaceted action groups have developed in many British urban areas, centred around feminist collectives, rape crisis centres, battered women's shelters, health clinics, black women's groups and groups of women in law, the media and other professions (see Bouchier, 1984). Feminists have turned to local councils for funding, access and space in order to maintain their activities, and (fearing hierarchy and male cooptation) have tended to prefer local-level dialogues to those at the national level.

Aided in part by the growing number of women in local councils mentioned above, since 1982 several local councils have created women's committees to take up issues of representation of women and women's interests (Goss, 1984). Such committees have been established in the GLC, in numerous London boroughs (including Camden, Islington, Southwark and Hackney), and in twenty-two other British urban centres (including Scotland). Virtually all of these constituencies are under Labour Party domination; support for some women's committees has come from local councillors, while for others the initiatives for committee establishment have emanated from the women's movement itself. In Leeds, for example, a local conference which drew together Labour Party women, trade union members and local women's groups (including Rape Crisis, Asian Women and the 300 Group) resulted in the formation of a Women's Resources Committee (Flannery and Roelofs, 1984). The greatest resources were those of the GLC, which in 1984 devoted nearly £8 million to funding local women's groups and projects (interview, Valerie Wise, July 1984).

The GLC Women's Resources Committee has attempted to involve a wide spectrum of women by holding open meetings and coopting women to represent such groups as lesbians, the disabled and trade unionists (Goss, 1984). Funding has been given to the Greenham Common women for day care and to a female transportation service, as well as to day care and health facilities — all to a generally hostile press reception (Flannery and Roelofs, 1984). A major thrust of the GLC Women's Committee was to foster multi-action centres for women, thus bringing some order to the centrifugal politics we have described, perhaps building on the women's action centres that already exist in many British cities (interview, Valerie Wise, July 1984).

Other women's committees have been established in the London boroughs of Camden and Islington, with varying degrees of success. The Camden group, with strong support from local Labour council-lors, has devoted considerable funding to women's efforts. A Women's Bus travels around the community to focus discussions and provide information and advice (Goss, 1984; Flannery and Roelofs, 1984). However, in Islington, as of 1984 the women's unit was all but defunded and defunct (interview, Hilary Potter, July 1984).

While the trend towards local-level support for women's efforts in Britain is still too new to measure — and it is worth recalling that the GLC was abolished in April 1986 by the Thatcher government — these efforts to provide linkages between traditional, socialist and radial feminist groups, and to seek to reach out to the vast number of British women who have heretofore been unaffected by the feminist movement, are notable. Whether local-level priorities will be reorganized and feminists given real power (as opposed to the customary advisory role), and a modus vivendi reached between feminist democracy and traditional hierarchical government struc-tures, as yet remains to be seen.

Conclusion

It is clear that the British feminist movement has succeeded in changing life-styles and consciousnesses, as well as creating a host of alternative services and community-based women's activities in (primarily) urban centres throughout the British Isles. The degree of activism and commitment are impressive, even to the casual observer. But with regard to other measures of 'success' — those related to the larger society and policy outcomes — the movement's achievements have been less impressive. Only a fraction of British women has been reached by the women's liberation movement in its various manifestations; the movement remains isolated, both by deliberate design and by the obstacles erected by British political and economic institutions. While the energy of British feminism has been able to achieve policy triumphs such as the mass demonstrations in the case of abortion rights (against the Corrie bill) and Greenham Common, the movement continues to exist on the fringes of British life. Its isolation from most British women has been reinforced by media emphasis on the movement's domination by anti-male radical feminists.

While public policy enactments related to such movement goals as equal pay, sex discrimination, abortion and domestic violence have reflected feminist concerns via trade union and Labour Party politics, the impact of policy change has been minimal. The major exception is in the area of abortion policy, where a coalition of trade unionists, feminists and Labour Party activists has effectively intervened to prevent a weakening of the existing law and also mobilized to weaken the impact of a restrictive interpretation by the Department of Health and Social Security after 1981. Furthermore, the EOC, TUC and women's groups have succeeded in expanding public consciousness around such issues as positive action and equal value (equal pay) (Atkins and Hoggett, 1984:198).

This chapter has suggested the significance of several major factors which appear to limit the role of British feminists: the closed and inflexible nature of British government, particularly the administrative process; the reluctance of key institutions such as political parties and trade unions to go beyond rhetoric in meaningfully sharing power; and the localized, purist nature of the women's liberation movement, which has failed to create coalitions and an enduring national presence. Whether these obstacles to success of the women's movement in Britain may yet be overcome will be a subject for future analysis.

List of abbreviations

CND   Committee for Nuclear Disarmament
CPAG   Child Poverty Action Group
CLPD   Campaign for Labour Party Democracy
EOC   Equal Opportunities Commission
EPA   Equal Pay Act
EEC   European Economic Community
GLC   Greater London Council
GMWU   General and Municipal Workers Union
MSC   Manpower Services Commission
NAC   National Abortion Federation
NCCL   National Council for Civil Liberties
NHS   National Health Service
NWAF   National Women's Aid Federation
SDA   Sex Discrimination Act
TGWU   Transport and General Workers' Union
TUC   Trades Union Congress
WAC   Women's Action Committee
WAG   Women's Action Group
WRRC   Women's Research and Resources Committee

References

Ashford, Douglas (1981) *Policy and Politics in Britain*. Philadelphia: Temple University Press.

Atkins, Susan and Brenda Hoggett (1984) *Women and the Law*. Oxford: Basil Blackwell.

Blondel, Jean (1974) *Voters, Parties, and Leaders*. Harmondsworth: Penguin.

Bouchier, David (1984) *The Feminist Challenge*. New York: Schocken.

Byrne, Paul and Joni Lovenduski (1978) 'Sex Equality and the Law in Britain', *British*

Journal of Law and Society, 5(2): 148–65.

Christoph, James P. (1974) 'Capital Punishment and British Politics: The Role of Pressure Groups', in Richard Kember and J. J. Richardson, *Pressure Groups in Britain: A Reader*. London: Dent.

Coote, Anna and Peter Kellner (1980) 'Hear This Brother'. *New Statesman*.

Coote, Anna and Beatrix Campbell (1982) *Sweet Freedom: The Struggle for Women's Liberation*. London: Picador.

Costain, Anne (1982) 'Representing Women', in E. Boneparte (ed.), *Women, Power and Policy*. Oxford: Pergamon Press.

Deckard, Barbara S. (1983) *The Women's Movement*. New York: Harper & Row.

EOC News (various issues).

EOC (1981, 1982, 1983) Annual Report. Manchester: Equal Opportunities Commission.

Eurobarometer (1983) 'Gender Roles in the European Community', *Eurobarometer*, 19 (Ann Arbor, Michigan).

European Union of Women (1982) *Seizing Our Opportunities*. London: EUW.

Flannery, Kate and S. Roelofs (1984) 'Local Governments' Women's Committees,' in Joy Holland (ed.), *Feminist Action*. London: Battle Axe Books.

Freeman, Jo (1975) *The Politics of Women's Liberation*. New York: McKay.

Gelb, Joyce and Marion Palley (1982) *Women and Public Politics*. Princeton: Princeton University Press.

Goss, Sue (1984) 'Women's Initiatives in Local Government', in Martin Boddy and C. Fudge (eds), *Local Socialism?* London: Macmillan.

Hills, Jill (1978) 'Women in the Labour and Conservative Parties'. Unpublished paper, prepared for PSA conference.

Hills, Jill (1981) 'Britain', in J. Hills and Joni Lovenduski, *Politics of the Second Electorate*. London: Routledge & Kegan Paul.

Inglehart, Ronald (1977) *The Silent Revolution*. Princeton: Princeton University Press.

Jennings, M. Kent, Klaus Aurbuck and Leopold Rosenmeyer (1979) 'Generations and Families', in S. Barnes and Max Kaase, *Mass Participation in Five Western Democracies*. Beverly Hills: Sage.

Jenson, Jane (1983) 'Success Without Struggle? The Modern Women's Movement in France'. Unpublished paper.

Kaase, Max and Alan Marsh (1979) 'Distribution of Political Action', in S. Barnes and Max Kaase, *Mass Participation in Five Western Democracies*. Beverly Hills: Sage.

Land, Hilary (1979) 'The Family Wage'. *Feminist Review*, 6: 55–7.

Marsh, David and Joanna Chambers (1981) *Abortion Politics*. London: Junction Books.

Meehan, Elizabeth (1983) 'The Priorities of the EOC', *Political Quarterly*, January/March.

National Council for Voluntary Organizations (NCVO) (1981) Information Sheet 6.

Parkin, Frank (1968) *Middle Class Radicalism*. Manchester: Manchester University Press.

Phillips, Andrew (1982) *Charitable Status*. London: Interaction.

Punnett, R. M. (1980) *British Government and Politics*. London: Heinemann.

Pym, Bridget (1974) *Pressure Groups and the Permissive Society*. Newton Abbott, Devon: David and Charles.

Quart, Barbara (1983) 'Dancing on the Missile Silos: Letter from London'. *The Nation*, 28 May: 655–63.

Randall, Vicki (1982) *Women and Politics*. New York: St Martin's Press.

Richardson, J. T. and A. G. Jordan (1979) *Governing Under Pressure*. London:

Martin Robertson.

Rivers, Patrick (1974) *Politics by Pressure*. London: Merlin Press.

Robarts, Sadye, Anna Coote and E. Ball (1980) *Positive Action for Women*. London: NCCL.

Robinson, Pamela (1982) 'Women's Action Group Committee Report'. Unpublished report.

Rowbotham, Sheila (1979) *Beyond the Fragments*. London: Merlin Press.

Scott, Hilda (1982) *Sweden's Right to be Human*. London: Allison and Busby.

Sebestyen, Amanda (1979) *Notes From the Tenth Year*. London: Theory Press.

Stacey, Margaret and Marion Price (1980), *Women, Power and Politics*. London: Tavistock.

Stott, Mary (1978) *Organization Women*. London: Heinemann.

Stott, Mary (1980) 'Can Women Put Politics Aside to Unite on a Common Platform?' *The Guardian*, 26 November: 11.

TGWU (1980) *Women's Handbook*. London: Transport and General Workers' Union.

TUC (1982) 'Women's Conference Report'. London: Trades Union Congress Women's Advisory Committee.

Wandor, Michelle (1972) *Body Politic. Stage 1*. London: Stage 1.

Whitely and Winyard (1983) 'Influencing Social Policy: The Effectiveness of the Poverty Lobby in Britain', *Journal of Social Policy*, 12: 10–11.

Wilson, Elizabeth (1980) *Only Half Way to Paradise*. London: Tavistock.

6
The women's movement, politics and policy in the Reagan era

Virginia Sapiro

Introduction

The latest phase of US feminism is now about twenty years, or a generation, old. Although it has not yet achieved the longevity of the previous era of sustained feminist activity — the suffrage movement, which lasted roughly from the decade of the 1860s to 1920, when the suffrage amendment to the Constitution was ratified — the current wave of feminism has made a lasting impression on US life.

One of the important questions that faces not just US feminism but women's movements world-wide, is what happens when a social movement with at least some measure of sympathy and support from governmental leadership confronts a change in the political climate that works against it. This is exactly what happened in the USA in the 1980s when President Reagan brought with him the first explicitly anti-feminist administration in memory. This chapter explores the relationship between the US women's movement and the Reagan administration, including the effect of the administration on the movement and vice versa.

Although the chapter will outline the shape of the movement as a whole, it will concentrate on a particular aspect of women's movement politics in the USA: its relationship to public policy on women and conventional electoral politics. This aspect of movement politics is especially important in the US context because of certain features of the political system that are substantially different from those found in most European countries. Two points bear special attention. First, although many feminists are very active in political parties, the women's movement as a whole has maintained its independence from political party organizations, preferring to label itself bipartisan or nonpartisan in an attempt not to be 'owned' or coopted by the party organizations. Second, and related, social movements and interest groups (and especially those outside the dominant economic interest groups of business and labour), as distinct from political parties, have tended to play a greater and more independent role in conventional politics and policy-making than is generally true in European political systems.

The women's movement and politics before Reagan
The women's movement grew in size and complexity through the
1960s and 1970s. The early patterns of development are well
documented in Jo Freeman's (1974) book on the origins of the
movement. The feminist movement was complex and diverse from
the start in that it grew from two general sources that became inter-
mixed. The first included women who held positions or were active in
the national and state government or political party organizations
(Tinker, 1983). Some had long been active in support of an Equal
Rights Amendment to the Constitution, which had first been
proposed to Congress in the early 1920s. Many were members of
state-level Commissions on the Status of Women which were formed
at the instigation of President Kennedy. A group of members of these
Commissions was responsible for the formation of the largest and
best known feminist organization, the National Organization for
Women (NOW).

NOW was formed by a group of delegates to a national meeting of
Commissions on the Status of Women in 1966 who were frustrated by
the constraints placed on them and the slowness of governmental
response. NOW became particularly active in pursuing legal changes
in the status of women including, especially, those that affect education, employment and reproductive rights. In the following years
many other national, state and local organizations pursuing related
goals were formed. One of the best known is the National Women's
Political Caucus (NWPC), which is dedicated to increasing the
influence of women in government.

The other strand of feminism involved women who were, on
average, younger and were involved in the social movements of the
1960s, including, especially, the civil rights, student and anti-war
movements (Evans, 1979). These women turned their often radical
politics to the concerns of women; they organized more at the local
level and often in a less formal way than the other strand of feminism.
Out of this base came the early emphasis on consciousness-raising
and organizations such as rape crisis centres and shelters for battered
women.

As Freeman points out, the women's movement quickly
mushroomed. While the movement as a whole had been held
together through the 1970s by a common desire to see the ratification
of an Equal Rights Amendment (ERA) to the Constitution, it was
also marked by the development of groups and organizations as
diverse — and sometimes as conflicting — as one can imagine.
Groups devoted to the specific concerns of black women, older
women and lesbians, among others, sprang up. Feminists formed
their own groups within many job classifications as well as business,
trade, labour and arts associations. The universities provided a

setting not just for organizations of feminist educators interested in the status of women as professional educators, but also for the growth of a new field of enquiry: women's studies. By the end of the 1970s most colleges and universities had courses on women, a very large proportion had formal women's studies programmes and a number offered undergraduate and even graduate degrees in women's studies. The expansion of academic feminism helped to promote the impressive growth of the feminist publishing trade, including the yearly publication of hundreds of new books on women and feminism, many offered through feminist publishing houses, and scores of feminist periodicals.

Feminists also organized around specific issues of special concern to women including education, employment and reproductive and marital rights; violence against women; the 'feminization of poverty' and child care. In almost every arena of human life, feminists were soon found attempting to exert their influence.

The women's movement was not, however, simply composed of leaders in selected areas of human concern. It became a truly mass movement which involved often impressive shifts in the consciousness and attitudes of women in the mass public. As Ethel Klein (1984) has pointed out, the post-second world war breakdown of longstanding gender roles in the family and labour market pushed women into a new understanding of their problems and their potential as women. As a result, the distinctions that Freeman (1974) noted between the 'older' and 'younger' or 'conservative' and 'radical' dichotomy in the movement blurred and broke down. (Of course, one reason the age distinctions are blurred is that the earlier 'young' faction is now in — or is rapidly approaching — middle age.) There are certainly clear differences and conflicts within the movement, but these range across the many sociological and ideological fissures familiar in other countries.

What was the impact of the women's movement up to the late 1970s? First and foremost, there was an impressive growth in feminist consciousness among US women and increasing popular support for more diverse social roles and a higher status for women (Klein, 1984). Second, there was a tremendous proliferation of groups and organizations aimed at improving the quality of life for women. Most cities and a large proportion of towns have at least some women-oriented services, including women's health and counselling centres, rape crisis centres, shelters for battered women and women's transit services. There was also a growth of businesses (often with cooperative structures) providing special services to women by women, including bookshops, restaurants, publishing houses, music companies and law firms.

A third area of impact, and the one that will serve as the dominant theme of this essay, is that of the women's movement on government and government policy. Unfortunately, while it is relatively simple to document change in governmental policy on women, it is less easy to determine the causal links between social movements and policy change. Much of this analytical work is yet to be done. Ethel Klein has offered a useful starting point by graphing the relationship among feminist activism, relevant bills submitted to Congress and legislative success (passage) of these bills from 1899 to 1980 (Klein, 1984:12). The lines show a rough correlation, but further research needs to be done.

From auxiliaries to individuals
Until the 1960s the principles of law and policy as they affected women were simple and straightforward. The gender division of life and labour into men's and women's spheres was regarded as essential to a well functioning society. Policy on women was based on an ideology that defined women as mothers and wives — or potential mothers and wives — within a patriarchal family system. The implications are two-fold. First, policy assumed that in the normal course of events women would serve as housekeepers and mothers, and would be dependent upon a husband for support. Men would make a living and women would make a home. The protection of men's independent rights and economic opportunities was therefore more important than the protection of women's. Women's income, like their labour, was defined as auxiliary.

Second, this ideology went further in its prescriptive values and argued that patriarchal families and family values constituted the core of a stable and well functioning social system. This view of the family hangs on regulating women's sexual, reproductive and work lives in such a way as to block their path to opportunities outside the family and to maintain their situation of being subordinate to and dependent on a man.

In the 1960s and especially the 1970s, law and policy on women changed substantially in some areas, while in others it was possible to see the beginnings of a change in the underlying gender ideology. Women began to be treated less simply in terms of their functional roles as family members and auxiliaries and more as independent autonomous beings with their own rights. The law began to state that, even if most women were found to perform certain roles, or to have specific and apparently gender-linked characteristics, the law must treat individual women as individuals. It also began to suggest that, even if governments continued to want to preserve traditional family values, this goal did not constitute a strong enough reason to interfere with women's rights as citizens. Policy-makers began to recognize that 'the' family was not perhaps as healthy an institution for women as it once seemed, and they therefore began, albeit slowly, to respond to problems such as wife-battering and marital rape.

The shift in governmental action took a number of forms in the 1960s and 1970s. Study commissions and special offices dealing with women's issues sprang up throughout the federal bureaucracy, and many agencies reserved special sums of grant money for research and development on women's needs and problems. This type of action, encouraged by the development of women's studies, provided a relatively painless way for an agency to show its concern for the status of women. The agencies also encouraged state and local action by providing grant money for special projects relating to women's problems. The network of rape crisis centres and shelters for battered women are only two examples of the kinds of projects that used federal seed money. Indeed, one could argue that much of the change in many women's policy areas that took place in those years was accomplished by a combination of federal money with local action, and was organized by feminists found at both levels. This is one reason why women's organizations are wary of the Reagan administration's desire to 'turn responsibility back to the states' by cutting such federal grants programmes.

Federal action to change women's policy fell primarily in two areas — civil rights and poverty relief — with the former being considerably more successful than the latter. What follows is a brief review of some of the most significant changes.

The 1960s witnessed the first federal statutes attacking sex discrimination. These statutes, which concerned employment discrimination, included the 1963 Equal Pay Act and Title VII of the 1964 Civil Rights Act. The former declared discrimination in pay illegal, and the latter declared discrimination in hiring, firing, benefits, promotions and job conditions illegal.

Although neither act had much impact until the 1970s for reasons discussed below, the cause of anti-discrimination was boosted by executive orders of both President Johnson and President Nixon. Elaborating on a technique used by earlier presidents, Johnson ordered that employers who held government contracts were not only to refrain from discrimination, as Title VII had ordered them to do, but also were to undertake 'affirmative action' to prove they were making all 'good faith efforts' to avoid discriminating in employment. The punishment for failure to comply would be the loss of government contracts. This policy is widely misunderstood to have called for preferential treatment of minorities and women over more qualified white males. The reality is that these programmes amounted to massive bookkeeping exercises to prove that employers had at least considered women and minorities, which probably scared some employers into action but which never ended up in the loss of contracts.

The era of real change

The era of real change in policy on women and its implementation began in 1971 and 1972. The shift is marked by three events, the first two occurring in the Supreme Court and the last in Congress and the executive branch. In 1971 the Supreme Court heard the first sex discrimination case arising from Title VII of the 1964 Civil Rights Act and, for the first time, declared an act of discrimination against women illegal (*Phillips* v. *Martin Marietta*). The Court's second critical action of the year is found in *Reed* v. *Reed*, in which the Court ruled an act of sex discrimination unconstitutional on equal protection grounds, and signalled its intention to scrutinize sex discrimination cases more strictly in the future.

The third critical event of the 1971–2 season was the acquisition by the Equal Employment Opportunities Commission (EEOC) of the power to litigate. The EEOC was the enforcement agency created by the 1964 Civil Rights Act, but it had little real power until this new congressional mandate. As a result, the government, through the executive branch, shared the burden of Title VII lawsuits with the victims of discrimination; the government itself could sue offenders.

The discrimination policies developed during the remainder of the 1970s were largely extensions and elaborations within this framework. The Supreme Court followed its own precedents, and when it seemed to falter, for example on the issue of discrimination against pregnant women, Congress put it back on track by writing an amendment to Title VII which specified that discrimination against pregnant women was illegal. The EEOC, like other agencies, was generally filled with advocates committed to the mission of the agency: the eradication of discrimination. They were slowed down considerably by inadequate resources, but they stayed on track even if the train moved slowly. The same can be said of other executive actions during the Carter presidency.

Apart from employment policy, the other important area in which women's individual rights were changed by federal action concerned their control over reproduction. These changes are due almost entirely to the judicial action of the Supreme Court in the 1960s and 1970s on issues involving constitutional rights. The well-known 1965 case *Griswold* v. *Connecticut* marked the turning point, because it not only declared unconstitutional state actions prohibiting the distribution of contraceptives to married people, but also set an important precedent for the future: the Court read into the Bill of Rights a constitutional right to privacy. The Court remained relatively consistent in its application of the view that the decision over whether to have a child is a part of the fundamental right to privacy. It expanded application of the principle to include women regardless of age or marital status and, further, to protect the right of a woman to have an abortion, at least during the first trimester (*Roe v. Wade*, 1973). The only decisions that most feminists interpret as inconsistent with the logic of protecting women's individual rights over reproduction revolve around the questions of equal protection for rich and poor raised by the abortion funding cases, in which the Court declared that states may withhold public funding for abortions, including those that are medically necessary.

As suggested above, the federal government has made efforts to alleviate the very special poverty problems that women face, although these efforts were sometimes half-hearted and resulted in little success. In accepting the patriarchal view that men are bread-winners and women are dependent upon those breadwinners, policy-makers have generally assumed that if men are helped they will pass on their improved conditions to women. This view is a variation of the more widely know 'trickle-down' theory. Thus far, it has not been found to work.

The biggest welfare programme in the USA is Aid to Families with Dependent Children (AFDC), which was a federalization of earlier state efforts and has been amended many times since its inception, particularly in the 1960s and 1970s. AFDC was designed to provide relief for impoverished children (and, after 1950, their caretakers) in families in which one parent is absent, disabled or deceased (Miller, 1983). From the 1960s to the 1970s the number of families (most of them headed by a woman) served by AFDC rose by 300 per cent, largely because the number of single mothers rose substantially owing to increasing divorce and illegitimacy rates.

To summarize, the situation Ronald Reagan found when he took office was one in which public policy and law at all levels of government were based much less on patriarchal principles regarding the treatment of women than they had been fifteen years earlier. In the conflict between individual rights of choice and the preservation of 'traditional family values', the former were beginning to win relatively consistently. Policy was having to take account of the fact that women who do not fit the traditional stereotype are now the rule rather than the exception, which in turn breaks down the support system for the traditional familial and gender ideology.

As suggested earlier, it is difficult to draw the causal connections between the women's movement and policy change. The evidence strongly suggests, however, that, while the women's movement was formed in part as a result of social and political change up through the late 1960s, the movement, including its representatives within the government, helped both to safeguard the changes that had taken place and to maintain the rate of further change. The earliest important legislation took place without a mass movement in place; but one can argue that the further and relatively rapid expansion of these efforts would not have occurred without the feminist movement.

The Reagan administration and women's policy and influence

An assessment of the Reagan era from the point of view of the women's movement can be summed up in a possible response to the old question, 'Do you want the good news or the bad news first'? The good news is that interest and participation in feminist politics has reached an unprecedented level and degree of professionalization since 1980. The bad news is that the renewed vigour of the movement can be attributed in large part to the fact that not only are the politics and policies of the Reagan administration the most explicitly anti-feminist in memory, but they have even been successful in rolling back some of the important changes that took place over the preceding two decades.

President Reagan and his allies wish not just to slow the tide of change but to reverse it. They are staunch believers in the patriarchal family and traditional values. Their view is in part a utilitarian one and in part a moral one. On the utilitarian side is the belief that, if adult citizens are matched in pairs consisting of a breadwinning male and a homemaking female, most dependents such as children and the elderly can be cared for without having to resort to public assistance. This care-giving is cheap for two reasons: the public coffers are not being tapped to pay for it, and the labour that such care requires is given 'voluntarily' by the women of the family. The match-up of homemaker with breadwinner also relieves the pressure on the labour market by reducing the demand for jobs and therefore unemployment. (This view is based on the incorrect assumption that the labour market is integrated and therefore that women usually compete with men for jobs.)

The moral view is simply that: a belief in the traditional values. Although many of Reagan's important allies in Congress and the interest groups (particularly those of the New Right) accept these moral values as a primary motive, it is not clear that a part of the moral stance, especially on the part of the President himself, is not also attributable to utilitarian purposes. These moral values support the utilitarian order described above. In some areas of the country there are about as many births to single women as to married women, partly because of the astounding rise in the number of births to adolescents in recent years. Families headed by young single mothers are more likely to become poverty-stricken than others. One way to decrease the number of people living in poverty is to reduce the number of these births.

How has the Reagan administration sought to implement its views on women's issues? In the first term of his administration, Reagan employed the usual techniques at a president's disposal: appointments, the regulatory process, the budgetary process, executive organization and various other means of influence. Following is a brief review of actions of the administration and its congressional allies on women's policy.

The platform on which Ronald Reagan was elected rejected two of the main objectives of the women's movement: choice in abortion and the Equal Rights Amendment. It was the first platform of a major party to be so explicitly antagonistic to feminism since women gained the right to vote, and it was the first since the 1940s that did not endorse the ERA. When Reagan took office the ERA was running near the end of its ratification process. A small number of additional state legislatures had to ratify by the deadline in 1982 or the whole process would have to begin again. The measure ultimately failed.

President Reagan has consistently claimed to support the idea of improving the status and opportunities of women. He has made no direct attack on the original legislation of the early 1960s. Early in his administration he attempted to show his interest by establishing and maintaining a number of offices and task forces charged with handling women's issues. In this respect he followed his predecessors, who did much the same thing. The difference is that Reagan staffed these offices not with feminists, but with activists in anti-feminist organizations. Most of his appointments to 'women's' offices were opposed to the feminist agenda, especially to the key demands such as the ERA and reproductive choice. The procedures of these offices often seemed designed to make haste as slowly as possible (Kirschten, 1982a, 1982b).

Most of the 'movement' on women's issues in the Executive Office seems to have been centred on the creation and movement of special offices and various shifts of personnel. And a considerable amount of these personnel and organizational changes in the executive branch seemed designed to forestall real policy change. The Women's Bureau in the Labour Department, for example, which is one of the oldest national agencies on women, had its staff cut by 28 per cent during the first year of Reagan's term (Kirschten, 1982a).

Turning to specific policy areas, the Reagan administration has worked hard to retard the pace of employment anti-discrimination policy. Michael Wines, writing in the *National Journal*, concluded that, 'taken together, the administration's actions — however well intentioned — can only be read as paring back both the scope and the pace of anti-discrimination efforts' (Wines, 1982: 537). Reagan and, not coincidentally, his key appointments in the Justice Department believe that rigid enforcement of anti-discrimination measures in the 1970s was divisive and 'overly intrusive' in its effect on the relations between employer and employee. As a result, they have written new regulations that limit both the scope of affirmative action policies and the types of suits they will undertake. In fact, very little work has been sent to the offices that deal with discrimination; staffs have been cut and cases that could have gone to court have been held up purposely.

In February 1984, the administration's point of view was upheld by the Supreme Court in an important case concerning Title IX of the Education Amendments of 1972. This law is supposed to do for education what Title VII does for employment. One of the questions involved in the case was whether, if a portion of a university were found to discriminate, federal funds must be withheld from the entire university or just from the offending portion. Previous administrations and the House of Representatives have all used the more comprehensive interpretation; the Reagan administration argued for, and the Court accepted, the more limited view of anti-discrimination sanctions.

The Reagan administration's opposition to abortion, and especially to public funding for abortion, is well known. Severe limitation on public funding was accomplished by Congress and the Supreme Court before Reagan's assumption of the presidency. Reagan wishes to go further. He is sympathetic with congressional attempts to circumvent the original abortion cases themselves, and Sandra Day O'Connor, the person he appointed to the Court as the first female Justice in US history, agrees. Reagan has supported the idea of a law that would declare conception the beginning of human life and thus, presumably, would condemn abortion as murder. Nevertheless, the Court has continued to expand the right to abortion.

The administration has been particularly active in trying to restore parental control over adolescents' access to contraception and abortion. The administration's view is that the government interferes with the privacy of the family by allowing minors to make their own decisions over reproduction without making sure the parents are involved. The administration has tried repeatedly to use its regulatory powers to achieve its ends. Linda Demkovitch notes that these efforts are significant in two respects. First, Reagan has been a strong proponent of getting government 'off people's backs' through deregulation, especially where people's private actions are concerned. Second, Reagan wants regulation, where it is deemed necessary, turned back to the states. One of the proposed regulations alone would have overturned the laws of thirty states plus the District of Columbia.

Efforts to regulate the sexual behaviour of adolescents gained at least some success through congressional action on the Public Health Service Act Amendments of 1981 relating to adolescent pregnancy and parenthood, otherwise known as 'the Teenage Chastity bill', which Reagan signed into law. This bill, which originally did contain language about the promotion of chastity, prohibited references to abortion during teenage counselling sessions that were part of federally funded programmes unless the parent and child specifically asked for information on abortion. Programmes funded by the Chastity bill included research on the 'causes and consequences of premarital adolescent sexual relations' and services to pregnancy prevention programmes, pregnant teenagers and teenaged parents. No funds can be used to pay for abortions, and they can be used for contraceptive drugs or devices only under very strict and limited conditions.

Reagan's attempts to cut back governmental social welfare policies have very direct effects on women. As many observers have noted, recent years have witnessed a 'feminization of poverty', in part owing to the rising number of single mothers. One poverty programme that has been subject to change during the Reagan era is Aid to Families with Dependent Children (AFDC): the administration relied heavily on the regulatory and budgetary processes to achieve its end of reducing the number of people receiving AFDC payments.

These are only some of the policy areas in which the Reagan administration has attempted, sometimes successfully, to turn back the tide of change on women's issues. Feminist groups have been dismayed at these actions and at numerous other indications of insensitivity to the economic and social conditions of women in the USA and abroad. One glaring example occurred in April 1982 when, in the course of explaining why the apparently high unemployment rates were not as serious as they looked, President Reagan attributed some of the size of the figures to 'the increase in women who are working today and two-worker families and so forth' (Kirschten, 1982b). Unemployment of women, it seems, is not real unemployment, or it does not matter as much as male unemployment.

The Reagan ideology on gender affects not only domestic but also foreign policy. Both houses of Congress joined feminist groups in criticizing the President in 1981 for his opposition to a voluntary international code on infant formula proposed within the World Health Organization (WHO). The WHO action came in response to estimates that up to one million infants die each year because of misuse of the formula in the Third World. Because of Reagan's view that the resolution violated freedom of speech, the USA stood alone against 119 nations that voted for the code. In 1981 the Reagan administration became infamous world-wide for arguing at an international conference on population problems that adoption of free market economies would be the only real solution to overpopulation in the Third World and that henceforth US foreign aid could not be used for any family limitation programme the administration found offensive, such as those including the use of abortion. Through their lobbying efforts on these and other administrative policies, the US feminist movement has shown its involvement not just in domestic politics but also in international politics. In some cases the President has appeared to respond positively to the agenda of the women's movement. Reagan pushed for changes in estate tax laws to ensure that women do not lose their homes or farms in widowhood. Although he has made sure that funds for child care have been cut since he took office, tax credits for child care expenses have been increased. The administration also filed a brief arguing that employers violate the 1964 Civil Rights Act by using sex-based actuarial tables in calculating life assurance payments and benefits. One of the greatest causes of poverty is the refusal of divorced husbands to pay court-ordered child support payments to their ex-wives. Realizing this, Reagan had built into the AFDC system the means for tracking down and forcing such men to pay. These efforts, however, are slight compared with the general resistance that Reagan has shown to the feminist movement.

Women's politics during the Reagan era
When people talk about changes in women's political activity they usually focus on mass-level politics, and especially the vote. By the late 1970s women and men were engaging in mass-level political action in roughly equivalent numbers. Women remain grossly under-represented among office-holders, although the proportion of women holding elective and appointive office has increased and the public has become more accustomed to the idea of women taking leadership positions.

After a slow start, President Reagan has appointed a somewhat greater number of women to government positions than did his predecessors. He placed women in some highly visible positions including, among others, the first female Supreme Court judge, two replacement cabinet members and the 'cabinet-level' ambassador to the United Nations, Jeane Kirkpatrick.

Having more women in government positions is not the same thing as increasing the power of women in government; nor does it necessarily improve the government's response to the women's movement. Women picked to serve in the administration are, as we have seen, screened for their ideological stands just as men are. For the most part, they are conservative and explicitly anti-feminist. As far as women's power in the current administration goes, Muriel Sibert for one, a stockbroker who unsuccessfully sought the Republican senatorial nomination in New York in 1982, confirmed that 'the women who represent the Republican Party at the highest levels of public life . . . have as much to do with leadership of the party as a mannequin has to do with the management of [a department store]' (*CQ Weekly*, 23 April 1983).

The gender gap
Probably the most interesting focus of attention for women and politics in the Reagan era is women's interest groups and gender differences in reactions to the President and his policies. Feminist groups sounded the alarm during the 1980 presidential election, although their support for President Carter tended to be lukewarm at best.

The major surprise of the 1980 election was not the Republican victory or its size, but the different voting patterns of women and men as groups: the 'gender gap'. Exit polls showed that 54 per cent of men and only 46 per cent of women voted for Reagan. The difference was the biggest on record. Interest in the gender gap grew after the election as it became clear that the difference of opinion was persistent. In the years since the 1980 election public opinion polls have revealed a relatively consistent gender gap, with men remaining more favourable towards the President, his party and his domestic and foreign policies than women.

Studies repeatedly show that the administration's stand on the ERA, abortion and similar issues does not entirely account for the gender difference. Kathleen Frankovic concluded from an analysis of poll data that the difference can be consistently attributed to views of militarism and peace (Frankovic, 1982). Men have been, among other things, more convinced than women that the Reagan administration's 'tough line' policy and rhetoric will help keep the country out of a major war. Men have been more convinced that war will not happen, especially if the USA builds up its arms.

An internal White House study concluded that Reagan's problem was two-fold: his defence and foreign affairs posture, and women's fear of losing government benefits (Bonafede, 1982). Women are, after all, disproportionately dependent upon the government because of their responsibility for children, their age profile and their higher levels of poverty.

Despite the persistence of the gender gap in public opinion, differences between male and female votes for Democrats versus Republicans in the 1982 and 1984 elections were only marginal. Interestingly, in those years another — and related — voting pattern emerged: the 'marriage gap'. Married people leaned towards Republicans, while people who were single for whatever reason leaned towards the Democrats (*Public Opinion*, February/March 1983: 32).

The response of feminist organizations

Feminist interest groups were spurred into unprecedented action during the Reagan era. They were frightened by the Reagan success and perhaps even more by the change of party hands in the Senate. They were determined to push the Equal Rights Amendment to ratification by its 1982 deadline, a goal they did not attain. They were encouraged, however, by the gender gap.

The major feminist organizations profited in members and money from the Reagan era. The National Organization for Women (NOW), the largest such group, grew by about 40,000 people between 1977 and 1982. A report in the early autumn of 1982 listed NOW membership as 220,000 people, and following the 1982 election membership was reported to be 250,000. Their budget grew from $500,000 in 1977 to $1.3 million. The National Women's Political Caucus (NWPC), organized to promote women's involvement in politics, was reported to have 60,000 members in early 1982 and 73,000 by the time the 1982 election was over. In contrast, Eagle Forum, the largest group organized specifically to combat feminism, reported 50,000 members at the end of 1982 (Kirschten, 1982a; Bonafede, 1982). The difference in size reflects a difference in strategic style. The feminist organizations try to include as many people as possible. Eagle Forum and other right-wing organizations would rather have a smaller core of dedicated workers and a large mailing list of those to whom they can send appeals for money.

Feminist organizations have become increasingly active in electoral campaigns. One can argue that feminist electoral partici-pation became truly professionalized in the 1980s. Both the NWPC and the Women's Campaign Fund (WCF, founded in 1974), not only helped to fund campaigns, but also worked on recruiting and training candidates. One of the debates that some of these groups face is whether to support any and all women, only women who are ideolo-gically acceptable or only women *and men* who are ideologically acceptable. Both the NWPC and WCF define themselves explicitly in terms of aiding women in a bipartisan effort, although their biases tend to run Democratic. The President of the NWPC during the Reagan years was Kathy Wilson, a long-time Republican activist, although a Republican who has repeatedly and publicly stated her desire for Ronald Reagan to leave the presidency to someone else. (Under her presidency a headline of the NWPC newsletter read, 'It's not the government we need off our backs — it's Ronald Reagan': Kirschten, 1982a.) NOW changed its policy in 1982 and decided that, while they will work to get more women into office, their main goal is to elect candidates with the correct policy views, regardless of sex. In 1982, 6 of the 109 candidates they supported were men running against women (Bonafede, 1982). In 1984 for the first time, NOW endorsed a candidate for the Democratic nomination for president, a decision also reached by the AFL–CIO (the federation of labour unions) the previous week: they endorsed Walter Mondale.

The amount of money involved in feminist politics in the Reagan era is impressive. In 1982 NOW gave almost $500,000 to congressional candidates and $1 million to state candidates. Fifteen per cent of these were Republicans. NWPC contributed $50,000 to congressional candidates, 88 per cent of whom were Democrats, and $500,000 to state and local candidates. The WCF contributed $271,000 worth of cash and services to 93 federal and state candidates (Bonafede, 1982). Beginning in 1982, the heads of many of the major feminist Political Action Committees (PACs) met regularly to compare notes and coordinate strategy for campaigns and donations. These are only a few of the feminist organizations involved in campaign politics. Many others organize workers, contribute money, carry out research on how to exploit the gender gap and participate in many other ways.

Whether or not these feminist campaign efforts made any difference is difficult to tell. Observers believe that there are at least a couple of races in which women's support did make a difference. Many women in politics feel the women's movement has been important in their careers for the encouragement and support it gave them. No doubt the feminist PACs and electoral organizations will refine their techniques as they gain more experience as professionals in the field.

Feminist organization in conventional politics is not limited to electoral activity. Feminist political organizations have sprung up and grown within government as well. Organizations of women judges and bureaucrats have become increasingly active during the Reagan years. Numerous newsletters are now available that are designed specifically to help women who are already involved in politics and government. The Congressional Women's Caucus, originally limited to female membership, expanded in 1981 to admit men, although their entrance fees are higher. The centrality of 'women's issues' in Congress is indicated by the number of congressional caucuses that have emerged during the Reagan era. Congressional caucuses are bipartisan groups of members of Congress who meet to discuss issues of common concern. The Congressional Women's Caucus (renamed the Congressional Caucus for Women's Issues) reached a membership of 125 by 1983, all but eight of whom were female. This caucus was originally opposed by the Pro-Life Caucus. In June 1983 two new caucuses in the Senate were founded within a day of each other: the conservative Senate Caucus on the Family and the more liberal Senate Children's Caucus. The feminist groups, joined by the many registered lobbyists for feminist organizations, push for favourable legislation.

Organization of women in politics has spread across the country. The striking aspect of feminist politics is the degree to which it transcends partisan loyalty. Most women's organizations have always claimed to be nonpartisan or bipartisan, although simply by the nature of their issue stands they have generally been heavily Democratic. Ronald Reagan has managed to make the women's movement more bipartisan in a sense than it was; many Republican women have been vociferous in their objections to Reagan's policies. Public opinion polls carried out in 1983 showed that the gender gap was as strong in the Republican as in the Democratic Party. Many Republican women didn't even try to go to their party's national convention in 1984 because they knew it would be so dominated by Reagan supporters that they would have little possibility for influence. The only clear voice against the nominee at that meeting was a woman's.

The women's movement became more active than ever in electoral politics in 1984. They were encouraged by Walter Mondale who, as a senator, had once sponsored a comprehensive day care bill that was vetoed by Richard Nixon, and who selected as his running mate a feminist woman, Representative Geraldine Ferraro.

The fact that the final vote tally showed a smaller gender gap than in 1980 should not be taken as an indication that the women's movement was weak in its impact on US politics. Feminists were activated in a way they had not been since the waning days of the ERA. At the same time, however, the anti-feminists were also activated. Ferraro became the particular focus of attack by anti-abortionists, including church leaders. Public opinion polls repeatedly showed that the public agreed more with the Democrats than the Republicans in their stands on 'women's issues'. But the involvement of activists is not the same thing as a mass vote, and agreement on a wide range of issues is not enough to tip the electoral scales. The election was decided not by these issues but by others, and others on which the President had greater support. The fact that Republican women leaders remained noticeably reticent in the autumn of 1984 indicates the continued strength of the movement.

Conclusion

The Reagan era has been a time of change. The direction of public policy has, in many respects, been turned around. In other cases the speed of change has been slowed. Some of these changes are due directly to Reagan's action, while some, such as abortion politics, have only been encouraged by him.

The feminist movement has come of age and matured in many respects during the Reagan era. Although grass-roots action and radical politics are still very apparent and important to the movement, the movement combines this with a very professionalized wing capable of mixing in big-time politics.

The continued strength of the women's movement is remarkable, given the visibility and influence of the opposition. At the national level the conservative and anti-feminist President has used his presidential power in the regulation and enforcement of law, appointments and the budgetary process against the feminist movement. His power has not been complete: the lower house of Congress remains Democratic; civil service procedures limit the power of the President over the bureaucracy; and public opinion on most women's issues has arguably been influenced more by the women's movement and real changes in women's roles than by the administration. Although the attitude of the Supreme Court could change as Reagan is able to replace retiring members, it remains relatively immune to political pressure.

On the local and state levels the New Right, a movement consisting of the traditional right wing as well as fundamentalist and conservative church people, has been very visible. These anti-feminists by no means constitute a homogeneous force; their tactics range from quite conventional lobbying through various forms of protest and demonstrations to violent action against abortion centres. It is unclear how much real influence these groups have. Pamela Conover and Virginia Gray (1983) conclude that their apparent successes have been greatest in the traditionally conservative and anti-feminist areas of the country — in other words, where there was little feminist change for them to turn back in the first place. They do, however, serve to drain the feminist movement of time and resources.

It is difficult to ascertain exactly what lessons European feminists can learn from the example of the government-orientated wing of the US feminist movement. Their strategies, successes and failures have been structured in many senses by certain relatively unique features of US politics, and especially by the structure and roles of US political parties and interest groups, as well as by the nature of the electoral system and divisions of governing power. At the same time, however, the coalition of 'radical' and 'conventional' politics, as well as the attempt of the women's movement to remain an independent force in political life, can offer lessons to others.

List of abbreviations

AFDC	Aid to Families with Dependent Children
AFL-CIO	American Federation of Labor — Congress of Industrial Organization
EEOC	Equal Employment Opportunity Commission
ERA	Equal Rights Amendment
NOW	National Organization for Women
NWPC	National Women's Political Caucus

PAC   Political Action Committee
WCF   Women's Campaign Fund
WHO   World Health Organisation

References

Bonafede, Dom (1982) 'Women's Movement Broadens the Scope of Its Role in American Polls', *National Journal*, 11 December: 2108–11.

Conover, Pamela and Virginia Gray (1983) *Feminism and the New Right: Conflict over the American Family*. New York: Praeger.

Evans, Sara (1979) *Personal Politics: The Roots of Women's Liberation in the Civil Rights Movement and the New Left*. New York: Vintage.

Frankovic, Kathleen (1982) 'Sex and Politics: New Alignments, Old Issues', *PS* 15 (Summer): 439–48.

Freeman, Jo (1974) *The Politics of Women's Liberation*. New York: Longman.

Kirschten, Dick (1982a) 'Hell Hath No Fury', *National Journal*, 6 March: 472.

Kirschten, Dick (1982b) 'The Presidential "Gender Gap" Looms as a Major Political Problem for the GOP', *National Journal*, 21 August: 457–60.

Klein, Ethel (1984) *Gender Politics*. Cambridge, Mass.: Harvard University Press.

Miller, Dorothy C. (1983) 'AFDC: Mapping a Strategy for Tomorrow', *Social Service Review*, 57 (December): 599–613.

Tinker, Irene (ed.) (1983) *Women in Washington: Advocates for Public Policy*. Beverly Hills: Sage.

Wines, Michael (1982) 'Administration Says it Seeks a "Better Way" to Enforce Civil Rights', *National Journal*, 27 March: 537.

7
From social movement to political party: the new women's movement in Iceland

Audur Styrkársdóttir

Introduction

Several features make the Icelandic new women's movement unique in an international perspective: the very successful Women's Strike in 1975, the election of Vigdís Finnbogadóttir as president in 1980 and the introduction of Women's Lists in the local elections of 1982 and the parliamentary elections of 1983.

As the political system and various social factors undoubtedly play a decisive role in forming social movements, this short introduction will give an account of the most important aspects of the Icelandic political system as well as of some of the social factors contributing to the rise of the new women's movement in that country.

The political system

Iceland became an independent country in 1944, having been under foreign rule since 1262. A parliamentary system of government was adopted. Forty-nine MPs are elected by proportional representation in eight constituencies. Eleven supplementary seats are then allocated to those parties that have had MPs elected in at least one constituency. These seats are distributed in order to make parliamentary representation of each party as proportional as possible given the prior distribution of the 49 seats. The total number of MPs is fixed at 60.

The Icelandic people elect a president every four years. The president supervises negotiations between the political parties represented in parliament when a new national government is to be formed. The president can also refuse to ratify bills passed by parliament: such legislation may take effect, but a national referendum must first be called to determine its fate. The president has never used this power to submit laws passed by parliament to a referendum. Thus in reality the presidency has been less powerful than the constitution indicates.

Over 60 per cent of Iceland's population of about 238,000 live in the two urban constituencies: Reykjavík, the capital of Iceland, and Reykjaneskjördaemi, on the south-west peninsula.

In local government and parliamentary elections the voter can opt for one of the lists of candidates for various offices entered by each political party in the relevant constituency, town or district. The voter can blank out names or change the rankings of candidates on the list she or he votes for; however, the electoral rules minimize the effect of such alterations. Thus, in general the choice of alternatives is very structured, leaving little room for change.

The political system has, however, undergone significant changes since the elections of 1971. Electoral volatility, for instance, has become a characteristic of the Icelandic party system. Increasing volatility may indicate that in general the relationship between social structure (e.g. class, region) and voting behaviour in Iceland has weakened over the last decade. It has been pointed out that the increasing fluidity in the electoral market may be reflected in changes in the party organizations and in the behaviour of individual politicians; and it may have contributed to the appearance of the Women's Lists in 1982 and 1983 (Kristjánsson and Hardarson, 1982).

A second factor of change within the Icelandic political system may also have contributed to the appearance of the Women's Lists. Following increased demands for greater political participation in the late 1960s, almost all political parties in Iceland to a greater or lesser extent adopted the practice of holding primary elections prior to the 1971 elections (except for the People's Alliance, which held primaries only in 1978–9). The primaries were intended to give the voter a chance to decide on the composition of the party list in local and parliamentary elections. The rules governing the primaries have varied, both over time and within parties. A major factor, however, has been the rules by which candidates are ordered on the lists. Participants in the primaries are asked to select a fixed number of candidates, mostly by number of preference (1,2,3, etc.) but sometimes without preference order.

These rules enable a consistent majority to govern the ordering of seats. Although a considerable number of those participating in the primaries want to support one particular candidate or candidates, there is little chance of putting her or him in a safe seat except by gaining the support of another big group, thus forming a plurality or majority for that particular seat. If, for instance, women want to elect a woman of a particular party in the primary election, they would, first of all, have to agree upon which woman/women to support and, second, would have to gain the support of a considerable number of men participating in the primary. Such alliances are, of course, extremely difficult to establish.

The primaries did not lead to a significant increase of women in local government during the 1970s: the proportion of women thereby elected increased from 3.6 per cent after the 1974 elections to 6.1 per cent after the 1978 elections. No increase of women was seen in parliament, with only three women MPs during the years 1971–83.

Social changes
Iceland has undergone significant social changes since the 1960s, especially in the entrance of married women into the labour market and in the increase in women's educational level. In 1964, 28 per cent of married women over the age of 16 held either full-time or part-time jobs (Sigurdsson, 1975); in 1980 the proportion of married women holding jobs in Reykjavík was 65 per cent (Karlsson, 1982).
The 1970s also saw a marked change in the educational level of women. In 1960, 24.8 per cent of those graduating from gymnasium were women; in 1983 this proportion was 59 per cent (*Hagtíðindi*, 1984). In 1970 the proportion of women graduating from the University of Iceland was 15.3 per cent; by 1980 this proportion was 40.9 per cent (*Árbók Háskóla Íslands*, 1979–80).
We should expect such profound changes to have marked implications for the role and status of women, although in the absence of comprehensive research it is not clear to what extent. This chapter is intended to deal with a limited number of these implications, namely, the most important features of the new women's movement in Iceland.

The turbulent years of 1970–5
During the period 1970–5 the new women's movement made its appearance in Iceland in the form of the Redstocking movement (Raudsokkahreyfingin). This movement caught the attention of the media and resulted in a successful revival of feminist issues on the political as well as the non-political agenda, culminating in the Women's Strike on 24 October 1975.

The formation and the organization of the Redstocking movement
In 1968 a group of young women, mostly schoolteachers, had formed a special group within the Women's Right Organization (WRO — Kvenréttindafélagid, founded in 1907). The formation of this group was initiated by the leaders of the WRO, who felt the need to recruit and activate young members. The group concerned itself mostly with sex roles as illustrated in children's books and textbooks. However, the new women's movement in Iceland really began with the formation in 1970 of the Redstocking movement, which was initiated by women who had few or no ties to the WRO or any other women's association in Iceland. Thus, the year 1970 is a more feasible starting-point for my discussion.
The Redstocking movement held its inaugural meeting in October 1970. The founders of the movement were young and well-educated women, many of whom had studied abroad and come into contact with or heard of similar movements in Denmark and the Dolle Mina

in the Netherlands. The Redstocking movement in Iceland was open to both women and men — unlike the WRO, which was open only to women until 1972, and unlike many similar movements which excluded men in other countries. During the first four years women of all political standings (and a handful of men) worked within the movement. Young, radical, well-educated women were, however, prominent. The Redstocking movement was intended to call attention to the low status of women in Iceland and to raise their consciousness and the consciousness of the population in general.

Unlike various women's groups in other countries, the Redstocking movement in Iceland did not form consciousness-raising or sex-therapy groups or engage in other activities that were seen as vitally important in the feminist movement elsewhere (that is, not until 1980, or two years before the movement ceased to exist). Instead, the members of the movement focused on parliament, state institutions and the labour unions. They pressed parliament for free abortions and for increased allocations to day-care centres; they collected evidence on sexual discrimination in the labour market and submitted such evidence to the labour unions and the state; they hammered on the political parties and the labour unions to change the way in which they operated and to show more consideration for women. A member of the Redstocking movement, a schoolteacher, influenced the new bill on school laws in 1973, which cites the equality of the sexes as one of its main aims.

The Redstocking movement thus worked inside the system, at least during its most prosperous years, and not outside it as did many feminist groups in other countries. The movement did not have any formal leadership, adopting a 'flat' structure with everybody equally responsible — or no one in particular. It has been maintained that such an organization, lacking formal leadership, would also lack the means with which to fight within the political system (Dahlerup and Gulli, 1985:36). But perhaps the organization has little to do with whether movements fight inside or outside the system. In the Icelandic case, at least, another important factor seems to have made up for the lack of centralized organization; the fact that Iceland in 1971–4 had a leftist government undoubtedly integrated the Icelandic new women's movement into the political system more than their European sister-movements. In 1971–4 the government was a coalition of three parties, two of them leftist parties — the People's Alliance (left socialist) and the Union of Leftists (a split from the People's Alliance in 1967) — and the third, the Progressive Party (centre party, formerly a farmers' party), adhering to a more leftist stand than before on many issues. One of the three women MPs, Svava Jakobsdóttir, MP for the People's Alliance, had close ties with the Redstocking movement and became its spokeswoman in parliament. Svava Jakobsdóttir introduced a bill in 1973 providing for equality between the sexes on the labour market, which was passed, and she spoke fervently for free abortions when that issue was brought up in parliament in 1973 and 1974; the Redstocking movement and the Women's Right Organization were the only women's associations that fought for the women's right to self-determination in abortion cases.

It has often been maintained that, internationally, the influence of the new women's movement was stronger on the abortion issue than on any other issue. I shall therefore describe this issue briefly with regard to Iceland.

The abortion issue in Iceland: a battle lost but the war won
In 1970 the Minister of Health appointed a committee to reconsider the old abortion law dating from 1935, wherein abortion was forbidden unless the life or health of the mother or the foetus was in danger. The committee was set up at the request of doctors who were beginning to be aware of a steadily increasing demand for abortions. This committee consisted of three males: two doctors and one psychologist. Various women's organizations demanded that a woman should be put on the committee, with the result that in January 1971 one of the males dropped out and a woman took his place.

The reconsideration of the old abortion law thus began shortly before the Redstocking movement entered the scene. However, the movement had a decisive influence on the bill, for in November 1971 yet another woman was appointed to the committee — this one a prominent figure in the Redstocking movement.

The committee prepared a bill on the abortion issue, granting the woman's right to decide on abortion. This bill was introduced in parliament in 1973 and immediately attracted nationwide attention. A number of organizations debated on the bill and sent their approval or disapproval to parliament. Only three groups were decidedly in favour of the bill: the Redstocking movement, the Women's Right Organization and the Association of Psychologists. The largest women's association in the country, the Union of Women's Organizations (Kvenfélagasambandid), claiming about 18,000 members, was split over the bill with the majority against it. The bill was not passed in parliament because one of the three parties forming the government, the Union of Leftists, stood against it.

In 1974 a new centre–right government was formed consisting of the Progressive Party and the Independence Party (conservative). This government appointed a new committee consisting of three males, two of them MPs, to reconsider the abortion bill, with the result that in 1975 a new bill was introduced and passed. The new law permits doctors to decide whether there are sufficient grounds for granting a woman an abortion.

Iceland had three women MPs in 1975: two of them were in favour of the new bill (both representing the Independence Party); one of them, Svava Jakobsdóttir, was against it — on the grounds that doctors should not decide on abortions, women should.

The Redstocking movement did not initiate the revival of the abortion issue in Iceland, and it was far from being the only women's organization concerned with this issue. However, the movement dominated the debate and greatly influenced the turn of events. The Redstocking movement and the Students' Union helped women contact British abortion clinics and hospitals, thus making it clear to the opponents of a new abortion law that women had access to other means if a new law was not passed. Although the Redstocking movement and the Women's Right Organization lost out on the self-determination issue, they in fact won the abortion issue: it was virtually uncontested by parliament or other state institutions that a change had to be made. In practice, doctors very seldom deny a woman an abortion, at least not in the capital of Iceland. Self-determination is therefore the practice in Iceland although the law states otherwise.

A change of direction in 1974

By 1974 its founders considered that the Redstocking movement had succeeded in raising people's consciousness. Its members felt that the movement was stagnating in an endless debate on who should do the dishes, and that it now needed a clear manifesto. In the summer of 1974 the Redstocking movement adopted its first manifesto with the following slogan: 'No women's struggle without class-struggle; no class-struggle without women's struggle'. Women holding other ideas left the movement.

The Redstocking movement now emphasized the importance of the struggle of the working classes. In 1974, 1975 and 1976 the movement arranged, with the country's two largest labour federations, conferences on the status of low-paid women. These conferences influenced the demands of the labour unions to the extent that both federations adopted a policy on child-care centres, and in 1980 the government signed a contract with the federations stating that by 1990 the number of child-care centres would equal demand. (This will not, however, be realized, since the government has not increased its contributions to child-care centres to any extent and has actually cut them since the formation of the centre–right government in 1983.)

After the adoption of a Marxist platform in 1974, the Redstocking movement became slowly more and more isolated, recruiting mostly members of small orthodox Marxist groups. In late 1982 the movement was formally abolished, with many of its active members having joined the Women's List in Reykjavík.

The Redstocking movement and, to a certain extent, the Women's Right Organization were the only organizations in Iceland that can be counted as part of the new women's movement in the 1970s. Other feminist groups were not formed until 1982, with the arrival of the Women's Lists. The Redstocking movement, however, inspired women of all political standings and led to a revival of feminist issues throughout the whole country. The ideas born within the movement greatly influenced the events that I shall discuss below: the Women's Strike in 1975, the election of Vigdís Finnbogadóttir as president in 1980, and, finally, the introduction of the Women's Lists in 1982 and 1983. Although the Redstocking movement has been dissolved, the wave that it unleashed has not broken; its ideas still live, as does — in this way — the movement.

The Women's Strike in 1975
When the Redstocking movement was formally founded in 1970, one of its spokeswomen put forward the idea that all married women in Iceland should stop their work for twenty-four hours in order to demonstrate the importance of their work inside and outside their homes. The idea was well received although the strike was not realized until five years later.

In late 1974 five women's organizations formed a joint committee in order to organize events during 1975, which the United Nations had declared International Women's Year. Among these five organizations were the Redstocking movement and the Women's Right Organization. The Redstocking movement's representative on the joint committee introduced the idea of a women's strike, of married, unmarried, young and old women, to call attention to the importance of women on the labour market.

In September 1975 the joint committee and individuals from about twenty-five women's organizations and labour unions elected a ten-member strike executive committee; by then it had been decided to strike on 24 October. The executive committee consisted of women from all political parties and women from the largest labour unions. Prominent was the chairwoman of one of the two women's labour unions in Reykjavík.

The executive committee organized a rally in Reykjavík on 24 October 1975, calling all women to attend. The number that turned up was a staggering 25,000, according to police records.

Rallies were held all over the country, and they turned out to be a great success. It was estimated that 90–95 per cent of Icelandic women answered the joint committee's call for a strike. The result was that the wheels of society came to a stop. An action of this kind was tried in other countries in 1975 (e.g. 'Alice Stays at Home' in the USA), but nowhere did women answer the call as unanimously as in Iceland, making this experience unique.

Several factors contributed to the success of the Women's Strike. The most influential was an effective and comprehensive organization. Women in almost all of Iceland's women's organizations worked fervently to make the strike successful. The labour unions were utilized — they actively supported the strike, and within each union propaganda for the strike was overwhelming. A special media committee was set up, with members writing articles in all newspapers calling upon women to show solidarity, and contacting the media to ensure favourable coverage before the strike. The newspapers in Iceland all have strong ties to the political parties, and having women from all political parties on the executive committee undoubtedly proved essential.

The presidential elections of 1980

When it became clear in late 1979 that the president of Iceland, the late Mr Kristján Eldjárn, would not run for another term in 1980, feminists began to wonder if the presidency could be filled by a woman. It is difficult to say where the idea originated; most likely a lot of people had it at the same time.

In February 1980 a group of women and men had found their candidate. Her name was Vigdís Finnbogadóttir and she was a director of one of Reykjavík's two theatres. After long consultation with friends, and after a number of people had officially urged her to do so, Vigdís agreed to stand.

The election was to be held on 29 June. The campaign started at the beginning of May with meetings throughout the country and mass media coverage. Vigdís's campaigners emphasized that her running for the presidency was an act intended to break the habit of having only men as presidents, and that women were as well qualified as men for the office. They underlined that, by voting for her, Icelandic women would revive the spirit of the Women's Strike in 1975 and that the Icelandic population, men as well as women, would make world history by electing her since no woman in the world had been elected president in a nationwide election. They also stressed that the choice was between a woman and three other candidates, who happened to be men.

For some decades it has not been the habit of the political parties or other organizations publicly to interfere in the presidential campaigns in Iceland. It is, however, well recorded that individuals within the political parties play a decisive role in these campaigns. In the 1980 presidential election some powerful members of the political parties worked for the male candidates. Vigdís's campaigners managed, however, to break through the party-lines and win the support of other powerful leaders within the parties. She won the election with a narrow 1.5 per cent lead, receiving 33.8 per cent of valid votes.

Vigdís Finnbogadóttir's election was not a women's affair in the sense that Icelandic women united behind her and Icelandic men behind the male candidates. However, women were more prominent than men in her campaign. Out of Vigdís's recorded twenty-four campaign offices throughout the country, fifteen were headed by women, and, according to one of her most active campaigners, women were decidedly more active than men in her campaign outside the Reykjavík area.

A lot of women who had at one time or another been active members of the Redstocking movement became active supporters and agitators in Vigdís's campaign. The Redstocking movement had won a major victory in changing people's attitudes towards women, for it was seldom contended during the campaign that Vigdís would not be able to run the presidency because she was a woman. Her political affiliations were, however, questioned, and it was pointed out that she had actively supported the campaign against the NATO bases in Iceland, this issue being one of the most controversial in Icelandic politics. Articles were printed in the biggest newspaper of the country, *Morgunbladid*, which is attached to the conservative Independence Party, stating that, because of her standing against the NATO bases, Vigdís was not the kind of president Icelanders needed.

On the lower levels of the campaign, one of Vigdís's active campaigners told me, certain unpublicized occurrences showed that, although Icelanders were ready at least to consider the possibility of having a woman as president, many of the old prejudices against women still lingered. Questions of a personal nature were put to Vigdís in campaign meetings which no one thought of putting before any of the male candidates. Also, during her first four-year term in office, Vigdís's actions were more scrutinized than the actions of former presidents, with her supposed 'mistakes' immediately catching the attention of the media. Her term expired in spring 1984, but she was re-elected without opposition.

The Women's Lists in 1982

Women have always been poorly represented in Icelandic local government and in parliament. The 1970s saw a small increase in the proportion of women in local government. Following the elections of 1978 this proportion went from 3.6 per cent (in 1974) to 6.1 per cent; in bigger towns the proportion of women went from 6.9 to 9.3 per cent. During the years 1971–83 only three women sat in parliament; before the elections of 1971 Iceland had only one woman MP (1963–71), and further back in the century we find either one woman MP or occasionally two, and sometimes none.

The first sign that Icelandic women were preparing to organize a battle for an increased number of women in local government and in parliament came from the Women's Right Organization in 1980. In this section I shall discuss events leading to the introduction of Women's Lists in the local elections of 1982, the election results and the ideology of the Women's Lists.

Preceding events

In October 1980 the Women's Right Organization organized a conference on women in politics, inviting all women in local government to attend. In that conference the possibility of a women's list was discussed. Although the majority of participants rejected the idea, it had been brought out into the open. A group of women working within the Redstocking movement plus a number of former activists and other interested women began discussing the idea of entering a Women's List at the local election in Reykjavík in 1982. Almost simultaneously, a group of women in the town of Akureyri began to discuss the possibility of entering a Women's List in Akureyri. The result of these discussions was the introduction of Women's Lists in both towns at the local elections in 1982.

The Redstocking movement participated informally in the discussions in Reykjavík until the autumn of 1981, when its leaders broke away, denouncing the whole idea as 'bourgeois'. The Redstocking movement was dissolved in 1982, by which time many of its members had become active in the Women's List movement. These women felt that the Redstocking movement had ceased to attract women and that certain mistakes had been made in its propaganda, such as denigrating the role of housewives, with the result that women as well as men had become prejudiced against the movement. Something else needed to be done in order to unite women in their struggle.

The election results

It is clear that during the election campaign the Women's Lists in Reykjavík and Akureyri were the lists the political parties feared the most. The election campaign was a trying one for the Women's Lists; all newspapers in Iceland have strong ties to the political parties and the press was dead-set against them.

The election was held on 23 May 1982. The Women's List in Reykjavík received 10.9 per cent of the valid vote and got two representatives elected on to the city council out of a total of twenty-one. In Akureyri the Women's List received 17.4 per cent of the valid vote and got two representatives elected out of eleven. This was a surprising and a very welcome result.

The total number of women on the city council in Reykjavík went from three after the 1978 election to eight after the 1982 election (in 1982 the number of city council representatives was increased from fifteen to twenty-one). The proportion of women on the city council went up from 20 to 38.1 per cent. In the town of Akureyri the number of women on the city council went from two in 1978 to three in 1983 and the proportion of women increased from 18 to 27.2 per cent.

On the whole, the proportion of women in local government went from 6.1 per cent in 1978 to 12.5 per cent in 1982, which was an impressive increase although the proportion is still devastatingly low.

The increase in the proportion of women in local government in 1982 is due first and foremost to an increase in women representing parties other than the Women's Lists. The fact that some women were preparing a Women's List affected voters in the primary elections and made them at least consider women when casting their vote. It is also clear that the political party leaders saw the Women's Lists as a threat; therefore they tried to influence the outcome of the primaries by taking a stand more favourable to women, for example, when speaking at party meetings.

The ideology of the Women's Lists
Among the things stressed in the Reykjavík Women's List manifesto was the following:

> Men and women hold different values due to the traditional division of labour between the sexes. Development of society is governed by the values of men — women's experience has not put any significant marks on this development. Now we face the near destruction of nature and all living things. Technology and pollution stemming from technology grows bigger and becomes an ever bigger threat to the basic needs of human beings. In this world there often seems to be no room for human interaction, human feelings, creativeness and interaction with nature. Humankind is threatened by an arms race that will lead to total destruction. This development must be stopped — women must unite in order to stop it. (Women's List, 1982)

The manifesto also stressed the powerlessness of women on all fronts — in parliament, in local government, in the labour unions. Women are in all the lowest paying jobs, stated the manifesto, and very few of them hold top positions. In addition, women must do all the housework and care for their children. The manifesto accused the political parties of showing no regard for women and of being run by a handful of power-hungry men. No party takes any notice of the special experience of women, the manifesto went on to say: if and when they do take up matters of interest to women, it is only to impress the voters and is usually tossed away after elections. Women have tried to work within the political parties with no result; therefore they must take matters into their own hands.

The manifesto also pondered the question of why women had not gained any significant influence in society, in spite of having equal rights and after greatly increasing their educational level. The manifesto answered with the following declaration:

> The reasons are undoubtedly many and complex. One of them could be the fact that women have not questioned the values governing society. But instead of agreeing upon the roles and values that men hold, as they have done until now, women are beginning to realize that their experience is a positive experience, something that has to be conserved and developed — not only for their own sake but for the sake of society. The Women's List wants to make use of the women's world of experience; it wants to make it visible, and, above all, it wants to make the women's world of experience as well integrated into society as that of men. Men and women can work together only when men adopt women's culture and experience, in the same way that women adopt the best from the culture and experience of men. (Women's List, 1982)

On a practical level, the Women's List in Reykjavík adopted a special manifesto on local government, stating among other things that power must be decentralized and given to the people at all levels of government. It also said that wages of women working for the city must be reconsidered; that child-care centres must be built for all children, and that changes must be made in the running of schools so that schoolchildren could get their meals there. (Icelandic schools are still run as if the mothers of schoolchildren are always at home to give them lunch.) The platform also emphasized the need for creative work for the town's teenagers and the need for new town planning ideas. More money should be given to the health care system, and the town council should designate a home for abused women. The manifesto of the Women's List in Akureyri ran along the same lines. So did the manifestos of the Women's Lists entered at the parliamentary elections in 1983.

The old and the new Women's Lists: similarities and differences
The ideology of the new Women's Lists in Iceland fits perfectly with the ideology of the women's lists that were entered at the local elections in Reykjavík in the years 1908–16 and at the parliamentary elections of 1922 and 1926. These lists were entered by the women's organizations and were sometimes were successful (Styrkársdóttir, 1978, 1982). This was exceptional compared with other European countries, where women entered politics during the first decades of the century with no success (see Dahlerup, 1977, 1978; Evans, 1976, 1977).

Both the old and new Women's Lists in Iceland emphasize that

women's consciousness is distinct from the consciousness of men —
women are, for instance, more peaceful and are concerned more with
social issues than men. It is also maintained that women have certain
distinctive interests that must be represented at the governmental
level. Whereas the Women's Lists, old and new, emphasize the
differences between women and men, the Redstocking movement
and feminists of the 1970s stressed similarities between the sexes.
Feminists of the 1970s maintained that the difference between the
sexes was due to different upbringing, and that the difference should
be eliminated in order to create a human race without social sex
differences. The Redstocking movement's adherents scorned values
that were seen as feminine values. The Women's Lists, old and new,
wanted to uphold those differing values, making them an integrated
part of society.

There are, however, marked differences between the old Women's
Lists and the new ones in Iceland. While the Women's Lists in
Reykjavík and Akureyri in 1982 were entered by women who had
either no ties at all to the women's organizations before or else had
ties only to the Redstocking movement (and, with very few exceptions, to the Women's Right Organization), the old Women's Lists
were entered by the women's organizations. The established
women's organizations in Iceland did not participate in the Women's
Lists of 1982, nor for that matter in the Women's Lists of 1983,
entered at the parliamentary elections. The Women's Right Organization, which in the 1920s and the 1930s was the head-organizer
behind the Women's Lists, refused to support the Women's Lists of
1982, using instead the general slogan, 'Women — choose women'.

The Women's Lists in 1983
Preceding events
The day after the local elections were held in 1982, one of the two
women elected from the Women's List in Reykjavík declared in a
newspaper interview that the behaviour of the political parties
towards the Women's List during the campaign would force women
to enter a Women's List in the next parliamentary election, which
was to be held in 1983. This was the first official sign of what was to
come — the entrance of Women's Lists in three constituencies in that
parliamentary election.

In late February 1983 a meeting was held in Reykjavík in order to
introduce the idea of a women's parliamentary list. About 500
women attended the meeting, and it was unanimously decided that
such a list should be entered. In this meeting a manifesto draft was
introduced, which ran along the same lines as the manifesto of the
Women's Lists in the local elections. It was also decided in this
meeting to talk to women in other constituencies in order to get more

Women's Lists entered. These talks led to the introduction of Women's Lists in two additional constituencies — one of which is near Reykjavík (Reykjaneskjördaemi) and the other including the town of Akureyri.

The election results

The Women's Lists in the parliamentary elections were ill-received by the political parties. Most of them were accused of taking a confused stand on the question of the NATO bases in Iceland — either supporting them (according to the opponents of the NATO bases) or being supporters of communists and the Soviet Union (according to NATO base followers).

The Women's List in Reykjavík received 8.4 per cent of the valid vote and got one representative. The Women's List in Reykjaneskjördaemi received 7.2 per cent of the valid vote and the Women's List in the north received 5.8 per cent of the valid vote. The total number of votes cast on the Women's Lists was 5.5 per cent of valid votes. This resulted in their gaining two supplementary seats, one from Reykjavík and one from Reykjaneskjördaemi, gaining a total of three seats.

Primaries were held within all political parties before the 1983 election — except for two new parties which entered the scene: the Women's Lists and the Union of Social Democrats (a split from the Social Democratic Party). In these two parties the lists were decided in general meetings open to all members. The primaries resulted in a minimal increase of women in safe seats. The 'old' parties had only three women MPs to boast of before the election: afterwards their number was four.

However, the two new parties, the Women's Lists and the Union of Social Democrats, got five women elected, three and two respectively. This leads us to speculate again on the effect of the primaries. As was mentioned before, a consistent majority can decide on the ordering of all seats in the primaries as they are conducted today in Iceland. These rules seem to be unfavourable to women and minority groups in general, as can best be seen in the low number of women MPs and the slow increase of women in local government. The choice of alternatives in general elections is very structured in Iceland. Given these two factors — a very structured election system and primaries in which a consistent majority can govern the ordering of seats — it becomes apparent that it is far easier to try your luck in elections by entering your own list than by entering candidates in the primaries of one of the established parties.

The fact that some women were preparing a women's list greatly affected the voting in the primaries before the local elections of 1982, but not in the parliamentary elections of 1983. It is a well recorded fact that the nearer you get to the perceived centres of power, the fewer women you see. Thus it is easier for women to do well in local elections than in parliamentary elections — and in primaries held before local elections than in primaries held before parliamentary elections.

The Women's Lists: a conclusion

It is too early, and not at all justifiable, to judge the results of the Women's Lists in Iceland, since the lists entered at the local elections have operated for only three years and their MPs have served only two sessions when this is written. Perhaps their most apparent result until now has been in reviving women's issues and lending them new perspectives. It is also clear that the political parties are very much aware of their existence and that they have been forced to take this into consideration in their propaganda.

The Women's Lists have conducted themselves as a leftist group, that is, as followers of the welfare state and sympathizers with the struggle of the working classes. They have taken a firm stand against the rule of the conservative Independence Party in Reykjavík, which after the election in 1982 gained control over the city. In the town of Akureyri the Women's List representatives form a majority on the city council with the representatives of the parties of centre and left, the Progressive Party, the Social Democratic Party and the People's Alliance. One representative of the Women's List served as the chairwoman on the city council for one term. The Women's List MPs have taken a firm stand against the centre–right government of the Progressive Party and the Independence Party which has, since coming to power in 1983, drastically cut wages.

It has been maintained that, if women are to have a chance of having a lasting effect upon the policy of institutions, one of the necessary conditions is a so-called 'critical mass' of women, preferably feminists (Haavio-Mannila et al., 1985:166). The proportion of women in the Icelandic parliament hardly reaches this so-called 'critical mass'. But with four women sitting in the Upper House of parliament (out of a total of twenty) and five in the Lower House (out of a total of forty), compared with only one woman in the Upper House and two in the Lower House during the years 1971–83, we could expect more emphasis on women's issues in parliament; especially since three out of nine women MPs are elected on lists basing themselves on women's issues.

Although not trying to change the code of conduct within parliament, the Women's List representatives have united with other women MPs on more issues than women MPs have done in the past. The three women MPs from the Women's Lists, the one from the People's Alliance, the one from the Social Democratic Party and the two from the Union of Social Democrats united several times during the parliamentary terms of 1983–4 and 1984–5 in the introduction of bills. The Progressive Party (centre) does not have any women MPs; the Independence Party (conservative) has two, but they have not taken active part in the introduction of bills with the other women MPs. (Their roles are, however, different from ordinary MPs: one of them is a minister and, as such, introduces bills concerning the policy of the government; the other is the chairwoman of the Upper House of parliament and her role is therefore restricted.)

The Women's List parliamentary representatives have also clearly influenced the topics discussed in parliament: they emphasize matters of interest to women and children, which have not been one of the major topics among MPs in the past, to say the least.

The proportion of women on the city council in Reykjavík is over 38 per cent and therefore perhaps does reach the so-called 'critical mass'. However, strict party lines have always determined the governance of the city, with a clear-cut division into majority and minority. The Independence Party holds twelve city council representatives out of twenty-one and therefore rules the city. Its four women representatives have not departed from the party line in any single important matter.

In the town of Akureyri the circumstances are different. Here all the city council representatives have always tried to reach an agreement in important matters, such as the budget. The Women's List in the town of Akureyri managed to put a significant mark on the budget of 1984, to cite one example: all single parents who are not able to use the town's day-care centres receive a certain amount of money from the city council for three, six or nine months, according to circumstances. This is unique to Iceland.

The proportion of women elected on to the city council in Akureyri was 27.2 per cent. However, alternate women members have taken seats on the city council a number of times, sometimes even managing to form a majority. Thus, when we are looking for proof of whether women change anything when gaining power, the town of Akureyri is clearly the place to study.

What future?
The Icelandic new women's movement is clearly an interesting one in an international perspective. Some things are unique in character, such as the very successful Women's Strike in 1975, the election of Vigdís Finnbogadóttir as president in 1980 and the appearance of the Women's Lists in 1982 and 1983.

Social and political factors have obviously played a decisive role in the appearance and formation of these events, although in the absence of comprehensive research their importance is not quite clear. Some important factors have been discussed here: the new women's movement in the form of the Redstocking movement was imported to Iceland by women who had studied or lived abroad or had heard of similar movements elsewhere. The political circumstances in Iceland, that is the leftist government in 1971–4, undoubtedly contributed to the movement's being practically integrated into the political and social system during those years. The new women's movement paved the way for profound change in attitudes towards and among women. These changes were most apparent in the Women's Strike in 1975 and the presidential elections of 1980.

It is too early at this point to predict the future of the Women's Lists in Iceland. However, it is clear that they have influenced the political system in an irreversible way: the political parties must show more consideration of women, both when deciding their lists (with or without primaries) and when deciding on political topics. Otherwise the Women's Lists will continue.

Surveys among Icelandic voters have shown that the Women's Lists have not lost any of the attraction they had in the elections of 1982 and 1983. They have, therefore, a good chance of doing well in the next elections. Many voters seem to trust these representatives, and so do many of those who will decide upon the future of Icelandic politics during the next years. In the summer of 1985 there was a lot of public talk among voters and political leaders alike of entering a joint list of the Women's List, the People's Alliance, the Social Democrats and the Progressive Party at the local elections in Reykjavík in 1986. This list would supposedly be headed by a representative from the Women's List. Even if this does not come to pass, the amount of trust in the Women's List demonstrated in Reykjavík by the idea is overwhelming. The Reykjavík Women's List has not decided whether to enter a list at the local elections in 1986: if they do their chance will be good; if they don't, they will at any rate have shaken the party system in Iceland irreversibly.

List of abbreviations
IP   The Independence Party (conservative)
PA   The People's Alliance (left socialist and communist party)
PP   The Progressive Party (centre party, former farmer's party)
SDP   The Social Democratic Party
USP   Union of Social Democrats (a split from the SDP in 1983)
WRO The Women's Right Organization (founded 1907)

References:
Arbók Háskóla Íslands 1979–80 (1982). Reykjavík: University of Iceland.
Dahlerup. Drude (1977) 'Et selstændigt kvindeparti?' pp. 149–92 in *Kvindestudier.*
      Oslo: Fremad A/S.
Dahlerup. Drude (1978) 'Women's Entry into Politics: The Experience of the Danish

Local and General Elections in 1908–1920', *Scandinavian Political Studies*, 1 (2–3).

Dahlerup, Drude and Gulli Birta (1985) 'Women's Organizations in the Nordic Countries: Lack of Force or Counterforce?', in Haavio – Mannila et al. (1985).

Evans, Richard J. (1976) *The Feminist Movement in Germany 1915–1933*. London: Sage.

Evans, Richard J. (1977) *The Feminists*. New York: Harper & Row.

Haavio-Mannila, Elina, et al. (1985) *Unfinished Democracy. Women in Nordic Politics*. Oxford: Pergamon Press.

Icelandic Statistical Bureau (1984) *Hagtidindi*, no. 4:69. Hagstofa Íslands: Icelandic Statistical Bureau.

Karlsson, Kristján (1982) *Jafnréttiskönnun í Reykjavík 1980–82*. Reykjavík: Jafnréttisnefnd Reykjavíkur.

Kristjánsson, Svanur and Ólafur Hardarson (1982) 'Problems and Prospects of Party Government in Iceland'. Aarhus: ECPR paper.

Sigurdsson, Jón (1975) 'Kventhjódin og thjódartekjurnar'. Unpublished paper, Kvennaársrádstefna ASÍ og BSRB.

Styrkársdóttir, Audur (1978) 'Analysis of the Women's Political Movement in Iceland 1908–26'. Grenoble: ECPR paper.

Styrkársdóttir, Audur (1982) *Kvennaframbodin 1908–26*. Reykjavík: Félagsvísindadeild H.Í. og Örn og Örlygur.

Vinnumarkadurinn 1980 (1982). Reykjavík: Framkvaemdastofnun Ríkisins.

Women's List (1982) *Kvennaframbodid*. Reykjavik: Women's List.

In addition to the above sources, various sources in Icelandic, including newspapers and magazines, have been utilized in this chapter. I have not cited this material specifically, but further information will be supplied on request.

8
Independence or integration: the women's movement and political parties in Finland

Riitta Jallinoja

Introduction

The independence of the women's movement has been a crucial issue to the movement all over the world. The very idea of autonomy has been that women can formulate their demands freely only when they do not have any other ideologically binding ties. However, this principle also has a more theoretical background, embracing the idea that all women form an independent social category. According to this view, women have certain common social features and certain common interests. In this respect, 'women' is analogous to such categories as 'working class' and 'ethnic minorities'.

This chapter will describe how the theme of independence/integration has been understood by the old as well as the new women's movement in Finland. The examples given will illustrate the lack of consensus among active Finnish women with regard to the question of independence/integration.

The purpose of the chapter is to investigate the ties of the Finnish women's movement to the country's political parties, especially since the 1960s. The results are based on my doctoral thesis, entitled 'The Active Periods of the Finnish Women's Movement' (Jallinoja, 1983). One of the principal — and to me surprising — findings was the fact that, despite its ever present aspiration for independence, both the first and the second wave of the women's movement in Finland have had close ties to the political parties. These ties seem to be closer in Finland than in other Western countries. One reason for this is the dominant position of political parties in Finland.

'Women' — an ambiguous category

The radical wing of the new women's liberation movement has declared that gender division is the most important of all social divisions. It has also been seen as an independent factor of exploitation (Firestone, 1972; Millett, 1971). This in turn means that no liberation movement apart from the women's movement can abolish the exploitation of women. Consequently, the women's movement cannot be united with other social movements, which, despite their otherwise good aims, practise patriarchal gender division. In extreme cases, this principle has led to total isolation from the rest of society, where men's hegemony is seen everywhere (Yates, 1975: 77; Solanis, 1970: 514–17).

Unlike the radical feminists, other groups of the women's movement in Finland have accepted political commitment. For example, many women of the new women's movement have adopted socialist views. For them the class struggle and the women's movement are closely connected; socialism is understood to be a necessary condition for the liberation of women. This view has drawn part of the new feminist movement relatively close to the workers' movement (Reed, 1971:65, Allen, 1970:13; Rowbotham, 1972:20). This perspective has been criticized, not only by the radical feminists but also by those who have been committed to political parties other than those of the left. As a result, cooperation among feminists in Finland has met with some difficulties.

Political ties do not constitute the only factor that has brought about ideological fusions between the women's movement and other social movements: on the contrary, many other ideas have mingled with the ideology of the women's movement — for instance, temperance, chastity, religion, nationalism, soft technology, vegetarianism, peace and self-help. These issues have been seen as closely connected with the interests of women and in that way have become part of the ideology of the women's movement at different times. They have even led the women's movement to become entangled with other social movements. Even if most feminists agree upon some basic principles of the women's liberation ideology, there is obviously disagreement about other issues, such as political connections. This has divided the movement into several organizations and groupings and at the same time has given outsiders the impression of a discordant movement, which in fact it is.

The main point here is that 'women' is not a totally unambiguous category. To put it simply, women are not only women: they belong to different classes, and they hold different ideological views. These differences tend to create varied strategies for the women's movement in terms of independence or alliances with other social movements and groupings.

The political parties in Finland

In Finland, the strength of the political parties can be understood only through its historical background. The formation of the political parties occurred in a fairly short time, at the turn of the century. Before that the political life was solely the business of a handful of men: over 70 per cent of the adult male population could not vote. In 1906 the Russian Tsar agreed to the establishment of a National Assembly in Finland, which at that time was part of the Russian empire. This parliamentary reform suddenly gave all adults, including women, the right to vote. In this kind of rapid and thorough change, people without almost any kind of political traditions had to evaluate political life through the recently formed parties. These parties very soon became forceful symbols of the new situation, and they structured the people's political and ideological thinking in general.

The process was strengthened by the fact that the independence movement, which was very important to Finland in those days, was also channelled into the political parties. In fact, two parties — the Finnish Party and its splinter party, the Young Finnish Party — were formed on the basis of the national issue. After Finland got its independence from the Soviet Union in 1917, a new kind of cleavage occurred. The class struggle, which had earlier been diluted by the struggle for independence, broke out and culminated in the Civil War in 1918. The 'Reds' were beaten, the 'Whites' won, and for a long time after that Finnish political life was characterized by the strict division into two politically hostile camps, the left and the right. In the 1930s the Communist Party was prohibited. After an underground period of more than ten years, it was again legalized in 1944. In short, the most important events in Finnish political history have been associated with the political parties.

The model of integration in the first phase of the women's movement
The Finnish women's movement in its organized form started in 1884, when the Finnish Women's Association (Suomen Naisyhdistys) was founded. Similar organizations were founded in the same year in Sweden and Norway (Dahlsgård, 1975). The first active period of the women's movement in Finland lasted until about 1908. During this period it can be characterized by the term 'the women's rights movement'. The main topics concerned equal rights and moral reforms. The movement was of a moderate nature (Evans, 1977). It eventually split into three separate organizations; the above-mentioned Finnish Women's Association, the Women's Rights League Union (Naisasialiitto Unioni, founded in 1892) and the Finnish Women's League (Suomalainen Naisliitto, founded in 1907).

The split of the women's rights movement
The split of the women's rights movement into three organizations was based mainly on political conflicts, though the movement was said to be completely non-political. The activists' individual ties, first to other political movements and then to the political parties, made it difficult for them to work together. In short, the process was as follows. From the 1860s until its independence from the Soviet Union

in 1917, Finland experienced a very strong national awakening. One of the main issues at that time was language. The upper class spoke Swedish and the mass of the people, Finnish. This divided the upper class (and soon also the middle class) into two hostile groups, Finnish-minded (Fennoman) and Swedish-minded (Svecoman). The former group consisted of upper- and middle-class people who, for example, began to speak Finnish and send their children to Finnish-speaking schools. In the 1880s the Finnish-minded were divided into two political groups, the moderates (the young wing) and the conservatives (the old wing). These political movements formed the base of the bourgeois parties founded at the turn of the century. All this was, in a crucial way, reflected in the women's movement.

The leaders of the Finnish Women's Association were of the conservative wing, the so-called 'old Fennomans'. When the split in the national (Fennoman) movement became openly acknowledged, the young and more liberal women began to criticize the older, more conservative wing, including the leaders of the Finnish Women's Association. The Swedish-minded women, who were mainly liberally oriented, joined this young front. As a result of these conflicts, the Women's Rights League Union (Naisasialiitto Unioni) was founded (1892). This common front of young Fennomans and Swedish-minded women broke up around the time of the first parliamentary elections (1907). The result was the foundation of the Finnish Women's League (Suomalainen Naisliitto), which became the organization mainly of young Fennomans. Thus, the split in the women's movement occurred almost completely along the lines of the contemporary political parties.

The cooperation between the three women's organizations was not great. The Finnish Women's Association and the Union were even hostile towards each other. What is more important, the issues that the organizations presented in public concerning women's status scarcely differed from each other. Thus, political preferences took priority over common women's issues, which were unable to unite the women's movement (Jallinoja, 1983:43–52).

From the women's movement to the political parties
Everything that has happened to the women's movement from the turn of the century onwards is an accurate reflection of the extent to which the Finnish women's movement has been tied to the political parties. The relationship has been fairly close. It has also furthered the weakening of the independent women's movement. The passivity made itself felt for the first time soon after the parliamentary elections in 1907. Many activists in the women's rights movement were elected to parliament. Table 1 shows that a considerable part of the women MPs were members of the women's rights movement.

TABLE 1
The proportion of female members of parliament belonging to one or more
of the organizations of the women's rights movement, 1907–20

Party	Proportion of female MPs in the women's movement %	Total number of female MPs
Bourgeois parties:		
Finnish Party/Coalition Party	67	12
Young Finnish Party (liberal)	100	6
Swedish Folk Party	67	6
Agrarian Party	25	4
Social Democratic Party	3	38

Source: Jallinoja (1983:105).

The other main channel the activists of the women's movement
chose to use was the women's organizations in the political parties
themselves. These were founded just before the first parliamentary
elections; many activists of the women's movement were among the
founders, and some even became presidents. Subsequently, the main
interest of these organizations concentrated on party-related activities, although women's issues were at hand all the time. When
making the choice to involve themselves in the political parties, the
representatives of the Finnish women's movement presented for the
first time the later often quoted idea that it is necessary to work where
'the real decisions are made'.

In the course of some years, however, women realized that the
political parties were neglecting women's demands for equality to a
great extent. A handful of women therefore recommended the
foundation of a Women's Party, but they did not succeed in their aims
(Östenson, 1957:7). As Alexandra Gripenberg, the president of the
Finnish Women's Association, put it, 'Let every woman find her
party among the existing political parties' (Gripenberg, 1907:7).

**The women's equality movement of the 1960s: its background in the
radical movement**
After the first parliamentary elections at the beginning of the
century, the women's rights movement seemed to be quite dormant
until the 1960s. All three organizations of the movement continued to
function, but only a few new members joined each year. This was still
the case in 1965, when women's emancipation once again became a
topical issue. Very few people knew anything about the old women's
organizations, which many decades before had enthusiastically

represented the women's rights movement. The average age of the members was now high: in the Union, for instance, it was over 70. The activities of these women were concentrated more on old women's retirement homes and Christmas bazaars than on current women's issues (Jallinoja, 1983:123–7). It is no wonder, then, that the new wave of the women's movement had to find other channels for its activities.

New activism for women's rights
The base of the new women's movement was what in Finland is called 'the radical movement'. This movement, which arose at the beginning of the 1960s, was similar to the New Left movement in other Western countries. At the beginning it was mainly culturally oriented, but little by little it became more politically oriented. It was mainly a movement of students and young professional people, and had no central organization. It first emerged as a peace organization (Sadankomitea) founded in 1963 as part of the new international peace movement formed by Bertrand Russell (Jallinoja, 1983:132–8). The foundation of this organization was indicative of the fact that the new generation had to create its own movement; the old organizations were not accepted, though their main ideas on the subject may have been quite similar. This was typical of the 1960s, and the women's movement was in this respect no exception.

Other important associations of the radical movement, and later also of the new women's movement, included two radically oriented organizations of writers (Eino Leino Seura, and Kiila). Opinion-forming journals also became central to the radical movement. In addition to its formal organizations, the movement made its mark in many informal activities, such as public debates and seminars. All this happened in the middle of the 1960s, when the women's movement finally emerged. The main position in the new struggle for women's rights was taken by 'Association 9' (Yhdistys 9), founded in 1966 and named after the number of its founding members. Association 9 was an independent women's rights organization. It succeeded in creating a debate in Finland about sex roles, partly by applying unorthodox and activist methods. Table 2 shows how many members of some central circles of the radical movement joined Association 9.

The activist members of Association 9 were even closer to the radical movement than its rank-and-file members. The nine people who founded the Association were all committed in one way or another to the radical movement. Some of them had already presented their ideas on women's issues in the leading newspapers, which meant that their interest in the status of women was well known. According to my interviews with participants, it took about

TABLE 2
The proportion of members of some groups of the radical movement that
joined Association 9 (in per cent)

Sex	Sadankomitea (a new peace organizations), 1965	The organizations of writers		Those who wrote in the opinion-forming journals, 1964–8
		Eino Leino Seura, 1960–70	Kiila, 1965	
Women	33	74	36	39
Men	13	15	12	12
The proportion of women members in these groups	28	8	27	18

Source: The membership lists of each organization for the above-mentioned years.

two years for their first ideas about women's position in society to crystallize into the founding of the Association. During 1964 the discussion was mainly informal and personal. Women in the radical movement had become dissatisfied with the insignificant part they played in the movement; as Table 2 shows, they formed only a minority of the participants in the groups of the radical movement (Jallinoja, 1983:128–32).

Critical books on sex roles soon indicated how to deal with the problem. This kind of literature appeared in the Nordic countries at the end of the 1950s. Because many Finnish people read Swedish, books from all the other Nordic countries were fairly widely distributed. Swedish-speaking women were among the first to become acquainted with the new books on sex roles. The debate started in Finland in 1965, when the sex role issue was presented in some newspapers and seminars (Jallinoja, 1983:146–51).

The ideology based on equality

The process through which the Finnish women's movement arose in the middle of the 1960s very much resembled the rise of the new feminist movement in other Western countries. Women were dissatisfied with the male dominance in the new radical movement. Their experience was greatly inconsistent with the emancipatory ideology of the New Left, the aim of which was to break all power structures in the world (Evans, 1980:45,83; Koedt, 1976:318; Burris, 1976:327). In spite of this obvious similarity, there was one important difference between Finland and most other Western countries, and this concerns the character of the women's movement that arose from the New Left movement (in Finland called the radical movement).

Association 9, which represented the core of the newly risen women's movement in Finland, based its ideology on the principle of *equality*, not on feminism as in other countries. Of course, equality may in principle include many different aims, but in Finland the new women's movement concentrated mainly on issues that revealed that women wanted to do all that men were allowed to do. The principle of equality was thus understood from the male perspective. One of the basic issues was women's, especially married women's, right to paid work. In relation to this issue, Association 9 demanded women's right to pursue their careers and to participate on all societal decision-making levels. An active woman who would participate in public life thus became the ideal (Jallinoja, 1983:151–7). In accordance with its ideology of equality, Association 9 was open to men also; in fact, 28 per cent of the members were men.

New women's organizations, similar in ideology to Association 9, were founded during the same period in the USA (the National Organization for Women, NOW, founded in 1966) and the Netherlands (Man–Vrow–Maatschappij, 1968) (Mølgaard, 1975:273–4). Unlike the Finnish organization, NOW was not an organization of the New Left movement: its foundation was based mostly on conflicts concerning public equality politics (Freeman, 1975:49).

Thus, while discussions of sex roles based on the principle of equality were not at all unknown in other Western countries during this period — the issues were typically raised by individuals engaged in scientific research or public policies — only in a few cases did this lead to the formation of an organized social movement as in Finland and the USA.

The social background of the women's equality movement
The fact that Finnish women started the new women's movement somewhat earlier than elsewhere, and with equality rather than feminism as the basic ideology, can be interpreted as a result of the socio-historical position of women in Finland. The most important factor is the long tradition of Finnish women being employed outside the home. As early as 1910, 39 per cent of the economically active population outside agriculture were women. Between 1920 and 1960 it was 41–42 per cent and in 1980 as high as 47 per cent (Finnish Statistical Yearbooks).

The high employment rate of Finnish women is related to a number of factors. First is the relatively high educational level of women. The proportion of female university students was 32 per cent as early as 1930, compared with, at most, about 20 per cent in other Western countries (*Komiteanmietintö*, 1935:19–20); it increased rapidly in the 1950s. By 1954 it was 45 per cent, and since 1964 it has been 49–50 per cent (Statistical Yearbooks). The high percentage of women studying at universities is due to the country's traditionally great respect for education. The national movement understood the high value of enlightenment: Finland's citizens, including women, must be educated, preferably in Finnish. All this created an atmosphere in which the value of education in Finland was if anything almost overestimated.

Partly connected with the high educational level of Finnish women and with their high employment rate is the fact that a relatively large proportion of them have remained unmarried. Even in the latter part of the nineteenth century, it was common among middle- and upper-class women to remain single: about 40 per cent of them were unmarried (Jallinoja, 1983:81). They formed the core of the first wave of the women's movement. In the 1920s this phenomenon became common among the population in general. For example, in the 1920s and continuing into the 1930s, the proportion of unmarried women in the age group 40–44 years was as high as 40 per cent in urban areas. In rural areas the percentage was about 30 per cent (Finnish Statistical Yearbooks). Most of these unmarried women worked outside the home. This meant that the number of women employed outside the home was comparatively high in spite of the fact that married women were mainly housewives, even in the working class (Population Census, 1920:58,41). Under these circumstances the employed woman became a rather common figure at an early stage, and this facilitated the acceptance of married women's employment.

The question of marriage and employment was especially difficult for female university graduates. Because of their education, the proportion of employed women was higher in this group than among women with less education. At a time when it was not so generally accepted for a woman to combine a career and a family, the choice of the former often meant the renunciation of marriage. As late as 1960, 38 per cent of female university graduates in the age group 30–44 years were unmarried. For *all* women in urban areas, unmarried women constituted 24 per cent in the same age group in 1960 (Population Census 1960:IX,II.) In addition to the fact that female university graduates were more inclined than other women to remain single, they also showed a greater tendency to work outside the home when married. For example, in 1960 the proportion of employed women among married female university graduates was 82 per cent; among registered nurses it was 58 per cent and among all urban married women in the age group 25–44 years it was 45 per cent (Population Census 1960:IX,II).

These socio-economic factors greatly contributed to the adoption of equality rather than feminism by the new women's movement. Association 9 expressed the core of this situation in its ideology. Above all, it demanded women's right to work outside the home even when the woman was married. The reputation of Association 9 is based mainly on this part of the programme. The feminist groups that emerged in the 1970s criticized the Association exactly for this position. The criticism is not quite fair, however, since the Association did in fact raise many issues that later became popular in the new feminist movement, first and foremost issues concerning women's private lives: Association 9 demanded sexual liberation for women, the equal division of housework between spouses and the right to free abortion. The last-mentioned issue resulted in the passing in 1970 of a new abortion law, which was quite liberal. However, in spite of these similarities with the new feminist movement, Association 9 evidently understood the issues pertaining to private life differently. Their model was mainly the life-style of men.

The new feminists also criticized the Association for its trust in the ability of the state to improve women's situation. Association 9 extensively turned to the state authorities when presenting its demands. A relatively great number of its members also strove to obtain posts in state and municipal offices, and to a large extent they succeeded. The success in the realization of their aims was measured by political resolutions made in accordance with these aims. The interviews that I conducted in 1980–1 show, however, that many activists of Association 9 gradually became frustrated at how little change had really occurred on the state level, in spite of their efforts. The feeling of failure was related to that felt with regard to the aims in the political parties.

In spite of the tendency of Association 9 to work for political reforms through the state, it also emphasized changing public attitudes towards women. Association 9 often took a public stand, and many scientific studies later showed that attitudes changed in accordance with the aims presented by the Association.

The politicization of the women's equality movement
Association 9's focus on public policy ran parallel to the change in the radical movement, which in general was becoming more and more politically oriented. The political parties became the natural allies of the radical movement.

The change in the political climate among students occurred at the beginning of the 1970s. The student council election at Helsinki University in 1966 showed that 90 per cent of the representatives of the student council had no connection with any political party. The next election (1968) brought the first signs of change: 25 per cent of the representatives of the student council were elected from party-related election lists. By 1969 the proportion was 33 per cent and by 1970, 78 per cent. In 1973 nearly all those elected (95 per cent) represented some political party. The largest groups were conservatives (32 per cent) and the People's Democrats (27 per cent) (*Helsingin yliopiston ylioppilaskunnan kalenterit*, 1966–73). The core of the student movement was now closely related to the Communist Party.

In Association 9, too, this tendency led to a demand for party alliance, because it was felt that the political parties were the most central decision-making organs. All parties were at first accepted as allies, at least in principle. But in 1966 there were already signs that activists in Association 9 were finding their home on the left. The parliamentary election of 1966 was a landmark of this change. The Social Democratic Party was the great winner of the election, and one of the male founders of Association 9, Arvo Salo (SDP), was elected to parliament.

During 1966–8, many activists of Association 9 gave their support to the Social Democratic Party and some of them even joined the party. This happened throughout the radical movement in general.

At the end of the 1960s, the radical movement began to turn to the Communist Party. It was said that, 'if you were a real radical, you would join the Communist Party'. The younger generation of the radical movement in particular demanded this, and at the very end of the 1960s this group took the leadership in the student movement. Their organization was the Academic Socialist Society (ASS), which was founded as early as 1925, but whose role in student politics had been marginal until the end of the 1960s (Jallinoja, 1983:179–84).

Because Association 9 was part of the radical movement, it experienced the same type of politicization. According to my interviews, before the formation of Association 9 most of its future activists were politically independent. The party commitment was established in 1966–70 and the winners in this respect were the Social Democratic Party and the Finnish People's Democratic League. This change in party orientation is illustrated in Table 3.

The strong commitment of the new Finnish student movement to the political parties influenced the fate of the women's movement not only by politicizing it but also in a more dramatic way. Association 9 ceased its activities in 1970. Activists had already demanded the dissolution of the Association in 1969. The main reason for this was said to be that now it was time to work where the real decisions were made. This view received more support in 1970, but not the majority of 75 per cent that was demanded for the dissolution of the Association. The solution was that the newly elected board simply did not continue its work.

The party orientation of women's groups meant the postponement of the rise of a new feminist movement, which since 1967 had gained increasing popularity among female members of the New Left in other Western countries. In Finland the tendency was in reverse. At the beginning of the 1970s any women's movement was considered irrelevant, because there were more important questions, such as the class struggle (Jallinoja, 1983:204–6).

The new feminist movement of the 1970s and 1980s: its late rise in Finland

The new feminist movement known as the 'women's liberation movement' had its roots in the USA, where it started in 1967 (Evans, 1980:200; Hole and Levine, 1975:113–14). From there it very rapidly spread to Europe; most of the Western European countries acquired their own new feminist movements in 1968–70. In Finland the movement was certainly known at the very beginning of the 1970s. For example, the women in the Academic Socialist Society talked about it in some seminars, but they were much opposed to it. One of the reasons for this was the new feminists' way of treating the woman question quite independently of class structure. According to opponents of the women's liberation movement, women and men do not form separate classes; on the contrary, working-class women have more in common with working-class men that with bourgeois women. All in all, women's issues were not considered important, and practically all women in the Academic Socialist Society were of this opinion (Jallinoja, 1983:205–6).

So at the beginning of the 1970s the situation in the Finnish student movement was not favourable to the new feminist movement. Most activities centred on the Academic Socialist Society, whose loyalty to

TABLE 3

Political party membership of 25 activists of Association 9 before its foundation, during its existence and in 1980*

Party	Before 1966	1966–70	1980
Social Democratic Party	6	10	8
Finnish People's Democratic League**	1	9	11
Swedish People's Party	0	1	0
Conservative and Centre Parties	0	0	0
Independent	18	5	6
Total	25	25	25

* The definition of activists was based on the following criteria: being members of the boards, and/or leaders of the working groups. The sample was random and represents 54 per cent of all activists defined in this way.
** The Finnish People's Democratic League consists of a number of socialist/communist organizations, of which the Communist Party is the most central.
Source: Jallinoja (1983:181)

the Communist Party was strong. The time of Association 9 was over. But in spite of all this, something was happening behind the scenes. Feminist ideas were, after all, getting support among some women.

The first feminist groups

In this situation, it is no wonder that the new feminist movement was finally created not by women in the Academic Socialist Society, but by women outside it. The first two feminist groups were founded in 1973, mainly by women who had belonged to somewhat marginal groups of the student movement. Some of them were Maoists (this group was really tiny in Finland), some belonged to less radical groups and some of them were completely outside the radical movement. The founding of the feminist groups came about when some women returned to Finland from abroad (France, Britain, Denmark and Sweden), where they had become acquainted with the new feminism. They were fascinated by the ideas they had heard and also by the whole atmosphere that they had encountered in feminist meetings.

The first year of these two groups was characterized by Marxism–feminism: Marxist books directed the way to handle 'the woman question'. This kind of orientation was also seen in the names of the groups, 'Marxist–Feminists' and 'Red Women' (Rödkäringarna). During this time they did not differ much from those women in the Academic Socialist Society who were interested in the question of women. But soon, feminist books began to give new views on women. Study circles became consciousness-raising groups, and public issues made way for private issues. Gradually new groups were formed, and in 1976 these groups founded an informal coordinating community called 'Feminists'. They became well-known publicly and met a great deal of resistance, even among women who were sympathetic to the emancipation of women. The new way of looking at the woman question seemed to be too strange and against all prior traditions of the women's movement. It is no wonder, then, that the number of women in these new feminist groups was never high: during the 1970s there were only about 200 participants in Feminist groups in Helsinki and fewer than 100 in other towns (Jallinoja, 1983: 198–202).

Feminists conquer the 'Union'

The Feminist groups were not the only place where the new women's movement appeared. The old organization, the Women's Rights League Union (founded in 1892), was taken over by new feminists in the middle of the 1970s. The old members of the Union very much opposed this coup d'état, but it seemed to be the only way to increase the membership. At the beginning of the 1970s members numbered about 100 in Helsinki; in 1975 there were 330; and by 1979, 1,018. New branches were founded in some other towns in the same spirit that had changed the character of the Union in Helsinki (Jallinoja, 1983:202).

The channelling of the new feminist movement into a formal organization was in fact in opposition to the ideas of second-wave feminism. The autonomous Finnish Feminist groups opposed this move, and they had a lot of conflicts with the Union on that score. The Union was not considered really feminist by the Feminists. The members of the Union defended their formal organization on the grounds that it made it easier to present demands to the authorities. The arguments the Union presented clearly indicated the differences between its members and the Feminists. The Feminist groups concentrated more on personal consciousness-raising, whereas the Union, even though it too adopted consciousness-raising, wanted to work as an interest group for women vis-à-vis the state and other authorities. The Union thus combined the new feminist ideas and the principles of the women's rights movement as embodied, for instance, in Association 9. This was perhaps more typical of what happened in Finland than in many other Western countries.

The Union has partly followed the same lines as Association 9. In a way, it has continued the work and the tradition of the Association. It has tried to influence state officials. It also has rather close relations with the political parties. Though the Union itself is non-political, many individual members belong to political parties. This ensures fairly good relations with the parties, and at least in principle the possibility of working with them. It has also made it possible for women who do not consider themselves 'real' feminists to join the new women's movement.

The positive relations between the Union and the political parties can also be seen in the willingness of the female members of parliament to join the Union. In 1966–79, 45 per cent of the women Social Democrats in parliament were members of the Union. The proportion in the Swedish People's Party was 67 per cent, in the Coalition Party (conservatives) 47 per cent and in the small Christian League 100 per cent. However, although so many female members of parliament have joined the Union, they are not active members there. Their membership is rather a sign of recognizing the ideas of the women's movement (Jallinoja, 1983: 41).

It should be noted that none of the female representatives of the People's Democrats belonged to the Union. This reflects the relation the communists typically have had to the women's movement. They are not attracted to the independent women's movement: their women's movement is openly and absolutely party-related.

The feminists and the communist women

Though the large women's organization of the Finnish People's Democratic League (the Finnish Women's Democratic League, FWDL, with 23,000 members) has outlined its programmes in accordance with the principles presented in the programmes of the head organization, it has also from time to time shown a willingness to adopt some ideas from the independent women's movement. In the 1960s it published a programme, 'Women, Men, Democracy' (Finnish Women's Democratic League, 1968), which was like a straight copy of the programme of Association 9. Not all members of the Finnish Women's League accepted this publication, for the very reason that in their opinion it related the League too closely to Association 9. In the latter part of the 1970s some new feminists tried to create contacts with the Women's League, which on its side showed some interest in a closer contact, particularly since many new feminists proved to be socialists. Some joint meetings were held and some articles were written by new feminists in the newspapers of the Finnish People's Democratic League. However, this venture was not a positive experience for the new feminists. The opposition to the new feminism finally turned out to be quite strong in the FWDL. The very foundation of this opposition can be found in the later officially approved programme, according to which 'women are not a separate social class; women belong either to the working class or to those who own the means of production' (Finnish Women's Democratic League, 1980:5). Apart from this, the programme is pretty much based on the principle of equality of the sexes. The new feminist issues relating to private life were not included; they were considered strange and remote from the 'normal' political agenda.

Feminism in the Social Democratic Party

In recent times the new feminism has influenced the Social Democratic Party not so much on the organizational level as on the personal level. Some female Social Democrats have adopted new feminist ideas and have tried hard to influence the programmes and decisions of the party. But the opposition in the party has been strong, even among women. In spite of this, Social Democratic new feminists have managed to present their views, for example in their magazine *Tietosisko*. In 1985 they published a report on sexual issues. This was a remarkable sign of the realization of the new feminist idea, according to which 'the personal is political'.

Personal issues on to the agenda

The new feminist groups, and little by little the majority of the Union, have done their best to change the ideology of the Finnish women's movement in the direction of the international new feminism. The effects were scarcely felt before the 1980s. Today the public debate on women's issues is based not only on issues of equality (though these are still present) but also on personal issues. The woman question has widened its scope to encompass all spheres of life.

The contents of the magazines of the Feminists (*Alkanainen*) and the Union (*Akkaväki*) roughly indicate the issues that have most interested these two groupings of the new feminist movement. Table 4 illustrates that both magazines have helped to bring the personal oppression of women on to the public agenda. The table also indicates some differences between the magazines. The Feminists have handled the woman question in more of a general way, for example by describing women's movements all over the world and by depicting the oppression of women in cultural and other spheres of life. The aim of these articles has been to raise women's consciousness of themselves as subjects. *Akkaväki*, the journal of the Union, has instead given more space to traditional types of equality issues, among which women's prospects at work and in public decision-making have been given a great significance. The differences between these two magazines, however, have been less than might be expected if we compare the programmes presented by the

TABLE 4

The articles of *Aikanainen* (journal of the Feminists) and *Akkaväki* (journal of the Union), classified according to the main topics of articles (in per cent)

Topics		*Aikanainen* 1977–81	*Akkaväki* 1980–82
I	Woman question in general		
	(no specification of the topics)	31	22
	The oppression of women in culture, etc.	14	3
II	Public life sphere (on the basis of		
	traditional equality principle)	21	33
III	Private life sphere (motherhood,		
	sexuality, battering, marriage, divorce,		
	love, homework)	18	20
IV	Special issues related to woman		
	question (peace, ecology, neighbourhood)	8	14
V	Other topics	8	8
Total	(%)	100	100
	(n)	(248)	(124)

Source: Jallinoja (1983:229).

Union and the Feminists. Later, *Akkaväki* altered its scope still further in the direction of new feminism.

Independence or integration

Throughout Finnish history, the basic tenet of the women's movement has been independence. Women have maintained that this is the only way to formulate freely the ideology of the movement. Dependence has far too long characterized the life situation of women. The women's movement has been one sign of women's aspirations to liberate themselves. The reality in the women's movement, however, has been somewhat different, with a recurring tendency towards integration.

From the point of view of the political parties

In order to understand this we must first take a look at those political parties having no close relations to the women's movement. At the beginning of this century it was the Social Democratic Party and the Agrarian Party that had no close ties to the women's rights movement, and later also the Communist Party, founded in 1918. It is very easy to conclude that this was because the women's rights movement was bourgeois. This is not, however, a valid answer, because it is tautological: rather, we must ask *why* the women's movement was bourgeois and therefore did not attract women in the Socialist and Agrarian Parties.

The Socialist and Agrarian Parties were more rigidly class-oriented than the so-called bourgeois parties. The former worked for workers and farmers respectively. The conservative parties never clearly referred to middle or upper classes in their programmes. Among supporters of the Socialist and Agrarian Parties, party loyalty was strong. Party interests had priority over all other issues. Among such issues was 'the woman question'.

Thus, if it was a class-based party, it could not easily embrace issues that were based on other than class cleavage. This has also been true later in history. It was the change of the Social Democratic Party from class-based party to general party that allowed for a closer relation with the women's movement. The party has become less and less class-oriented at the same time as the leadership in the party has moved from workers to university graduates. The party now wants to be a general party in the same way conservative parties have always wanted to be. The first signs of a closer relation with the women's movement were seen in the 1960s.

Among the old political parties, only the Finnish People's Democratic League and the Centre Party (the former Agrarian Party) are today almost completely without marked relations with the women's movement. To this class-oriented party category now also belongs the party of small farmers, the new Finnish Agrarian Party (founded in 1966). The degree of class orientation of a political party has thus influenced the closeness of the relations that the party — or, one should say, the female party members — has been ready to establish with the women's movement. This has also meant some conflicts between the party organizations and some feminists who have wanted to establish close relations with these class-oriented parties; feminist ideas have not been so well accepted in these parties.

This tendency is universal, but it is more severe in societies like Finland where the class struggle has had strong manifestations. The tendency is further strengthened if the role of the political parties has for one reason or another been strong. This has also been the case in Finland.

From the point of view of the women's movement
We find a slightly different picture when we look at it from the point of view of the women's movement. The women's movement has been more interested in establishing contact with the political parties than vice versa. But the emphasis on contacts with the political parties has varied over time. At the beginning, the movement more strongly emphasized independence. Later, the close relations that the women's movement originally had with other ideological, but eventually politically oriented, social movements enabled many women to look favourably at some kind of integration. The ideological roots of the women's movement determined which allies to choose. The main argument for integration, presented both at the beginning of this century and in the 1960s, was that the real decision-making takes place in political parties.

The important word here is 'real'. It sounds as if the women's movement is not something real. This view stems from the fact that it is the party apparatus that functions as one of the most important power mechanisms. In order to have influence in society, it is necessary somehow to be close to the parties. In other words, members of the women's movement sooner or later look for channels that contain strong political power.

But by integration, the women's movement did not mean a complete merge or absorption into the dominant power apparatus. Rather, the strategy of integration was regarded as a means to transform the aims of the women's movement into reality. In practice, however, this strategy tends to weaken the position of the women's movement itself. This is a tendency that has been obvious in Finland since the turn of the century.

The situation has changed in recent years, however. There are signs that the political parties have lost some of their power. This can be seen in the dissatisfaction that people show with the parties. New social movements are also a sign of this change; they have tried to show that it is possible to be an influential power even outside the party apparatus.

The new feminist movement has chosen the way that is common to all new social movements. It is trying to exert its influence outside the party apparatus. In Finland, however, this principle is perhaps not as evident as in other Western countries, even though the tendency is there. If we analyse the political ties of individual activists — not of the movement as such — we find that in the 1970s the proportion of politically independent persons was highest among Feminists (Table 5). But in spite of this, it is worth noting that, even among Feminists, membership of political parties has been rather common (mainly in the Finnish People's Democratic League), though even these women emphasize their independence vis-à-vis the party. 'Independent socialist' is an often used term in this respect.

According to my interviews, however, the relation to the political party is often ambivalent. Feminists have emphasized their independence with respect to the party, though they are members of the party; in practice this has meant that socialist Feminists have not been anxious to present themselves as candidates for parliamentary or local government elections. This has been the borderline that has distinguished Feminists from those women who have joined the Union, the formal organization.

TABLE 5
The proportion of supporters of different political parties among Feminists and activists of Association 9 and the Women's Rights League Union*
(in per cent)

Party	Feminists	Association 9	The Union
Social Democratic Party	5	32	36
Finnish People's Democratic League	55	48	18
Swedish People's Party	—	—	18
Conservative and Centre Parties	—	—	—
Emphasizing one's political independence	40	20	28
Total (%)	100	100	100
(n)	(20)	(25)	(11)

* Most of the supporters of some party were also members of it. The figures are based on interviews with the activists. For information on Association 9 see Table 3. Most of the Feminists interviewed belonged to the first two groups, Marxist-Feminists and Red Women. The sample was random and represents 43 per cent of all members of these two groups. The sample was completed with a few randomly selected members of younger Feminist groups. The activists of the Union are the members of the boards for the years 1973–9. The sample is random and represents 50 per cent of all activists defined in this way.

But this borderline *has* been crossed. For the Feminists, the formation of the Greens (not yet a party but an informal group which, however, has two representatives in parliament) has enabled them to join a political party and yet avoid the unattractive old parties. Because a number of Feminists also consider it important to try to influence public policy, some of them have joined the Greens by presenting themselves as candidates in municipal elections on the election lists of the Greens (in 1984). It is, however, too early to say whether the new feminist movement in the long run will follow the path of the earlier women's movements in this respect. In all its historical phases, the women's movement in Finland has first stressed its independence and then gradually begun to seek integration. The political parties have then become among its principal allies. In general, the stronger the party apparatus is in a society, the more probable the alliance will be.

References

Allen, Pam (1970) *Free Space. A Perspective on the Small Group in Women's Liberation*. New York: Times Change Press.

Burris, Barbara (1976) 'The Fourth World Manifesto', in Anne Koedt, Ellen Levine and Anita Rapone (eds), *Radical Feminism*. New York: Quadrangle/New York Times Book Co.

Dahlsgård, Inga (ed.) (1975) *Kvindebevaegelsens hvem, hvad, hvor*. Copenhagen: Politikens Förlag.

Evans, Richard (1977) *The Feminists. Women's Emancipation Movements in Europe, America and Australasia 1840–1920*. London: Croom Helm.

Evans, Sara (1980) *Personal Politics. The Roots of Women's Liberation in the Civil Rights Movement and the New Left*. New York: Vintage Books.

Finnish Women's Democratic League (1968)   *Naiset, miehet ja demokratia* (Women, Men and Democracy). Helsinki: FWDL.

Finnish Women's Democratic League (1980) *Naisten oikeudesta, syrjinnästä ja tasaarvosta* (About Women's Rights, Discrimination and Equality). Helsinki: Suomen Naisten Demokraattinen Liitto (Finnish Women's Democratic League).

Firestone, Shulamith (1972) *The Dialectic of Sex. The Case for Feminist Revolution*. London: Paladin.

Freeman, Jo (1975) *The Politics of Women's Liberation. A Case Study of an Emerging Social Movement and Its Relation to the Policy Process*. New York: Longman.

Gripenberg, Alexandra (1907) *Suomalaisen puolueen naisille. Suomalaisen puolueen naisvaliokunnan kirjasia VI.* (To the Women of the Finnish Party). Helsinki: Suomalaisen Kirjallisuuden Seuran Kirjapaino Oy.

Hole, Judith and Ellen Levine (1975) *Rebirth of Feminism*. New York: Quadrangle/New York Times Book Co.

Jallinoja, Riitta (1983) *Suomalaisen naisasialiikkeen taistelukaudet* (The Active Periods of the Finnish Women's Movement). Helsinki: WSOY.

Koedt, Anne (1976) 'Women and the Radical Movement', in Anne Koedt, Ellen Levine and Anita Rapone (eds), *Radical Feminism*. New York: Quadrangle/New York Times Book Co.

Komiteanmietintö (1935) (Committee Report). Helsinki: Valtioneuvoston Kirjpaino.

Millett, Kate (1971) *Sexual politiken.* Stockholm: Rabén & Sjögren.

Mølgaard, Kika (1975) 'Det nye kvindeoprør i Holland', in Dahlsgård (1975).

Östenson, Ebba (1957) *Svenska kvinnoförbundet 1907–1957.* Helsinki: Tryckeri Ab. *Population Census* (1920 and 1960).

Reed, Evelyn (1971) *Problems of Women's Liberation, a Marxist Approach.* New York: Pathfinder Press.

Rowbotham, Sheila (1972) 'Women's Liberation and the New Politics', in Michele Wandor (ed.), *The Body Politic. Writings from the Women's Liberation Movement in Britain 1969–1972.* London: Stage 1.

Solanis, Valerie (1970) 'Experts from the SCUM (Society for Cutting Up Men) Manifesto', in Robin Morgan (ed.), *Sisterhood is Powerful. An Anthology of Writings from the Women's Liberation Movement.* New York: Vintage Books.

University of Helsinki Students' Union (1966–73) *Helsingin yliopiston ylioppilaskunnan kalenterit* (University of Helsinki Students' Union calendars). Tapiola: Weilin & Göös.

Yates, Gayle (1975) *What Women Want. The Ideas of the Movement.* Cambridge, Mass.: Harvard University Press.

III

THE RISE AND CHANGE OF THE NEW WOMEN'S MOVEMENT

9

Emergence of the feminist movement in Turkey

Sirin Tekeli

Introduction

Turkey is one of the countries that new feminism, the ideology of the women's liberation movement, has reached only recently. The movement, which has existed for over a decade in the West, reached Turkey after the 12 September 1980 military intervention, which temporarily suspended democracy and brought political life to a complete halt. Feminism soon became a central issue, leading people to believe that it will occupy an important position on the political agenda of the country during the 1980s. It also led to intense polemics. The purpose of this chapter is to consider the meaningfulness of feminist ideology from the point of view of Turkish society, bearing in mind that it is too early to speculate about the movement's impact or evaluate its activities, mode of organization and so on as the ideology is still in the process of being formulated.

Is feminism meaningful to Turkish women?

Is feminism in Turkey, as one observer believes, a 'temporary fashion' originating from the West (Cemgil, 1984), or is it an ideology that would inevitably have been put on the agenda at some stage in the historical development of Turkey? Turkish women have finally decided to look at their own condition more closely: is this so very unexpected a development at a time when Western women, perhaps less oppressed than the women in the Middle Eastern and Mediterranean societies, have formulated a new ideology, created new forms of political struggle and reached a considerable level of effectiveness by being aware of their own oppression? In her famous research on the social and cultural geography of a region including Turkey, Germaine Tillion describes the women there as 'the last colony': 'In this era of decolonization, the vast feminine world is still like a colony. The Mediterranean woman, frequently abused in spite of laws, sometimes sold, often beaten, forced to work and whose assassination may sometimes remain unpunished, is the slave of our times' (Tillion, 1966:99). Tillion also found out that this many-sided, complex and profound oppression is not seen solely in the southern and eastern parts of the Mediterranean, where the Islamic religion is dominant, but is also encountered in Spain, southern Italy and Greece — that is, in the northern part of the Mediterranean where the Christian religion is dominant. She comes to the conclusion that this oppression is a product of a certain family structure prevailing in the region, the origin of which goes back to prehistoric times.

A similar explanation has been put forward by Emmanuel Todd, the writer of one of the most interesting anthropological works of recent years. He finds that the endogamous family seen in the Mediterranean region is also the determinant of the main areas where the Islamic religion will spread. In this kind of family, one definitely anti-feminist in nature, the price of physical protection for women is social non-existence (Todd, 1983:152–75).

But feminist movements of varying strength have appeared in all of the countries situated in the northern part of this region. Why should it, then, be a bewildering issue in Turkey? According to Tillion's thesis, the cause of women's oppression in Turkey cannot be the Muslim religion. Of course there are other Muslim Mediterranean countries that have not yet experienced a similar movement, and furthermore, Khomeini's Iran has witnessed developments in the reverse direction. But Turkey has a special place among Islamic societies: it is a country that has made the first and perhaps the most comprehensive reforms in the status of women and has accepted secularism as the founding principle of the state.

Should not all these differences from societies whose political systems are still based on the Islamic law result in a different kind of consciousness in women? I believe they should. For any ideology to emerge, its content or its message must be meaningful to a certain group in society, and when the issue is feminism, that particular group is those women who are oppressed, and feel themselves oppressed, because of their sex. The extent of this oppression, and its increase or decrease in time, will influence the sensitivity or responsiveness of women to the content of the ideology. Therefore, the first thing to do in considering the meaningfulness of feminist ideology from the point of view of Turkish society is to determine whether the 'material conditions' of the ideology exist. In more concrete terms, the following questions should be answered: (1) Are the Turkish women oppressed, and, if so, how? (2) What are the mechanisms of this oppression, and which are the mediating institutions? However, the existence of the material conditions, that is, the necessary conditions, is not sufficient for the emergence of that ideology. This leads us to ask another series of questions: (1) Why did feminism appear in

Turkey only in the early 1980s, and why couldn't it have developed earlier? (2) What were the obstacles to its development? (3) What are its actual limitations? (4) In which segments of society can it be expected to develop, and how?

In this chapter I shall first describe very briefly the change in the status and specific life conditions of women within the context of historical transformations in Turkey. I shall then examine the obstacles of a historical nature that feminism as an ideology is facing. Finally, I shall briefly describe the characteristics of the Turkish feminist movement, now in the process of formation. I hope that I shall be excused for being extremely optimistic from time to time, as I myself belong to the movement.

The oppression of Turkish women: historical heritage and socio-economic change

In order to understand the present position of women in Turkey, the most meaningful periodization of the past would be as follows: (1) the structure of the Pre-Tanzimat Ottoman society; (2) the process of 'Westernization', starting with Tanzimat and continuing until the end of the first world war; (3) the first years of the republic and the single-party regime; (4) the period of 'fast' social change starting after 1950 and coming to the present.

During the last hundred years there has been very little change in certain basic institutions affecting the real status of women — the most important of which is the family — although some important changes in the legal status of urban women have occurred. Family sociologists have observed very little change in the rural family during the last hundred years (Duben, 1984).

The Pre-Tanzimat period

In the Pre-Tanzimat period the Ottoman Empire was a powerful, centralized state based on economically self-sufficient family production. Political power was in the hands of a bureaucratic elite which received the agricultural surplus in the form of tax revenues (Keyder, 1979:4). Ottoman society was segregated according to two basic differentiations — that of *millet* (nation), with regard to religious differentiation, and that of gender — as opposed to Western societies, where class was the main determinant of social structure (Şeni, 1984). The legal and social status of women was defined by Sharia, the Islamic law which also legitimated the whole state system. According to Sharia, women were not legally equal to men, although some of their rights were under guarantee. With regard to testifying before a court of law, she was worth half a man, and with regard to family law, which permitted four wives, she was worth even less (Ortaylı, 1984:82). In all social strata, women's life centred around the family. In the rural areas she would work on the land of the economically self-sufficient family farm and then prepare the crop for consumption; that is, she would perform the necessary manufacturing processes for the preparation of food, weaving, sewing and so on. In the urban areas, within the bureaucratic elite she lived in the family, completely isolated both from the production process and from social life. Women were segregated from men, forming the 'harem' among themselves, and their only responsibility was housework and child-rearing. Economically they were absolutely dependent on males, either their fathers or their husbands. The state often issued decrees (*ferman*) regulating the behaviour of women outside their homes, such as the days of the week they could go out and the style of garments they should wear. These decrees permitted a very limited area of activity to women. In Ottoman society, therefore, both in rural and urban areas, women were subject to the absolute authority of men through the mediation of the institutions of state, religion and family.

The process of 'Westernization'

In the nineteenth century the Ottoman Empire was forced to make administrative reforms, borrowing some of the Western institutions as a model. The Ottoman elites came to realize that the Empire was deteriorating compared with the rapidly developing Western powers with their growing capitalist economies. Among those reforms, the 1839 Tanzimat Fermanı (the Tanzimat Decree) constitutes a turning point in the number of novelties it stimulated (Berkes, 1974).

The process of 'Westernization' that started with Tanzimat led to changes that also affected the status of women. These changes could be seen both in large cities, which began to establish commercial ties with Western capitalism, and in rural areas like the Aegean coast, Çukurova and Amik in the southern parts of Turkey, where production for the market (especially of cotton) had begun. The 1858 Land Reform gave equal inheritance rights to girls and boys, and secondary schools and teachers' and midwifery schools for girls were opened. Reformist intellectuals of the period began to criticize the lower status of the women in the family. Such legal, institutional and ideological changes gave women the opportunity to see the world outside their homes, at least in large cities like Istanbul and Salonica. And at the end of this process, in the atmosphere of relative freedom created by the revolution of 1908 (the Young Turk Revolution), the first feminist women entered the scene. Educated women from the intellectual circles of the cities started publishing magazines expressing their grievances against the deep oppression of women. They formed the first women's associations (Tekeli, 1982:196–201).

The process of change that started with Tanzimat did not affect a large number of women; but, by allowing a series of 'first steps' and by providing a break from the traditional society, it was qualitatively perhaps more important than the changes of the following periods. And yet, although it set the stage for them, it had some very obvious limitations. It was the Western world that was the centre of attention; new styles of life — although limited to in-house relations — were being copied from the West. These new models, which had affected daily life only through imitation, were not adequate for the formation of a new self-consistent self-identity of women. The 'alafrangalaşma' (becoming like the Western people) of this period, which lacked a material basis as it did not correspond to women's economic independence from marriage through work, and which took them out of the 'harem' but did not free them from dependence on their families, became the preferred subject of almost all the literature produced during that period and was heavily criticized by many novelists and essayists of the period (Moran, 1983). The Ottoman intellectuals saw that the traditional family structure oppressed women, gave them no chance to improve themselves and therefore played an indirect negative role in the underdevelopment of the country. But they would give up neither the political system nor the religion. Nor could they think that the relations between the sexes in the family should be reformed and made more democratic. They wanted women to be better educated; but for them the purpose of this education was to enable women better to perform their traditional role in the family: educating the children. Giving women the chance of developing their own independent identity and freeing them from men's control was never dreamed of.

The young Turkish republic

Great transformations materialize in periods of intense crisis. In Turkey the drastic changes in the daily lives of women were a product of the war years, a time that also led to the fall of the Ottoman Empire. The Balkan wars of 1912 and 1913 and the first world war forced a great number of women to go out to work and earn their living as manual workers or civil servants in order to compensate for the absence of their husbands who were away at war. In the same way, the first time that Turkish women became involved in politics — not counting the political plots prepared in the harem of Ottoman palaces — was during the years after the first world war when parts of the country had been occupied and the national struggle for independence started. Women then participated in a series of activities outside their traditional roles: they organized public meetings, addressed the masses, founded Defence of Rights associations and fought actively in the war (Tekeli, 1981, 1982).

But the activities of this period did not last for long. When the war ended, without showing any reluctance, the women returned home and resumed their traditional roles. A similar change was observed in Western societies at this time. And so the first wave of feminist movement was over (Evans, 1976).

The problems facing the young Turkish republic were very complicated. Turkey had come out of the war losing land and, more important, people. She was now a backward agricultural country amidst a capitalist world, her agriculture based on small family productions. Under these circumstances, the biggest contribution that was expected from women was their having as many children as they could to compensate for the loss of manpower in the war. In those years the agricultural enterprises were small and land was relatively ample; therefore in rural areas, for the economic survival of the family both women and children had to participate in the production process. Large families were not a burden but an advantage at this time. The state therefore encouraged population increase. These conditions resulted in a substantial decrease in the number of unmarried people until the beginning of the second world war, and the birth rate went up to 9.1 children per family on average (Özbay, 1984; Shorter and Macura, 1982).

Those were years of intense suffering. Women kept on giving birth to children at the expense of their own health, at a time when the mortality rate among children was very high. They would then work in the fields and do the housework so as to be able to feed and dress their crowded families, with only the help of the other female members of the family. In spite of all these endeavours, they were deprived of all kinds of rights (education, inheritance, etc.), and on top of everything else, they would certainly be beaten if they were seen to be revolting against traditional relations. No research has been done on the widely practised wife-beating in Turkey; the most important source of information on this widespread practice and its 'legitimacy' is literature (Akatlı, 1984:16).

Yet at the same time, in addition to the drastic reforms that modified the structure of the state, including the foundation of a republic to replace the old monarchy and the acceptance of secularism, the government was preparing the most radical 'women's revolution' ever attempted in Muslim–Mediterranean societies. The vestimentary reform of 1925 'prohibited' the wearing of the charshaf and the veil, symbols of religious oppression. The Civil Code adopted in 1926, which was translated from the Swiss Civil Code, replaced the Islamic law and gave women 'almost' equal status to men. (However, the husband remained by law the head of the family and the wife still needed his permission to seek a job outside the home.)

These new 'rights' given to women by the secular republicans carried a symbolic meaning in their fight against the religious authority that had formed the legal basis of the previous Ottoman state (Tekeli, 1981). When the attempt of 'transition to a multi-party democracy' failed with the brief Free Party episode in 1930, the enfranchisement of women was taken up again for symbolic reasons (Tekeli, 1981). In 1931 women were enfranchised for local elections, and in 1934 they were given equal political rights for national elections. In the first elections following this constitutional modification (in 1935), the number of women deputies (18, or 4.5 per cent) in the parliament was higher than in any of the Western democracies except Finland (Tekeli, 1982).

The intransigent 'Jacobin' administrators who had enacted these radical changes, shaking the settled traditions and culture of the society, knew very well that the number of women who would actually take advantage of these rights was not more than a handful. Almost all of them were concentrated in urban areas, in bourgeois or petit bourgeois (civil servant) families. The republican regime would honour and respect those 'exemplary—distinguished—elite' women who were educated, had professions, and practised them without ignoring their traditional duties both as supporting and obedient wives and as good mothers. They were given a duty, a mission, and they felt the 'power of a big, modern nation' behind them (Professor Topçuoğlu's memories; cited in Ozankaya, 1984).

These women, who considered themselves as the representatives of the period's 'state feminism', experienced the excitement of being pioneers of modernization so passionately that they could not realize that their own position did not reflect the real conditions of most Turkish women. And so they were led into a tragic 'schizophrenic' illusion: the new identity of these women was not one that they had selected themselves, but an ascribed one. And the ascriber was the state. (In a sense, the Ottoman heritage was still alive.)

The period of fast social change after 1950

During the period between the two wars, the accumulation of capital achieved via the exercise of etatism had proved successful and had led to the emergence of a group of entrepreneurs, ready to start up their own businesses in both rural and urban areas. At the end of the war, in the early 1950s, the country's rapid economic development, seen in conjunction with its growing integration with world capitalism, resulted in important changes in Turkish social structure. These structural changes can be itemized as follows: agricultural modernization in rural areas; the gradual breaking up of small family enterprises; the emancipation of rural labour and especially landless families from the land; growing urbanization, as a result of migration to cities; the revival of commerce and industry in urban areas; and fast social mobility.

All these changes influenced, directly or indirectly, the position of women both in their families and in society. However, it is not possible to claim that these changes have ameliorated the position of women in general, resulting in a decrease in the heavy oppression of the preceding period. On the contrary, some of these changes have led to conditions such that women's oppression has become even deeper in some social strata.

The effects of the modernization processes were different in the rural and urban areas. In the rural areas, during the first stages of capitalist development and the adoption of a market-oriented economy, when there was ample arable land there was an increase in the number of family enterprises producing agricultural goods and selling the excess produce in the market (Boratav, 1981). As time went by, small landowners saw that this kind of production was insufficient to provide them with a living and so some members of the families started to do wage work in others' fields as well as their own. And when even this additional kind of work proved insufficient, they started to do wage work that was not agricultural. However, this process did not lead to the complete breaking up of small family enterprises. In fact, in rural areas these enterprises are still quite common today, as the capitalist system of production has not yet fully developed.

What concerns us most here is that this breaking up of the family production process has affected men and women in different ways. As research shows, when small family production was insufficient for the living of the family, it was the men who did wage work, both in the agricultural sector and elsewhere; the women then either stuck to their old position as unpaid family labourers or completely got away from production and attained the status of 'housewife' (Özbay, 1984: 45).

This situation is clearly reflected in the statistics on population and the workforce recording the fall in the ratio of women's participation in the labour force. In 1955, the ratio of women in the labour force was 43.1 per cent. At the end of the twenty years during which the above-mentioned changes occurred in rural areas, this rate fell to 36.2 per cent, and by 1980 it was 33.7 per cent. But a very important majority of the women who were recorded in the population statistics as 'working' still had the status of 'unpaid family helpers' (91.2 per cent of all working women in 1955; 86.6 per cent in 1975), the large majority of which was concentrated in the agricultural sector.

The meaning of these indicators is very clear. In capitalist societies, the transition to wage labour results in the inclusion of women in exploitative relationships like men, but also puts an end to their gender-specific oppression rising from their imprisonment in domestic labour (Alzon, 1972; Young et al., 1981). In Turkey, the breaking up of the family enterprises has sometimes led to an increase in the women's propensity to pass on to wage labour, but often women have broken away from the production process altogether: this has increased their dependency on the family and the husband and thus made them subject to more oppression.

In the urban areas there are two strata, which at first sight seem to live under quite different and opposite work, social and family relationships: working-class women or, as defined in some research, the *gecekondu* women, and women from the middle classes.

Women who have come to urban centres from rural areas make up a great majority of the *gecekondu* women. As research shows, in Turkey migration to urban centres has occurred in two stages. Between 1950 and 1960, males who had abandoned agricultural work for waged labour outside agriculture came to the cities, leaving their families behind. Between 1965 and 1970, having created the necessary conditions enabling them to support their families, the mass of first-wave immigrants brought their wives and children to the cities. The *gecekondu* women's coming to the city was an extremely passive act, subject entirely to the male's decision. The dependency of these women on their men increased after they started to live in urban areas. The number of *gecekondu* women who have entered factories as workers is quite limited; indeed, statistics show a very small increase in the overall number of women wage workers. This means that a lot of immigrant women have instead assumed the status of housewives and have been completely detached from the production process. The only job these working-age women can find is household work. And their availability as maids enables the working middle-class women to carry on with their professions. 'Shortly, the situation can be defined as the exploitation of women by women' (Öncü, 1981:185). This kind of low-paid work involves no special knowledge or skill and is a mere extension of the work they learned to do back in their villages; lacking any social security and performed in the isolation of separate houses, it has no 'emancipatory' function at all.

In the urban areas, those women who have been able to break out of the circle of the classical household roles include those working in sectors like ready-to-wear goods, textiles and food, which have a relatively high propensity to employ women workers; women of the lower middle classes, working as secretaries, banking clerks and teachers; and women of the upper classes, who are university graduates working in professions. The proportion of women belonging to the first two of these groups is low compared with the developed capitalist societies. In the 1970s the ratio of women working in urban activities to the total urban population was around 10 per cent. As a growing percentage of the working population is employed in jobs outside agriculture, the ratio of women working in non-agricultural jobs to the total of working women has gone up to 10.4 per cent in 1970 from 3.5 per cent in 1950 (Kazgan, 1981:134). On the other hand, the ratio of women in professions like law and medicine is higher than that in Western societies. According to an optimistic estimate, two-thirds of women university graduates actually practise their professions (Öncü, 1981:187). Class structures special to underdeveloped societies are the main factors explaining why these women, in many cases daughters of the first generation of 'elite' women, who believed they were the representatives of the republican ideology, were able to get high-status professions fairly easily. In societies like ours, bourgeois classes with a short history and precarious position tend to have a stronger class prejudice as opposed to gender prejudice; and for professions with which their class is traditionally associated, they prefer the presence of women from their own class to the presence of men from lower classes, hence keeping 'the professions' within their class (Öncü, 1981:189). These women, few in number, owing to their class position, would appear to be the most emancipated representatives of their sex: they have prestigious professions, economic independence, high status.

To a large extent, these women have also emancipated themselves from marriage and the family, which preserves its patriarchal and oppressive nature in all strata. 'In large cities not only "artists" but also white-collar young women, whose families live in the same city, are now starting to live in separate apartments, two or three of them sharing the rent' (Kıray, 1984:71). Such novelties are quite revolutionary with respect to traditional culture, but for the present they are most exceptional and in general represent a temporary situation which ends with marriage. Marriage is still, in all strata of society, believed to be *the* institution that will allow women duly to perform their gender roles. Unmarried and childless women are regarded as having something wrong with them, and it is believed that they do not achieve their full identity. For both sexes, but especially for women, the family remains a very basic, fundamental institution. The most obvious evidence of this is the very high marriage and low divorce rates found in Turkey. Until recent years the proportion of unmarried women was only about 1–2 per cent even in urban areas, and in 1976 the gross divorce rate was 0.35 per 1,000 people. This is the lowest rate recorded among the Mediterranean Islamic countries (Levine, 1982:326).

On the other hand, having paid jobs outside the house has not much changed these women's roles within the house. Although they work as much as men do away from home (part-time work is not common in Turkey), work has not brought them emancipation. It would even be hard to say that they have gained economic independence; the average wage level of women is two-thirds that of men. In general, the money that working women earn goes directly into the family budget as 'additional income', and even pocket-money cannot be spared (Çitçi, 1982:226). The widespread use of 'mechanical slaves' and the commercialization of such home-made goods and services as ready-to-wear garments, tinned food and dry-cleaning could make daily housework easier. But in Turkey, relatively fewer women than in Western societies make use of these. Therefore in many families, when the couple returns home after eight hours of work, it is the woman who goes into the kitchen to prepare food and the man who lies on the sofa to read the daily newspaper; it is the woman who feeds the children and puts them to bed and the man who plays with them for a little while before they go to sleep. As a result, it is estimated that the weekly work done by women is twice as much as that done by men, sometimes even more — at least ninety-five hours per week.

Many young professional women are led to sacrifice their principled decisions of carrying out their professions to the rationality of home economics; they withdraw from working life because the costs of the daily maid and the fees of the day nursery exceed the money they themselves are earning.

We can conclude that apart from the handful of women from the upper classes, who work in high-status jobs, earn relatively high incomes and often can rely on the security of inherited property, the oppression of the majority of women in Turkey continues, and even seems to be intensifying with time, in spite of the important political and social changes wrought since the last days of the Ottomans.

A final but striking proof of this oppression is the fact that, even today, Turkish women do not have full control over their bodies. The control of the state, the husband and the father over a woman's body continues to exist in varying degrees, just as in the past. The situation in rural areas is especially oppressive. In the first place, fathers let their daughters marry very early in life for the sake of the bride money; then, the husbands continue to want more children until they have at least one son, as cultural mores require.

The policy of population increase adopted during the first years of the republic prohibited abortion and did not allow the use of contraceptive techniques. At the end of the second world war, when a population explosion occurred in Turkey as in most of the underdeveloped countries, the government's pro-population-increase policies were not immediately changed. The first alteration in this field occurred only in 1965, when the use of modern contraceptive techniques was permitted although abortion was still prohibited. Ten years later it was realized that this change in policy was not having the desired consequences and that rapid population increase had become a serious obstacle to economic growth. But, under the pressure of their conservative electorates, no civil government attempted a further reform. So it was only during the recent military regime that the government turned to more radical measures. Abortion was finally allowed by an amendment of law adopted by the Advisory Assembly in May 1983. Under the circumstances of the day, the involved parties, particularly women, did not have anything to say about the text of this amendment, which contains certain restrictions conflicting with women's interest. For example, the new law permits abortion within twelve weeks without requiring any medical reasons — but requires the written consent of husbands (from married women). After the law became effective in early 1984 under the military rule, it was discovered that the hospitals are not sufficiently equipped to cope with the demand. Long waiting lists have forced women to have abortions in private doctors' offices at high cost, as was the case, illegally, before.

Factors inhibiting the development of feminism

If in Turkey economic relations and other realities, such as traditional beliefs, norms and values — realities that are sometimes as material as economic relations — prepare the conditions for the oppression of women, as all the previously discussed data show, then why hasn't 'feminist ideology', defined as the criticism of women's oppression and the expression of the commitment to overcome it, formed and developed on this material basis? What are the reasons behind the delay in its emergence? What are the inhibiting mechanisms? In order to answer these questions fully we need to conduct systematic research centred around questions such as: What is an ideology? Who produces it? Under what circumstances? How do people become aware of its relevance? Who is opposed to it, and why? What are its means of communication? What sort of organizations help its development?

I shall propose a few hypotheses as the first steps of research into these issues. Put simply, I believe that the factors inhibiting the development and growth of feminism in Turkey are not much different from the factors leading to the oppression of women in Turkey. The same reasons have been the cause of both the oppression and an unawareness of this oppression. It is possible to classify these reasons into two categories, roughly defined as structural and ideological obstacles.

Structural obstacles

Among the structural obstacles, the first would probably be the underdeveloped capitalism in Turkey. The extensive nature of the family production unit in the rural areas, which absorbs the female labour force as unpaid family help, is a function of an agricultural economy that is still not completely integrated into the capitalist market. In urban areas, as a result of the lack of capital accumulation, the underdeveloped structure of the industry does not offer the necessary job opportunities for the female labour force. In comparison, all the Western countries in which feminism developed from the middle of the nineteenth century, becoming an active social movement in the early 1900s and revived in the late 1960s to occupy an important place among the radical opposition groups, are industrialized and/or agriculturally developed capitalist societies (Mitchell, 1971; Freeman, 1975; Michel, 1979).

One of the most important consequences of the existing underdeveloped economic structure in Turkey is the degree to which women need to depend on the family structure. The extent of this dependency is a remnant from the patriarchal structures of the Ottoman society; not only have such traditional values shown very little change, but they have actually intensified in parallel with the country's transition to a modern society. So the position of the family in Turkish society, with its economic foundations and patriarchal ideology, is the second structural obstacle inhibiting the development of feminism. In contrast, in societies where feminism has developed, the institution of family has gone through important transformations, especially after the second world war; it has shown a tendency towards disintegration and has been partly replaced by a series of alternative relationships, such as living together without getting married, being together without living together, single-parent (woman or even man) families, married couples living in different locations because of work, homosexual couples, communes and the like (Kandiyoti, 1984).

In Turkey, the family has remained such a widespread and alternative-less institution that it continues to be the only valid form of love, reproduction and security even when it loses its economic function. Therefore, in Turkish society it has become impossible for people, and especially for women, to have an identity independent from that of the family. Outside its protective cocoon, the woman becomes a 'marginal', an a-social person. And yet the family is a most conservative institution, in which role definitions change very slowly.

Education can be taken as a third inhibiting factor in its own right, though it is an extension of the two previously mentioned structural factors and is effective in interrelation with them. The economic resources necessary to afford widespread secondary and university education are quite limited in Turkey. Moreover, families tend to allocate their savings for the education of their sons rather than their daughters. As a result, the only level at which girls and boys receive an equal, nationwide education is primary school; at other levels there are marked inequalities, to the disadvantage of the girls (Özbay, 1981). This situation hinders the development of women's consciousness, as it is well known that an increase in the number of well-trained women with university degrees has had an important effect in the revival of feminism in West European countries (Mitchell, 1971).

In most Western countries, the starting point in a growing awareness of the oppression arising from sex discrimination was an exclusion from political responsibilities and the assignment of 'womanly' roles during the 1968 students' movements, even though both sexes tended to have the same educational background. In Turkey, however, as mentioned before, most women university graduates did have the support of their class in practising their professions, and, because of the 'elitist' role ascribed to them, have been very well treated in most jobs. This situation has prevented them from being aware that they form a privileged segment, and thus has made it impossible for them to perceive that their sex is one of the most oppressed of society. When asked by newspapers to make an evaluation of the situation of women in Turkey, most of these professional women said, 'In our society women are in a better position, more respected and get more equal treatment than women in Western societies.' A large number of 'elite' Turkish women, therefore, regard feminism as an 'unnecessary' ideology for their country.

Political and ideological obstacles
In addition to these structural factors, the political/ideological developments experienced in Turkey during the last fifty years have had specific inhibiting effects on the development of feminism. It is useful to point out once more that the 1980s was not the first time that feminism was heard of in Turkey: the issue had first been raised by Turkish women at the beginning of the century, during the 1908 revolution: at that time they had produced publications demanding equal rights and had founded feminist associations. Women also found a place for themselves in the short-lived atmosphere of democracy and freedom prevailing, at least, in the big cities of the Ottoman Empire.

The role of the internationally effective women's organizations (and particularly that of the suffragettes) in the first wave of feminism (as in today's) should not be ignored, either. Women belonging to the newly developing bourgeois classes, well educated and speaking a foreign language, had the opportunity of following developments in the Western world and especially those of the bourgeois feminist movements abroad. This short period of democracy came to an end when the Union and Progress Party came to power and established its dictatorship. Then came the first world war, and the early feminist voices were silenced under these catastrophic circumstances.

Second, it is important to stress that the women's 'revolution', imposed from above by the single-party regime during the first years of the republic, 'had not left much for feminism to say'. The transformation in the status of women realized by the state during the fifteen years between 1920 and 1935 represents one of the world's foremost examples of what northern European researchers call 'state feminism'. The important reforms carried out in the fields of family, education, clothing and political rights had two main effects on women. First, women's status improved substantially, even beyond their demands, as the passivity of the Women's Union shows: the Union did not voice an opinion on any of the bills concerning women that were presented to parliament in the early 1920s (Tekeli, 1982:207). Under these circumstances, most of the 'feminists' of the previous period had become the militant 'Kemalists', and for the prominent women of this generation 'feminism' and 'Kemalism' became synonyms. Second, under the single-party regime, reforms were always made from above by the decisions of the high-ranking administrators, and mass participation in the making of these reforms was hardly encouraged, if not dissuaded. We know, for instance, that the modest campaign started by the Women's Union to support women's political rights was hindered by the authorities of the single party (Tekeli, 1982:211). Therefore, among women, as in many other segments of the society, an attitude was engendered of expecting everything from the state and not having to engage in any social activity to improve their condition. This pattern of special interaction between the state and women that was formed during the single-party regime continued after the transition to the multi-party democracy in 1946; it exists even today. The most recent example of this attitude is the Abortion Law of 1983, which was prepared under the military regime without any public debate.

This pattern was so well assimilated by women that, even at times when almost all the segments in Turkish society were forming pressure groups aimed at promoting their specific interests (from the 1960s on), women were not able to form any similar organizations. The existing women's associations (Turkish Women's Union, Turkish Association of Mothers, Turkish Association of University Graduate Women, Association of Professional Women, etc.) were organized to defend the vested interests based on those rights acquired under the single-party era, rather than to extend them and make them more widespread. The main corpus of their activity comprised 'communiqués' published on official days of the republic to praise the 'Kemalist reforms'.

On the other hand, the large number of women who did not belong to these 'Kemalist elites' were under the influence of traditional beliefs formed by Islamic values. According to Islam, the woman's place is the home and her only social function is being a loving wife and a good mother. It was quite difficult to expect women who had assimilated these values, and nothing but these values, to revolt and demand an improvement in their condition. On the contrary, when social change accelerated after 1950, a tendency in the reverse direction was observed among these women. Afraid of losing their traditional identities, and as a reaction to the imposed modernization and secularism, women, especially those living in small towns and the *gecekondus*, showed a tendency to cover themselves up. This covering-up symbolized a demand to return to Islamic values and to the style of life prescribed by Islam for women. These women that Islam 'mobilized', therefore, not only did not demand an extension of their rights, but on the contrary were hostile to the message of the feminist ideology.

Orthodox leftism
Finally, in addition to these two basic ideologies that take women away from feminism, we must look at the relationship between feminist ideology and leftist ideologies; this played a critically important role in society, in spite of the fact that it affected smaller numbers of people compared with the two other dominant ideologies.

It is well known that leftist ideologies in general favour equality, freedom, solidarity and change. Therefore the groups most likely to give support to the demands of feminism are situated on the left of the political spectrum. But it is also a fact that, in many new left groups of the late 1960s, men tried to ascribe traditional roles to the young women active in their groups. This distance, or contradiction, between the ideological discourse praising equality of the sexes and the traditional relationships has played an important role in the emergence of the women's liberation movement in the Western societies (Mitchell, 1971). A similar phenomenon was observed in Turkey, but in a more inhibiting way, as this attitude of leftist men had had an oppressive/dissuasive effect on the militant women for years.

Turkey in the late 1960s saw the emergence of many youth organizations under the influence of the revival of leftist political groups in the West. It is interesting to note that, of those politically oriented movements that mushroomed in Turkey (Maoism, Trotskyism, Gueveraism, Focoism and so on), the only absentee was feminism. Even more interesting, a relatively large number of young women were active in these youth movements, in spite of the fact that Turkish women tend to have a relatively low rate of political participation (Tekeli, 1982:237). But all these leftist organizations, whether pro-Moscow, pro-Peking or some other denomination, looked at women's problems from a most orthodox point of view and considered any inclination of women towards feminism as a 'bourgeois deviation', and therefore as a prospective threat to 'class solidarity' and to their respective political forces. When these female members formed affiliated organizations to mobilize women, they tried to preserve the traditional image of the self-sacrificing 'mother–wife–sister' instead of giving them the opportunity to become aware of the oppression arising from this very role of women in Turkish society. And most of the women who were the leaders of these 'women's organizations' addressed their masses with a 'domineering–masculine' tone, in line with this orthodox view. The leftist organizations in Turkey were not democratic enough to let their women diagnose their problems themselves and develop a suitable strategy to fight against their oppression. In this, they too had been influenced by the other two widespread ideologies effective on the society (Samim, 1981).

Under these circumstances, it is not at all surprising that feminism was taken up in Turkey only very recently, after the 1980 military coup. Most of the feminist women had come from the above-mentioned leftist movements and were still close to the left. And the most immediate and oppressing ideology for them was neither Kemalism nor Islam, but the 'orthodox leftism'. Paradoxical as it may seem, the closing down of the leftist organizations together with all other political parties after the 1980 coup produced an emancipatory effect on women.

The feminist 'movement' in the early 1980s

The ban on politics at the end of 1980, under the rule of the new military regime, led to an awakening of interest in political problems, which used to be regarded as 'marginal'. The issue of women's oppression suddenly was placed at the head of a series of problems including the status of the individual in politics, the relationship between art and politics and so on. In addition, in a number of both leftist and rightist circles whose political rights had been restricted, 'democracy' as such, which before the 1980 coup was not considered as seriously as it might have been, was taken up as a central issue. The demands of women for 'equality, freedom, solidarity' brought the feminist point of view naturally to the forefront of the fight for democracy.

Thus, starting from 1981, the feminist way of thinking gained substantial grounds in daily life — through informal meetings and through discussions in the daily newspapers and the weekly, bimonthly and monthly reviews and magazines. This new issue aroused interest mainly among the very well educated, middle-class urban women, all with professions, mostly married and approaching middle age. Another distinguishing characteristic of this group of women was a high propensity to divorce, compared with society on the whole. They defined themselves primarily not with reference to the family but, like men, with reference to work, social problems, politics and so on, like their sisters in the West whose many sociological particularities they shared (Carden, 1977; Freeman, 1975). These women, who are quite a few in number, have revolted against the life-styles of their mothers. But there is a very important difference distinguishing them with their sociologically 'elite' characteristics from the other elite women Turkey has had so far: today's feminists in Turkey believe in the liberation of women through the liberation of the sex as a whole, not through their own individual emancipation; hence the increasing importance they give to 'solidarity'.

It is still too early to write about the 'history' of the struggle that a handful of women has been waging since 1982, and none of us (involved women) yet knows if such a modest start will eventually lead to a real 'movement'. Edgar Morin once said, 'In the world in which we live, the only way of being optimistic is to hope for the improbable.' Even if we believe in the profound truth of this premise, we also believe that it may not be void of importance to attempt to determine the patterns formed so far.

The feminist women in Turkey organized in small groups, thereby relying on their own experiences rather than taking the Western model as an example. A politically decentralized and federative structure was adopted from the very beginning. As the small groups included mostly 'intellectual' women from the leftist groups, they were split between two opposing objectives: the purely feminist one of forming consciousness-raising groups, and that of 'carrying on ideological struggle' by means of publications.

The 'Istanbul group'

To realize the stress caused by this dilemma, when resources, manpower and accumulated consciousness are limited, it is sufficient to look at the experience of the 'Istanbul group'. The women who joined this group, after the first failed attempt to produce specialized publications about women offered by a non-feminist but non-profit-oriented publishing house, YAZKO, in early 1982, were more oriented towards consciousness-raising. But after a year's experience in this direction, they were tempted again by the offer they got from the weekly magazine *Somut* that YAZKO was publishing. In the beginning, feminist women were given a full page in this magazine, where 'women's issues' were dealt with autonomously. Later, following a change in management, this full page was reduced to a half-page and the autonomy was lost. The experiment lasted for six months, in 1983. The group that assumed the responsibility for publishing the 'feminist page' rejected a hierarchical organization and worked as a 'structureless–leaderless collective'. Therefore it faced both the problems arising from 'structurelessness' and the difficulties of working with a publishing house that had different ideological and organizational principles. The official status of 'autonomy' granted by the magazine soon became an empty word as the editorial board became more and more critical about the substance of the page. At the same time, a 'non-structured, leaderless collective' appeared to be disfunctional, as it became more and more difficult to find enough material worth publishing.

Therefore this first bitter experience of getting acquainted with public opinion and being subject to criticism from all directions could not last for long. The group once again withdrew from publishing into small consciousness-raising groups with a view to creating new resources, summoning energy and formulating a better strategy. The following year (1984) this materialized in the foundation of an 'independent and autonomous' corporation: Kadın Çevresi (the Women's Circle) in Istanbul. This multi-purpose organization is for the time being engaged primarily in publishing, and its first two books were published at the beginning of 1985. The 'Book-club', the publishing collective of the Women's Circle, is run by about fifty women, working voluntarily, democratically and with self-sacrifice. In other big cities such as Ankara and Izmir, other collectives with similar purposes have been formed.

Starting from scratch
In concluding, we cannot avoid asking some questions: With the Women's Circle, are we confronted with just another 'social movement' like those that were active around the issues of 'solidarity–cooperation–mutualism' and 'local governments' in the recent past — social movements that appeared and disappeared as a *feu de paille* because in Turkey the institutions of the civil society have always been relatively weak compared with those of the state? Or are we witnessing the birth of a new sort of movement, one starting from scratch and aimed at ending the centuries-old oppression of women, and presently encouraged by the country's frail attempts to return to democracy, by the increase in urbanization and the literacy rate, by the rapid increase in the tendency towards university education among girls, by slow but continuous socio-economic development, including the setbacks like the current recession, which has obliged women to work and earn money, and by the emergence of indignant and angry young women who believe in finding a solution not by 'individual' liberation but by a collective

revolt against the oppressive structures?' Last but not least, we must not forget the moral support that the 'Young (female) Turks' hope to solicit from the international solidarity network that Western feminists are creating in the Old and the New World! Only the coming years will show us if this 'start from scratch' will lead us somewhere.

The first form of this chapter was published in Turkish in the February–March 1985 issue of *Yapıt Dergisi*. I am grateful to the publishers who let me refer to the article for this enlarged English version. I would also like to thank Fidan Türkent who helped me in translating the article.

References

Akatlı, F. (1984)   'Türk Romanında Aile', in *Türkiye'de Aile'nin Değişimi, Sanat Açısından İncelemeler*. Ankara.

Alzon, C. (1972)   'La Femme potiche et la femme bonniche', *Partisans*, no. 68.

Berkes, N. (1974)   *Secularisation in Turkey*. Montreal.

Boratav, K. (1981)   *Tarımsal Yapılar ve Kapitalizm*. Istanbul.

Carden, M. L. (1977)   'Le Nouveau Mouvement féminist aux Etats-Unis', in Andrée Michel, *Femmes, sexisme et société*. Paris.

Cemgil, A. (1984)   'Feminizmin İçyüzü', *Düşün*. Eylül.

Çitçi, O. (1982)   *Kadın Sorunu ve Türkiye'de Kamu Görevlisi Kadınlar*. Ankara.

Duben, A. (1984)   '19. ve 20. Yüzyıl Aile ve Hane Yapıları', in *Ailenin Değişimi, Toplumbilimsel İncelemeler*. Ankara.

Evans, R. (1976)   *The Feminists Movement in Germany, 1894–1933*. Sage. Beverly Hills, California.

Freeman, J. (1975)   *The Politics of Women's Liberation*. New York.

Kandiyoti, D. (1984)   'Aile Yapısında Değişme ve Süreklilik: Karşılaştırmalı Bir Yaklaşım', in *Türkiye'de Ailenin Değişimi, Toplumbilimsel İncelemeler*. Ankara.

Kazgan, G. (1981)   'Labour Force Participation, Occupational Distribution, Educational Attainment and the Socio-economic Status of Women in the Turkish Economy', in N. Abadan-Unat (ed.), *Women in Turkish Society*. Leiden.

Keyder, Ç. (1979)   'The Political Economy of Turkish Democracy', *New Left Review*, no. 115.

Kıray, M. (1984)   'Büyük Kent ve Değişen Aile', in *Türkiye'de Ailenin Değişimi, Toplumbilimsel İncelemeler*. Ankara.

Levine, N. (1982)   'Social Change and Family Crisis', in Ç. Kağıtçıbaşı (ed.), *Sex Roles, Family and Community in Turkey*. Bloomington, Indiana.

Michel, A. (1979)   *Le Féminisme*. Paris.

Mitchell, J. (1971)   *Women's Estate*. London.

Moran, B. (1983)   *Türk Romanına Eleştirel Bir Bakış*. Istanbul.

Öncü, A. (1981)   'Turkish Women in Professions: Why So Many?' in N. Abadan Unat (ed.), *Women in Turkish Society*. Leiden.

Ortaylı, İ. (1984)   'Osmanlı Toplumunda Aile', in *Türkiye'de Ailenin Değişimi, Toplumbilimsel İncelemeler*. Ankara.

Özakın, A. (1981)   *Genç Kız ve Ölüm* (a novel).

Ozankaya, Ö. (1984)   'Laiklik Öncesi Dönemde Şemseddin Sami'nin Aile Düzenine İlişkin Görüşleri', in *Türkiye'de Ailenin Değişimi, Toplumbilimsel İncelemeler*. Ankara.

Turkey 199

Özbay, F. (1981) 'Women and Education', in N. Abadan Unat (ed.), *Women in Turkish Society*. Leiden.

Özbay, F. (1984) 'Kırsal Kesimde Toplumsal ve Ekonomik Yapı Değişmeleri', in *Türkiye'de Ailenin Değişimi, Toplumbilimsel İncelemeler*. Ankara.

Samim, A. (1981) 'The Ordeal of the Turkish Left', *New Left Review*, no. 126.

Şeni, N. (1984) 'Ville Ottomane et représentation du corps féminin', in *Turquie, Les Temps Modernes*, July–August.

Shorter, F. C. and M. Macura (1982) *Population Growth in Turkey, 1935–1975*. Washington.

Tekeli, Ş. (1981) 'Women in Politics', in N. Abadan-Unat (ed.), *Women in Turkish Society*. Leiden.

Tekeli, Ş. (1982) *Kadınlar ve Siyasal-Toplumsal Hayat*. Istanbul.

Tillion, G. (1966) *Le Harem et les cousins*. Paris.

Timur, S. (1972) *Türkiye'de Aile Yapısı*. Ankara.

Todd, E. (1983) *La Troisième Planète: structures familiales et systémes ideologiques*. Paris.

Young, K., C. Wolhowitz and R. McCullagh (1981) *Of Marriage and the Market*. London.

10
The women's movement in Spain and the new Spanish democracy

Maria Angeles Duran and Maria Teresa Gallego

Introduction

For Spain, 1975–85 was a turbulent decade. It was a time of hope, euphoria and subsequent disillusion. The transition to political democracy began at an unfortunate time in history, coinciding with the worldwide economic crises of the 1970s. The new feminist movement that emerged in Spain during this decade was shaped by, and was itself part of, contemporary political and social changes. In this chapter we distinguish between three periods in the short history of the new feminist movement in Spain: the period of expansion (1975–9), the period of scattering and decline (1979–82), and the third period from 1982 to the present, in which feminism reached the institutions, but lost its strength as a movement.

The historical background for the women's movement in Spain

Let's begin with history. What is now Spain has undergone many changes during the past two thousand years. It has been a country inhabited by very different tribes (some of them were called 'ginecocratics' by Estrabon), a Roman province, a Visigothic monarchy, a mosaic of Christian and Muslim medieval kingdoms, an empire with colonies all over the world in the sixteenth and seventeenth centuries, a defeated, divided and underdeveloped country in the nineteenth century, and a fiery battlefield on which half the population fought against the other half during the civil war of 1936–9.

Today's Spanish society has been shaped by such upheavals, and under the thin layer of modernity lie the vestiges of ancient times (Fagoaga and Savedra, 1981; Scanlon, 1978). The social position of women still shows traces of the old pre-Christian and pre-Roman Mediterranean cults as well as the more obvious vestiges of Roman institutions like 'tutela' and Christian ideology and organizations. Moreover, there is a denied but latent Muslim presence. There also exists a permanent orientation towards America, a profound sense of regional differences, expressed among other ways in the family laws, and an overwhelming remembrance of the civil war, in which the values and roles assigned to women and family were completely different in the two camps. In spite of legal conditions, women are powerful in the family and the extended family remains strong (via matrilineal relationships).

The civil war was followed by the authoritarian regime of General Franco (1939–75), and in the 1940s the official ideology of women was very similar to that of contemporary Italy and Germany (Gallego, 1983). Things changed slowly during the 1950s and very quickly during the 1960s, when Spain experienced a far-reaching socio-economic change through processes of industrialization, urbanization, migration and international tourism. Some important legal improvements in the position of women took place in 1961 and 1966, but other inequalities remained. However, the important change was the acquisition of educational and economic independence for future generations of Spanish women.

After the death of Franco, in the very short period of three years, a new democratic parliament approved a new democratic constitution (1978) whose article 14 forbids discrimination on account of sex. Political parties, even the Communist Party, are now legal; general elections are a normal practice; and women are free to vote and to be elected for various kinds of political positions. But the percentage of women in parliament continues to be very low — in 1985 it was 6 per cent. Of the 52 provinces, only 3 have a woman governor. And in the civil administration only 5 per cent of the senior posts are filled by women.

1975 and onwards: economic crisis and political change

The beginning of the 1970s — the end of the Franco period — was already seeing some important political changes. Inside the Catholic Church many changes took place, and important portions of its hierarchy, organizations and members (almost everybody in Spain is baptized as a Catholic, and during the first years of the Franco regime the Catholic Church was strongly allied with the ruling political forces) took a stand in favour of a political transition to democracy and a responsiveness to new, egalitarian ideas about women. New organizations appeared: associations of parents, consumers, neighbours and housewives, in which women made up a large proportion of the membership. These associations were much smaller in numbers than the traditional associations of housewives or 'Catholic Parents', but their growing activity and better organization gave them more weight socially.

The transition to political democracy began at an unfortunate time for the economy. The difficulties in connection with the entry of women into the political life of present-day Spain arise not so much from legal barriers as from the absence of economic and social conditions that would make this feasible. The traditional division of economic roles between men and women is still in force: in 1983 only 28 per cent of the women who could be employed were actually in the workforce, and, of the total working population, only 30 per cent were women. The unemployment rate is higher for women (20 per cent) than for men (15 per cent), and in the public and the private sphere the funding for services that are of direct benefit to women — day care centres, holiday services, modernization of domestic equipment — has been reduced. Between 1975 and 1985 the economic situation of Spain worsened.

The fact that there are about 3 million unemployed persons has had very little effect on the division of labour in the home: men out of work have taken very little part in domestic tasks, and at the same time the difficulty of finding jobs has discouraged millions of women, who do not try to find work even if they would like a job. To maintain standards in the home, the only solution has been to increase the amount of work done at home so as to get the most out of the lower-quality goods and services available. For work outside the home, the working week was fixed by law in 1983 at forty hours (though this is often exceeded by moonlighting, travelling time and so on); the average working week of a housewife is often twice as long or more. Although women have achieved full legal status, and although most unmarried women now work outside the home, the majority of women are still economically dependent on the money earned by their husbands (Duran, 1985).

The sum of these two conditions — the need to do long hours of housework and women's economic dependence on their husband's earnings — still place women in a position of social inferiority, a situation made more general by the transition from the patrimonial type of economy to one of wage-earning.

Legal changes for equality
In Spain, with no great effort and in less than ten years, women attained the basic legal reforms it took other democratic countries more than forty years to achieve. With the approval of the constitution in 1978, all legal obstacles to women voting, being nominated for election or participating in the government have been removed. There is only one exception: preference is given to male heirs to the throne, diminishing women's possibilities of becoming head of state. At present, the possibility of incorporating women into the armed forces is being studied. The Catholic Church has not modified its decision to exclude women from the priesthood and consequently from the church hierarchy.

The three latest modifications of the law affecting the family are of great political importance even though they belong to the civil law. The constitution affirms the equality of husband and wife (articles 32 and 39) and the equality of children born in or out of wedlock. In 1978 the prohibition of information, diffusion and sale of contraceptives was removed, and little by little health centres have been set up to provide guidance on family problems. Abortion was a crime punishable under the law (article 413 of the Penal Code) until 1984, when parliament passed a law legalizing abortion under three special circumstances: if the mother's life is endangered, in the case of rape, or in the case of a malformation of the foetus. Opinion polls conducted at the time the bill was presented in 1983 showed a majority in favour of it, though it was bitterly opposed by the conservative opposition. The feminists were disappointed in the bill, because they consider it too restrictive and because the cost of an abortion is not covered by the health service. At present, the estimates of the number of abortions vary considerably, between 60,000 and 400,000 per year.

Poor women have their abortions in Spain, middle- and upper-class women usually go to Britain or Holland for them. That is why only poor and working-class women have problems with police, health or legal authorities! In 1985 the first legal abortions took place in Spain, under enormous pressures and resistance from the health workers, the majority of whom refused to carry out their duties on the grounds of moral objections. Even after approval by parliament, it is very difficult to apply the law, and both women and the doctors involved in the first cases of abortion are suffering from a massive campaign launched against them by medical and conservative associations.

Civil divorce has been allowed in Spain since 1982. Before then, there was only the possibility of an ecclesiastical declaration of nullity of marriage. Even in 1984, 90 per cent of all weddings were church weddings.

Who brought these changes about?

All of them have been claimed by the feminist movement, but no one could say that the movement was the unique or even the major force behind these changes. In many cases it was the Socialist Party that presented or got these reforms through parliament, although a centre party (Unión de Centro Democrático) proposed the divorce law, and the Communist Party (Partido Comunista de Espana) took the initiative to propose a more comprehensive abortion law. Rightist parties agreed to legal changes for equality within marriage, and centre parties also agreed to a more liberal divorce law. Only the restricted abortion bill presented by the socialist government found strong opposition in parliament, though it is supposed to cover only 5 per cent of the abortions actually taking place in Spain. Huge demonstrations filled the main streets of the cities protesting against the bill, in response to a call by the Confederación Católica de Padres, a national, Catholic confederation of parents in which women form the majority of the active membership. (This confederation is chaired by an influential Catholic woman.) By comparison, demonstrations in favour of a more comprehensive abortion bill were rare, and consisted almost exclusively of feminist women.

The feminist movement is ideologically far removed from the rank and file of Spanish women. Political leaders in Spain pay more attention to public opinion polls than to the actions of the different groups, and even the Socialist Party supported in parliament only those of its own electoral promises that, according to opinion polls, were widely accepted by the majority of the population. There is no doubt that the small groups or individuals who define themselves as feminists play an important part in drawing attention to women's problems and influencing public opinion through the mass media. They are a ferment, a symbol, but also a distant mirror in which most Spanish women do not recognise themselves.

Women in organizations and women's organizations

Throughout its history, Spain has never had any massive organized women's movement to press for political equality or integration. After the civil war the political system was a one-party system, and during the 1940s 'Sección Femenina' (the name commonly given to the women's section of Falange) reached more than 600,000 affiliated members, a figure never before attained by any organization in Spain. During the 1950s, after the beginning of the decline and bureaucratization of Sección Femenina, the Catholic organization of women, Mujeres de Acción Católica, obtained a similarly impressive number of members. But neither of these organizations was feminist (such a position was specifically rejected by the former), or fought primarily for equality for women. In 1977 the political system changed; the 'Movimiento' (a later political organization of the former Falange) was legally dissolved and with it its women's section (Gallego, 1983).

In 1982 an inquiry among 2,000 women showed that only 9 per cent were members of any type of association, whether cultural, local, religious, a parents' association or a sports club. Only 1.8 per cent were members of a women's association, 1 per cent were members of a trade union, and 0.7 per cent were members of a political party.

In another inquiry carried out among 2,000 women in 1984, in which women evaluated on a scale from 0 to 10 their interest in different items, politics got an average of only 2.39 points while family got 9.82 and religion 7.20. In the same inquiry only 8 per cent answered positively to the question, 'Do you think that politicians are interested in women's problems?' The breakdown of answers was as follows: 28 per cent, 'I don't know'; 36 per cent, 'They are not at all interested'; 7 per cent, 'They are interested'; 1 per cent, 'They are very interested' and 2 per cent, 'There are no specific women's problems' (Duran, 1985).

According to such data, we could hardly conclude that most women in Spain view their participation in formal political life as a real advance or improvement in their social position. Is participation in the political machinery an effective way of obtaining equality, freedom and social change? Or is it a new, profound way of obeying a political system that does not offer a real change for women?

None of the main parties has offered a revolutionary change in the economic structure of the country, which is based on the division of labour between men (outside the home) and women (inside the home) (Duran, 1979). And if a small political group or party were to offer such a change (as the Feminist Party tries to do), the population would turn its back on it, denying votes and help. People either distrust the revolutionary alternative or simply think it is not feasible.

Dimensions of the new Spanish women's movement
During the period of great political changes in the mid-1970s, a new women's movement emerged in Spain. The movement succeeded in calling attention to women's subordinate position, but it never had many actual members (Gonzalez, 1979).

In 1985 more than 600 women's groups were recorded in Spain, and a fifth of them explicitly consider themselves feminist. Most of them have a very loose organization, and the membership is difficult to define because there are no internal rules defining it. Many have fewer than a dozen members, share a meeting room with other groups or institutions, and do not have a calendar of regular activities. Since the beginning of record-keeping (1975) many of the earlier groups have disappeared and not all the new ones have been recorded. Although no data about the number of women affiliated or working with feminist groups are available, it is reasonable to suppose that it does not reach 0.1 per cent of adult women.

At this point, the question is how to define the boundaries of the women's movement. For this purpose an analytical distinction may be useful. There are three analytical dimensions to the movement: the moral or axiological, the cognitive or theoretical and the political or active.

The moral dimension of the women's movement
Top priority on the feminist axiological scale, that is, the scale of feminist goals, goes to equality. But what kind of equality?

The debate between followers of the 'equality feminism' and those of the 'difference feminism' has caused a break between some of the more active, vanguard feminist groups. The former variety stresses the need for homogeneity in the social roles of men and women, while the latter claims the right to be different from men although equal in dignity and social value. For Spanish feminists, equality value surpasses the limited field of the woman–man relationship and becomes a sort of worldwide equality: of classes, of races, of peoples.

However, some small groups and individuals involved in the movement do not back the equality moral: they regard women as better than men. And this feeling is not so new in a country where the cult of the Great Mother Earth existed (before Roman times) and where the cult of the Virgin Mother Mary is so deeply rooted.

Other values traditionally ascribed to women in Spanish society (altruism, beauty, erotic appeal, motherhood) are partly accepted and partly rejected by people in the movement, but there is little explicit reflection on them. At the same time, some values traditionally ascribed to men (intelligence, independence, culture) are assumed as key values in their own lives by most feminists as well as by many women who do not see themselves as feminists.

The cognitive dimension of the women's movement
The cognitive dimension of the movement concerns its system of ideas and theories, its cosmogony.

A rejection of the openly anachronistic ideas about women is the first stage in the creation of a feminist view of the world, but there are many further steps to negotiate. The efforts of some women's groups in Spain have centred on trying to build a feminist culture, or at least a non-sexist culture and educational system.

Some of the problems encountered in this connection include the struggle between different theoretical viewpoints (the mainstream of theoretical thinking began with very schematic Marxist arguments, but it later gained depth and width), the absence of empirical, ad hoc designed research, the lack of operative concepts and indicators, the dependence on foreign press channels, the fear of contributing to a 'market of ideas' or an 'intellectual ghetto' and so on.

During the past few years this side of the movement has experienced a great development, and dozens of debates, research programmes, seminars or symposiums have been carried out. The creation of a feminist view of the world is a long-term goal. However, since the range of 'feminist compromise' among people involved in research and discussion is very wide, the result is considered modest by those of the more radical positions.

The political dimension of the women's movement
With respect to the political or active dimension, the women's movement is a specific kind of organization aimed at social change. How should we define the boundaries of the movement? Should we

limit it to the few women participating in autonomous feminist groups? Should we include women — and men — who consider themselves feminist in a more or less vague way, even if they have never had contact with any feminist group or have left organized militancy? And what about those (relatively numerous) women who say 'I am not a feminist' but nevertheless would agree with the goals of most feminist groups? In any case, even the feminist groups that tried to be and to appear as mass movements did not attract more than a few thousand members.

Some of the main problems facing the movements/organizations in Spain include the choice between marginality, active resistance and innovation; the choice between short- and long-term changes; the means used for getting resources and influencing public opinion; the degree of individualism tolerated at the leadership level and the internal coherence and discipline required in the group; the struggle between centralization and spatial decentralization; and, last but not least, the character of the relations with the civil administration (the state), which is at the same time the main employer and the main provider of funds (aids, rent-free offices and so on) for the movement.

All these options decide the strategy of the groups, their potential allies, enemies and structure. In the mid-1970s it seemed possible that a new kind of social organization could have been born in Spain, capable of uniting the efforts of all the small feminist groups and concentrating the energy of the sympathizers. It did not happen. Now, the movement continues to expand and gain expertise in developing the moral and cognitive dimensions, but the possibilities of creating a great, strong feminist organization seem to have vanished.

Chronology of a decade

The first decade of an organized Spanish women's movement falls into three main periods. The changing political context of this decade was decisive for the development of the feminist movement; the general political and social changes shaped the outcome of the feminist activities (Gallego, 1985; Threllfall 1985; Moreno, 1977).

The first period (1975–9) was characterized by the creation, expansion and organization of the movement. During the second period (1979–82) the movement was divided by strong internal disputes and divisions. The third period (1982–5) covers the decline and fall of the organized movement and the rise of many micro-organizations all over the country, and the general acceptance of the feminist question by institutions in which, however, there is very little feminine representation.

The period of expansion (1975–9)

When December was springtime

From 6 to 8 December 1975, two weeks after the death of General Franco, the first great event of the new women's movement in Spain took place. It was the First Congress of Women's Liberation (I Jornadas por la Liberación de la Mujer), held in Madrid and attended by 500 women from different parts of Spain, some as representatives and others as individuals.

In those days the political transition from dictatorship to democratic government in Spain appeared uncertain and fragile, and all the groups of the opposition were appealing to the government for a general amnesty and extensive political reform. Such was the political climate in which this First Congress of Women's Liberation arose. Some of the women's organizations present had been formed years before and were connected with the clandestine political parties.

The congress was held in secret, and it is in this context that the main ideological positions debated there must be understood: whereas one section maintained that the themes of discussion should be strictly feminist, another considered it more important to deal with the political situation. It was the second view, called 'political', that was supported by the majority against the first, 'radical', view, and it was decided to create a feminist organization capable of defending in its own right the specific claims of women's rights and at the same time able to take part in the general struggle for democracy.

The division between the 'political' position (also called 'class-struggle feminism', because of its main theoretical point of 'double militancy' owing to its main strategical option) and the 'radical' position (also called 'single-militancy feminism') should not be overestimated. What really constituted the difference between the groups was their desired relations with the political parties and their influence on the political system; but basically they all accepted the viewpoint that women's oppression was of economic origin and that the class-based society had to be overcome.

As an example, we quote a text by one of the feminist collectives of the radical position: 'Feminism is political because as a revolutionary movement it upholds the destruction of capitalist and "macho" society, not only with a change in the method of production but also in social relations, ideology and the whole culture.' Such a programme was obviously shared by socialist and communist feminists, though their methods and strategies were different.

In May 1976 the First Catalan Women's Congress (I Jornadas Catalanas de la Dona) was held in Barcelona, attended by 4,000 supporters. This congress was widely reported even though it was limited to Catalonia. After much discussion the congress agreed on a position of 'socialist feminism' or 'class-struggle feminism', and this has remained constant in Spanish feminism, whether expressed by individual women or by small organized groups.

Nobody at that time had any experience of normal political practice. For the groups of women that had struggled for democracy in their political parties and trade unions, with no lessening of their feminist convictions, it was logical to assume that these organizations would take up, as part of their responsibility, the rights and claims of women. This confidence was not shared by the 'radical' minority of feminists, who demanded that priority be given to the feminist questions. The 'radical' feminists expressed bitter opinions with respect to many of the political proposals put forward by the first democratic governments.

In the shade of Utopia

The pre-election period until June 1977 was singularly utopian and euphoric. Throughout 1976 and 1977, the feminist movement was prominent in the media and in every kind of meeting, whether political or intellectual. This was due partly to the activity of the women's movement and partly to the country-wide election fever with its collective excitement and exhortations to participate and help bring about social and political changes.

Women realized that this was the moment to state their claims with full force and to have their demands recognized and incorporated into the party programmes. And of course the political parties, eager for recognition and for votes, were quick to see the potential in the women's issue. Even if it were a mere formality or pure demagogy, every party, from left to right, paid some attention to women's interests, though naturally with widely varying opinions.

Very briefly, the proposals of all the political parties of the 1977 election campaign can be grouped as follows. In the non-fascist right-wing parties we find a recognition of the formal equality of men and women and the intention to improve the education of women and to protect the family. The Liberal and Christian–Democratic Parties made similar promises and added some specific proposals such as the much-needed reforms of laws affecting the family and an increase in social services.

The Socialist and Communist Parties, at least in their election programmes, were the only ones to incorporate nearly all the demands of women, advocating strict equality of the sexes before the law, in the labour market and in the family and also the creation of services of a collective nature, with a view to socializing domestic work. Contraceptives and abortion would be made available under the national health service. They promised to end unemployment, too.

The election promises were high-flying but unrealistic, in many cases owing to political inexperience and the urge to get away from the worn-out apparatus of the Franco regime, which transformation was to be more difficult than was realized at the time. Moreover, the political parties underestimated the strong opposition on the part of powerful economic groups, Catholics and traditionalists, who saw a threat to their system of privileges and beliefs.

Main groups in the expanding period
During those years, the feminist groups were very numerous and held very differing attitudes. It is practically impossible to list them all since no reliable data are available; but we can divide them into two categories according to the characteristics mentioned above, the double and single militancy.

The double-militancy position
Women's Democratic Movement (Movimiento Democrático de Mujeres). This group came into existence in 1963 in Madrid and Barcelona and gradually spread to Zaragoza, Valencia, the Basque Country and Galicia. It may be considered the only women's group devoted to organizing public opinion in Spain in the 1960s and early 1970s. The leading members were women of the Communist Party, and the initial activities were related to the problems of political prisoners and workers. Although not basically feminist, it did devote special attention to women's problems and gradually attracted the support of younger women from the universities and trade unions. Many of its members infiltrated the legal, conservative National Federation of Housewives' Associations (created in 1968), but they were discovered and even expelled by the police from the meetings.

The group had to resolve internal divergences between one section that gave priority to the work of the Communist Party and the other one, which preferred to concentrate on the struggle of women as individuals suffering oppression and discrimination. But after all, this group played an important part in organizing the first Congress of Women's Liberation, and after this event it adopted a more radical feminist programme, taking the name of 'Women's Liberation Movement' in place of the old one.

Women's Democratic Association (Asociación Democrática de Mujeres). Formed in Madrid in 1976, most of the Association's members were connected with the Labour Party of Spain (Partido del Trabajo de Espana), a leftist, Maoist-oriented party. It defined itself as 'unitarian' (the search for unity among the different groups and positions of the feminist movement) and independent of political parties. At the end of 1977 it formed the Federation of Feminist Organizations of Spain, which immediately became opposed to the platform already created by the Women's Democratic Movement, whose aims were very similar. The result was a series of splits; of these, the most important resulted in the creation of the Union for Women's Liberation, founded that same year.

Front for Women's Liberation (Frente de Liberación de la Mujer). Formed in Madrid in January 1976, the members of the Front ranged from moderate socialists to communists, but many of them were not party militants and the group really allowed its members to choose whether or not they wanted to belong to political parties and trade unions. The basic ideological principle of this group was that the capitalist system gives rise to a specific oppression of women, and its aim was to create a socialist society where women's demands were satisfied. It was an effort to unite all those who considered women's liberation as related to the class struggle but not dependent on it, and certainly was not something to be postponed until socialism should triumph. Most of its members were professional university women. It had some influence on public opinion, though this was mainly limited to Madrid. From 1978 internal differences arose and the group broke into three divisions. A year later it disappeared completely.

Other groups. There were other small, less important, organized groups, connected in some measure with different political movements. Among those were the Republican Women of Madrid (Unión de Mujeres Republicanas de Madrid); the Free Women (Mujeres Libres), an anarchist group that had existed during the civil war; the Popular Union of Women (Unión Popular de Mujeres), a branch of the illegal group Antifascist, Patriotic and Revolutionary Front (FRAP); and many other local groups.

The single-militancy position

These groups took the name of 'feminist collectives' when they began to appear in January 1976. As women were considered a social class antagonistic to men, they were opposed to any political militancy and therefore advocated struggling exclusively in feminist organizations and creating a feminist party. The first one was the Feminist Collective Seminar of Madrid (Seminario Colectivo Feminista de Madrid), which became divided a few months later. Then followed the Feminist Collective of Barcelona, and also in that city the group LAMAR (Anti-authoritarian Struggle of Antipatriarchal and Revolutionary Women). There were feminist collectives in several other cities of Spain, some of them connected with professions such as the press, theatre, lawyers and so on. Groups like Self-Help, Independent Conscience and Lesbian Collective appeared in Madrid, Valencia and Barcelona.

All these groups were made up of small numbers of women, mainly professional women, who had a certain influence through their collaboration with the mass media and especially with the review *Vindicacion Feminista*. They paid a lot of attention to the theoretical analysis of feminism and rejected the political parties, the relationship with the public institutions and even the 1978 constitution. They did not recognize as feminist those women who collaborated with the political parties. They thought women needed to take power into their own hands for achieving liberation as a different social class. They did not get supporters among working-class women, and after some years of activity they gradually disappeared.

The period of scattering and decline (1979–82)
The main event of this period was a general meeting of the feminist movement held in Granada in May 1979, attended by more than 3,000 women from all over Spain. The two main tendencies that had appeared since 1975 turned out to be irreconcilable; neither was accepted as representing the movement, and no agreement could be reached even with regard to basic requirements. Besides the dichotomy of double and single militancy, the debate on 'equality' v. 'difference' feminism was sour and intense. There was never any attempt to arrive at a real theoretical analysis of either of these two concepts. Broadly speaking, the idea of equality was adopted by the section of double militancy that advocated the formation of a political platform demanding women's rights and liberties for women and eliminating all the barriers encountered by women.

The women who advocated 'difference' feminism were involved with the radical groups. They excluded any pact with other organizations, extolled exclusively feminine qualities such as motherhoood, and advocated the return to a separate sphere of femininity. The meeting, as a result of discordance, revealed the complete disintegration of the feminist movement/organization, and many women decided on personal transformation as the only road to liberation.

The fact that most of the basic legal claims of women, except the right to legal abortion, had been recognized contributed to the decline of the new women's movement in Spain. It lost its appeal. From 1980 on there were none of the previous mass mobilizing events; instead, there began a process of forming loose assemblies of women in different provinces, rather individual in character. The movement fell to pieces.

Women's committees in political parties
The women's committees within the political parties should also be mentioned. These groups contain women who feel strongly feminist. They have lasted through all stages of the movement since 1976. Thanks to their activity in the political parties, not only in the day-to-day running of the organizations but also at the special meetings,

congresses and conferences, the parties incorporated some of their demands into their programmes and proposals in parliament.

The right-wing and centre parties did not have women's committees whereas the left-wing parties did. At the beginning of democracy there were numerous political parties; these were much reduced in number after the first elections in 1977 owing to the electoral system and the preferences of the electorate. On the extreme left the Communist Movement (MC) survives. It has a Leninist orientation and has never got parliamentary representation, but it is the party with the relatively highest level of feminine participation and political activism.

Many of the pioneer feminists were connected with the Communist Party (PCE) during the Franco regime; when it was made legal in 1977 a Women's Committee was set up. The work carried out by the committee received more support from the leaders of the party than from the rank and file. Later the PCE suffered a severe internal crisis, and from 20 parliamentary seats in 1979 it dropped to 4 seats in 1982. The Women's Committee, strongly autonomous inside the party, was linked to the fraction of the party that supported a renewal, and when this failed there was an exodus of militants, among them the majority of the members of the committee. However, this committee and the Women's Committee of the communist-oriented trade union (CC OO) retain a prominent place among the women's groups in Spain today.

The Socialist Party (PSOE) had been less active during the Franco regime, and until 1976 did not contain any feminist groups. At the party congress of that year a small group of women formed the collective 'Woman and Socialism' (Mujer y Socialismo). Their task was to prepare pamphlets, meetings and talks on women's situation throughout the party. The work of this committee, whose members also took part in the autonomous feminist movement, especially in the Front for Women's Liberation, was regarded dubiously by Socialist Party members, both men and women. Some women refused to be connected with it, afraid of the possible negative effect of the 'feminist' label on their political careers.

In spite of this, at the twenty-ninth conference of the Socialist Party in 1981 a feminist was appointed to the executive committee, and some proposals made by Woman and Socialism were approved, among them the de-penalization of abortion and its inclusion in the public health service. At the thirtieth conference (December 1984) a feminist remained on the executive committee and some improvements for women inside the party were obtained and written into the by-laws.

Since the socialist victory in the local elections of 1979, Woman and Socialism has been very active in setting up small centres of information and assistance for women in every town. It was this committee that set up the first family planning centre in Madrid in 1977 and pressed for the opening of a new health centre.

The Feminist Party

The Partido Feminista de Espana was formed in 1979 but legalized only in 1981. It held its first congress in 1983. It did not enter any candidates in the general elections of 1982, and its radius of action is mainly Barcelona, although it claims to have members in many other provinces. It publishes a magazine called *Power and Freedom* (*Poder y Libertad*). It is now the main symbol of the 'radical' position, but its social or political influence is slight.

Third period: from 1982 to the present
Feminism reaches the institutions

After the legal dissolution of the feminine section of Falange (1 April 1977), a new sub-department for women's affairs was created at the Ministry of Culture, and many of the civil officers of the huge, defunct organization were transferred to this ministry. At this time the ruling party was the Democratic Centre Union (UCD), a centre party, and the relationship between this sub-department, called 'Feminine Condition' and the feminist movement knew varying periods of cooperation and antagonism. In September 1983, after the socialist victory in the 1982 general elections, this sub-department was transformed into the 'Women's Rights' Institute' (Instituto de la Mujer) at a higher administrative level. Its budget was increased by a factor of ten, and a socialist, feminist woman, a former member of the Front for Women's Liberation, was appointed to head it.

The main goal of the Institute is to implement the principle of non-discrimination written into the new constitution. Although the creation of the Institute is the main event for the women's movement in the past few years, it cannot go much further than the politics of the government, and this causes tension regarding controversial themes like abortion. Besides, it can press for legal changes but not for the creation of new jobs demanded by millions of unemployed women and housewives discouraged from job-hunting. Its budget is still not large enough to reopen the closed day care centres or provide most of the services consistently demanded by the feminists.

According to the new political structure of the Spanish state after the 1978 constitution, seventeen autonomous regions have been recognized. Some kind of Women's Departments exist in some of them. In the near future several autonomous regions (CC AA) will create a Women's Rights' Institute at their level in the process of transferring authority from the state to the autonomous governments. There are also women's committees at many town halls. Most of the efforts of all these institutions dedicated to women are directed towards obtaining legal assistance, health care and public debates on women's problems.

The creation of women's studies should be mentioned here. The first groups were formed in 1978 at the autonomous Universities of Madrid and Barcelona. Other universities have similar groups, for example in Madrid, Barcelona, Valencia, Granada, Alicante, Navarra and Zaragoza. Some of them are small groups, little more than debating societies, whereas others, such as the Women's Studies Seminar at the autonomous University of Madrid, offer courses and organize annual symposiums attended by several hundred teachers and researchers.

Other cultural and feminist institutions include the feminist bookshops (in Madrid, Barcelona, Valencia, Zaragoza, among others) and the Feminist Atheneum of Madrid. There are several reviews, including *La Mujer Feminista* (Feminist Woman), *Langaiak*, *Tribuna Feminista* (Feminist Tribune) and *Mujeres* (Women), the last of which is edited by the Women's Institute.

We can also mention some recent events that are important for the women's movement. In January 1983 the first general meeting of what was called 'Feminist Socialism Current' (Corriente de Feminismo Socialista) took place in Madrid. The meeting was attended by 500 women from all over the country who represented a great variety of opinions and ideology. They agreed on the attempt to discover new means of bringing pressure to bear on institutions. It was impossible to draw up practical programmes or proposals, but two years later this position had a growing number of supporters and there were more attempts to find some way of working together.

In February 1985 a new kind of symposium on women's situation was celebrated in parliament, with the participation of parliament members (women and men).

In October 1985 a 'radical' feminist woman was elected by parliament as a member of the new and important institution, Consejo del Poder Judicial, an independent council to supervise the courts.

Concluding remarks

In Spain, the new women's movement managed to attain in less than ten years the basic reforms that were achieved in other democratic countries between the end of the second world war and the 1970s. The reforms can be summarized as follows: (1) basic equality of women before the law; (2) equality with men in civic rights and liberties, even if in practice there are still many inequalities; (3) the suppression of obviously sexist regulations; (4) the awakening of public opinion to the situation of women, first by making people aware of the inequality that existed and then by obtaining a general condemnation of the old values and prejudices that maintained it: in all sectors of public opinion there is now at least a formal recognition of the rights of women; (5) the inclusion in the programmes of the different institutions of some of the claims of women; (6) the creation by the government of a special department to protect women's rights; (7) the adherence by the government to the recommendations and rules of the international organizations (ILO, UNESCO, United Nations) and (8) a number of campaigns of different types, some public and some private, to throw light on women's problems.

Of course, all these achievements that are essential in any democratic country are merely the basic condition for overcoming one of the outstanding incongruities of a democratic system. But they are far from constituting a real level of equality. It is a well-known fact that it is easier to fight against and overcome the most obvious obstacles of patriarchy (which also upset the system itself) than to stand up against the sexist and undemocratic content of all social relations: the so-called 'invisible patriarchy'. This task makes it much more difficult for women to draw up suitable projects and strategies.

At any rate, the future of the women's movement in Spain is uncertain. The opportunity for a real, immediate, fundamental change has been lost. Perhaps the surviving, weakened feminist groups constitute the seeds for the new organizations. Or perhaps the new 'institutional feminism' will be able to fight simultaneously against bureaucratization and traditional resistance to change. We see similar developments in all of Europe. It is possible to conclude that although the women's movement seems to be in a crisis, the aims that produced it are not: women's rights remain an unattained goal.

References

Duran, M. A. (1979) 'Ideología política y modelos familiares', *Revista Espanola de la Opínion Pública*, 50: 53–74.

Duran, M. A. (1985) *Informe sobre la desigualdad familiar y doméstica*. Madrid: Centro de Investigaciones Sociológicas.

Fagoaga, C. and P. Savedra (1981) *Clara Campoamor. La sufragista espanola*. Madrid: Subdirección General de la Mujer, Ministerio de Cultura.

Gallego, M. T. (1983) *Mujer, Falange y Franquismo*. Madrid: Ed. Taurus.

Gallego, M. T. (1986) 'Los movimientos feministas en Europa', in M. Mella (ed.), *La izquierda en Europa*. Barcelona: Ed. Teide.

Gonzalez, A. (1979) 'El feminismo en España, hoy'. Madrid: Zero–Zyx.

Moreno, A. (1977) *Mujeres en lucha*. Barcelona: Anagrama.

Scanlon, G. (1978) '*La polémica feminista en la España contemporánea, 1868–1974*'. Madrid: Siglo XXI.

Threllfall, M. (1985) 'The Women's Movement in Spain', *New Left Review*, no. 151: 44–73.

11

Is the new women's movement dead?
Decline or change of the Danish movement

Drude Dahlerup

Introduction

On 8 April 1970, a group of no more than fifteen Danish women marched down the main pedestrian street of Copenhagen. They were audaciously and grotesquely dressed, caricaturing the commercialized image of women as stupid sex objects. On their route they shouted feminist slogans at fashion shops and cosmetics stores. At the main square of Copenhagen they took off all their artificial female attributes — bras, roll-ons, artificial eyelashes and wigs — and threw them into a wastebasket on which was written 'Keep Denmark tidy'. Later the same day the group went to Tuborg, a brewery, handing out leaflets demanding equal pay.

In the 1980s, this action does not seem very shocking; but in 1970 it made headlines in the newspapers. This marked the start of the new women's liberation movement in Denmark.

In 1985, when this is written, feminist action is no longer visible in the streets. What has happened? Some people will argue that the movement is in decline, others that it is as vital as ever. But there is no doubt that the new women's liberation movement, which started around 1970 in most Western societies, has changed since the golden days of the first years. This chapter will seek to analyse the changes in the Danish new women's movement from 1970 to 1985, and discuss the causes of these changes. The conclusion is that the new women's liberation movement is still vital, but that it has undergone considerable change. I distinguish between a social movement at large, social movement organizations and social movement events. These concepts have proved helpful for empirical research of changes in social movements.

The rapid change of the social movements of the 1960s and 1970s calls for research into what is here called 'change' in social movements (which still remain movements), the 'transformation' of social movements into something else (for instance, an interest organization or a political party), and the 'decline' of social movements — when a movement has lost its force and simply fades away.

The concept of social movements
Empirical research into social movements is made difficult because of their very nature. They are multifarious, amorphous and fluctuating. In this chapter, social movement is defined as a *conscious, collective* activity to promote *social change*, with some degree of organization and with the commitment and active participation of members or activists as its main resource.

A few other characteristics should be added. To be termed a 'social movement', the activity must represent certain fundamental interests, must last for some time, and must have a certain size and several component parts. It is characterized by a combination of spontaneity and organization. It is common to characterize a social movement as an *emerging* interest. Since social movements may be very old (like the women's movement), it is probably more accurate to define a social movement not as an emerging interest, but as interests that, by definition, are not incorporated into routine politics. Social movements are marginal to the political decision-making processes. A social movement represents a protest against the established norms and values, and usually includes an attack on the power structure itself. Because it does not possess institutionalized power, it often uses direct actions and disruptive tactics. In this, the social movement differs from the routine politics of interest organizations.

Tarrow (1983) introduces the concept of 'movement events', that is, protest formations such as demonstrations, strikes, marches, boycotts, occupations and obstruction. Protest events may be organized by more conventional organizations also, but social movements make extensive use of such tactics. The general public as well as political decision-makers often get their main impression of the movement's ideas through movement events. In this way, the movements are dependent on the mass media which can spread, but also distort, the messages.

Today, even the smallest organization likes to call itself a 'movement'. But a social movement is more than just an organization: here it is understood as an entity of activities by organizations, groups and followers who share a commitment to some common cause.

The distinction between 'social movement' and 'social movement organization' (Zald, 1979) is appropriate here. A social movement always has one or more organizations or centres. In fact, it often has several centres. And the movement is more than its organizations: it represents endeavours to reach beyond its own boundaries.

It is not the loose organizational structure itself that makes it a movement. The loose, flat structure is characteristic mainly of the movements of the 1960s, 1970s and 1980s, not of earlier ones. Rather, it is the constant and successful effort to reach beyond its own circles that characterizes a movement. The purpose is not merely to keep the organization going, but to change people's way of thinking, to change certain political areas, to change everyday life and maybe even to challenge the basic power structure of society.

Consequently, it is not possible to recognize a social movement as such until it has existed for some years. Only then is it possible to assess whether the core groups have been able to reach beyond themselves and their own circles. The label 'social movement', as it is used here, is reserved for actions that last at least for some time and manage to cause some social change.

It follows from this conceptual discussion that the borderline between the movement and its surroundings is never sharp and is constantly changing. This makes it difficult to define the limits of the movement.

Contrary to the resource mobilization approach to the study of social movements, notably the work of MacCarty and Zald, Tarrow argues that organization may lie at the end rather than the beginning of a causal chain from 'protest' to 'solidarity' to 'formal organization' (Tarrow, 1983:7). In their book on poor people's movements, Piven and Cloward go further and challenge the notion that social movements must have a kind of organization and articulated goals before they are recognized as social movements in the literature. What about massive school truancy, or rising worker absenteeism, or mounting applications for public welfare, or spreading rent defaults — are they not social movements? (Piven and Cloward, 1979:5). According to my definition, they are not. This does not imply that such trends are not important, nor should they be neglected by social scientists. But to me, the focus of social movement theory is to study how people get together in a conscious, collective effort to change the world — or a bit of it.

The new women's movement in Denmark

Like its sister movements in other Western countries, the Danish new women's movement represents a challenge by a new generation of women to patriarchal society. The movement was new, unexpected, anarchic, diffuse and loosely organized. It mobilized a lot of energy and flower power of a new generation of women, predominantly young women from the new middle class.

The new women's movement reached Denmark in 1970. It was inspired by events in the USA, Britain and Holland and emerged as a rather large, autonomous movement based on small groups, only loosely connected. Compared with the movements in the other four Nordic countries, the Danish movement was rather anarchic and put a lot of emphasis on creating a counter-culture.

The background of the new women's movement
As in most other Western nations, the activists of the new Danish women's movement came primarily from the new middle class. First university women joined in, then came schoolteachers, pedagogues, nurses, social workers and so on.

This revival of feminist protest is rooted in the fundamental changes that have occurred in women's position in Western industrialized countries since the second world war. During the period of economic boom, this new generation of women, better educated than any generation before them and enjoying greater personal freedom (including sexual freedom, because of the pill), entered or planned to enter the labour market but found themselves up against the old image of women as housewives (the unpaid madonna) or sex objects.

They also began to feel the burden of women's double workload. While the twentieth century's division of work between the wife as housekeeper and the husband as breadwinner did have its problems, it was, at least for a while, accepted by both parties. In contrast, it is obviously unacceptable that the wife should still be chiefly responsible for all the household tasks in a family and a full-time wage-earner as well. The inequality has become very visible, both at home and in the labour market, where women are paid less than men and end up in more menial jobs. This new development contains the potential for revolt by women.

The social change in women's position and women's resources explains why a new generation of women started to revolt. To understand what triggered off the movement at this particular time and in this particular form, however, we need other explanatory factors.

Jo Freeman (1975) concludes that three factors seem to be essential for a new movement to emerge:

1. a pre-existing communication network or infrastructure within the social base of the movement;
2. the susceptibility of this network to the new ideas;
3. a situation of strain or crisis that actually triggers off the movement.

In the US case, according to Freeman, the New Left had created a communication network which allowed women to reach each other. This new network of women was in fact cooptable to the new ideas of feminist protest, since these ideas represented only the logical consequence of the claims to equality and participatory democracy of the New Left. A situation of strain came when women, who were later to become leading lights in the new women's movement, personally experienced discrimination against themselves as women and were met with sexist comments and ridicule when they tried to raise the question of women's position within the New Left (Freeman, 1975).

What happened in Denmark resembles the US experience. The Danish new women's movement also came out of the student movement and the New Left in general. The network created within the New Left was essential for the emergence of the movement. But the universities formed centres of communication too; the women who pulled off the very first happening of the movement were almost all from the Department of Literature at the University of Copenhagen.

No single event or situation of strain seems to have triggered off the Danish movement. Instead, I would add a fourth factor to Freeman's list:

4. international diffusion of ideas.

The immediate impetus to start a new women's liberation movement in Denmark came out of a large meeting on 6 April 1970, where three Danish journalists talked about the creation of new women's movements in the USA, Britain and Holland. In the same way, the new ideas soon spread to other big cities and to the periphery of Denmark.

The new movement and the other women's organizations

The new women's movement was neither the first nor the only feminist grouping in Denmark when it started in 1970. A traditional women's rights organization, the Danish Women's Society, had existed since 1871. During more than one hundred years, this feminist organization has worked hard to better women's position, focusing on effecting change through political reform. It has always acted as a pressure group and as an expert group with respect to women's issues. For a century, it has been a 'watchdog' on feminist issues. Several times during this period offshoots have emerged from the Society, often initiated by more radical feminists, as for instance in the 1880s, 1900s, 1930s and 1960s.

In all five Nordic countries, this type of women's rights feminism is still in existence. Therefore, contrary to the emergence of the successful National Organization of Women (NOW) in the USA, the Nordic countries did not get any new women's rights type of organization. But, surprisingly, the old organizations did not gain in membership during the 1970s: quite the contrary.

Feminist organizations are, however, not the only women's organizations in Denmark. In fact, they are among the smallest in membership compared with the many other kinds of women's groups: housewives' organizations, farmers' and smallholders' wives' associations, humanitarian societies, women's religious organizations and temperance societies. Within the political parties women have formed separate sections since the 1930s. Compared with

Norway, Sweden and Finland, the Danish women's sections in the
parties have always been rather weak. And this is important, given
the central role of political parties in the Nordic political systems.
Around 1970, women's sections within many political parties in
Denmark were dissolved — in the name of equality! (Haavio-
Mannila et al., 1985: Ch. 2). Because of the special structure of the
Danish trade union movement, a large union exclusively for un-
skilled women workers constitutes the fourth largest union within the
Trade Union Congress of Denmark (Cook, Lorwin and Daniels,
1984). Most of these women's organizations would not call themselves feminist, although they all join under a large umbrella organization, the National Council of Danish Women (founded in 1899),
which pushes for reforms for women and children. Most of these
organizations found the new women's liberation movement much
too radical and a threat to the serious work of their own organizations.

The new women's movement represents a protest not only against
patriarchal society, but also against the old, prudent kind of feminism
focusing on political reforms. Some of the first activists of the new
Danish movement came from a radical youth organization of the
Danish Women's Society; they later formed an independent organization which demanded free abortion and organized trips to
abortion clinics in Britain and Poland. Other parts of the new
women's movement had in fact never heard of the 'old' feminist
organization — nor did they care!

The new feminists — those who cared at all — saw the split
between old and new feminism as a political split between a liberal,
politically neutral feminism and a leftist feminism. This was no doubt
the fundamental difference between the old and the new wing of the
womens' movement in Denmark. The 'old' feminists, however, also
experienced the split as a generational conflict, and they were —
rightly — critical when the new activists not infrequently acted as if
they were the first feminists in history.

The ideology of the new movement
The ideology of the new women's movement is based on a radical
vision of a totally different society, a society without any oppression.
The Danish movement stands for an *anti-capitalist* feminism: the
oppression of women must be understood and confronted as a major
force in itself. But the oppression of women is also an integral part of
the exploitation and oppression of capitalist society. The oppression
of women is not just a relic from pre-capitalist society, but has
become integrated into the very structure of capitalism in new forms
of oppression. Destruction of class society is therefore seen as a
necessary, but insufficient, condition for the liberation of women —

contrary to the ideology of classical and, to some extent, also newer Marxism.

The new feminism rejects the neutrality of the women's rights feminism vis à vis class society. In fact, it is the first large *autonomous* feminist movement to describe itself as anti-capitalist or even socialist (as some Danish women's groups openly do). Previous feminists had either been part of the labour movement or autonomous and 'neutral' — and consequently were termed 'bourgeois' by socialist women.

The new women's movement includes a vision of a participatory, direct democracy in which everybody participates in decisions that concern themselves, and where decisions are made by consensus. This idea also shaped the organizational structure of the movement. The principle of participatory democracy was to be put into practice in the movement itself, and this was translated into the principle of having autonomous groups, only loosely connected, as the basis of the movement.

The new women's movement came out of the New Left, and in many ways the New Left remained the main group of reference for the movement, first and foremost in its many ideological discussions and splits. 'No women's struggle without class struggle, and no class struggle without women's struggle', goes a central slogan of the movement. Sometimes it was expressed like this: 'Women's struggle is class struggle, and class struggle is women's struggle'. These two slogans have been used interchangeably although their meanings are in fact far from identical.

The ideology of the new movement was based on a revaluation of womenhood. Like the 'Black is beautiful' of the militant black movement, so the new women's movement wanted to teach women, including the participants themselves, to value women's actual experiences and feelings and to build up women's collective strength. This is a challenge to patriarchal society, in which both men and women themselves are taught to disregard women's capacities. The new ideas were reflected in the movement's anti-hierarchical organization, the principle of rotation with regard to functions and the rejection of any leadership.

The idea of revaluing womenhood is not without contradictions, and, just as has happened in the women's movement throughout its entire history, this idea also created discussion and conflict in the new women's movement. It was clear to the new movement from the start that revaluing women did not imply a revaluation of the traditional role of the housewife. On the contrary, this role model was rejected, although the importance of the unpaid work of the housewife was stressed. Neither was the new 'career-woman' considered a model: like her male counterparts, the new women's movement disliked her.

'We are not fighting for women's right to an ulcer', it was said. Having 50 per cent of leadership positions occupied by women only means that women participate in the oppression of other women and men. And a 50 per cent female workforce in the most heavy and filthy jobs is no ideal, either.

Liberation, not equality, is the goal. This implies a criticism of traditional feminism, which cites equality between women and men as its goal. Even if traditional feminism also wants to revalue women, it is true that many of the campaigns to get women into the same positions as men have run the risk of supporting the image of woman as an insufficient male.

'The private is political' is another slogan of the new women's movement, in Denmark as well as in other countries. This does not imply that the political institutions were considered capable of bringing fundamental change to the position of women. 'Political' is here a much broader concept, and the meaning of the slogan is that problems previously considered private and a result of individual shortcomings are now seen and discussed as social problems and subject to collective action by women.

The new women's movement brought taboo issues into broad daylight: incest, battered wives, rape, women's neuroses, men's domination of sexuality, the unequal distribution of housework. These issues were discussed side by side with the shortcomings of public day care facilities, sex segregation in the labour market, abortion, unequal pay and women's powerlessness.

The new women's movement in Denmark has always been for women only — partly to give women a chance to learn to speak out without the often oppressive presence of men, partly as a means of creating a collective base for women. 'Sisterhood is powerful!' While the Danish Women's Society has always been open to men (although few came), the new movement had to throw male sympathizers out from their first meetings.

The new women's movement has often been criticized for separatism. The fact is, however, that most movement activists do live with men, and work with men on a day-to-day basis. The movement in fact creates just one single base for women in a male-dominated society.

Some circles within the movement, however, began establishing all-women communes, where they could live and raise children without male interference and dominance. It was the lesbian circles of the movement that most consistently developed this new way of living, which became a challenge to patriarchal society — and in some ways also to the heterosexual women of the movement.

During the first years of the new Danish movement, the term 'feminism' was often used for what has been labelled 'radical feminism' in other countries. According to the critics, this kind of feminism saw the causes of women's oppression in the patriarchal structures only, thus denying the capitalist exploitation. In fact, nearly all women in the movement were and are left-wing-oriented, and the disagreement only concerned the priority that should be given to the class struggle versus the gender conflict. Also, all activists were critical of the insufficient theory of women's emancipation in classical Marxism as well as in neo-Marxism.

Eventually, following the decline of the New Left, radical feminism has expanded. Ecofeminism, feminist astrology, matriarchal groups and witchcraft groups have developed, in their attempt to find a new meaning of womenhood. Their critics within the movement accuse the radical groups of encapsulation around an uncritical cult of womanhood. Others see this new trend as the real radical feminism, radical in the sense of a fundamental rethinking of society.

The strategy of the new movement

The new women's movement has never considered the state the main target of its activities, except for matters like abortion legislation. The activities have first and foremost been directed towards women, towards the general public and towards the labour market. Especially during its first years, the movement considered the state a kind of enemy and itself as being 'outside the system'. Being predominantly leftist, the new movement has seen no reason to avoid issues just because they are politicized by the political parties — a constant problem for the 'neutral' Danish Women's Society.

Table 1 gives some clues to the differences between the traditional women's rights feminism and the new women's liberation movement in the 1970s. In the 1980s, the gap between these two kinds of

TABLE 1

Variations in relations with the state among the two major branches of the feminist movement in Denmark in the 1970s

	Women's rights movement	Women's liberation movement
State as enemy	no	partly
Feminism as non-partisan	yes	no
Political reforms the main strategy	yes	no
Seeking integration	yes	no
Actual integration	marginal	—
Following the rules of the game	yes	no
Using direct action	no	yes
Ideology	equality	liberation

feminism seems to be narrowing because of changes in both branches.

The development of the new Danish women's movement, 1970–85

The Danish women's liberation movement has changed considerably during its fifteen years of existence. It is not easy to understand the direction of or the reasons for these changes. The development may be described in three stages: (1) period of direct action; (2) proliferation and a new feminist counter-culture; (3) decline of the Redstockings; new centres and further specialization.

Stage 1: period of direct action

The first three or four years of the new women's movement in Denmark were marked by enthusiasm and spontaneity, by the raising of new issues in public debate, by experiments with new forms of organization, by direct actions, and by extensive discussions and splits over ideology and strategy.

Especially during the first year, the movement engaged in many direct actions. The media coverage was extensive and made the movement known to the general public as the 'Redstockings', a name borrowed from the New York Redstockings. Some examples of this sort of creative, disruptive, non-violent actions are as follows:

— During a big open-air public meeting of the Social Democratic Party about 'Equality in the 70s', a few Redstockings interrupted the speech — transmitted direct on TV — of the chairman of the Danish Trade Union Congress in order to demand equal pay now. 1 May 1970, in Copenhagen.
— On Mother's Day a group of women entered a public bus and refused to pay more than 80 per cent of the fare because women get only 80 per cent of the salary of men. They were — peacefully — arrested and fined, but they refused to pay more than 80 per cent of the penalty. May 1970, in Copenhagen.
— Dressed as a bride, a woman took the floor during the matriculation ceremony at the University of Copenhagen, welcoming the male students to this the best 'bride fair' of the world. At the university's front building, the statues (all men, of course) were complemented by living statues of women representing all the functions men need and use in order to make it in the academic world: the cleaning woman, the mother, the secretary, the mistress, the Muse. September 1970, in Copenhagen.
— During a beauty contest a group of Redstockings interrupted the event, conducted by a popular TV host, and protested against the exploitation of women as sex objects and women competing for the benefit of men only. Summer 1971, in Aarhus.

Other actions included the interruption of a parliament meeting to demand equal pay, an action against the World Bank, the occupation of a bar closed to women, an action against a traditional women's magazine.

Creating these kinds of events does not require many women, as one can see. But the media coverage was extensive: this was something new, unexpected, disruptive, audacious, breaking the rules of how women ought to behave. Media coverage was essential to the new movement in order for it to spread the message; but the activists soon realized that the media, especially the boulevard press, were using the movement for their own purpose, often distorting the ideas of an action. The movement soon learned from its US counterpart to demand to talk to women journalists only. During this period, every single action was subject to long discussions and disagreements within the movement about the right strategy.

During the first year, the movement spread from Copenhagen to Aarhus, Odense and a few other big cities. In each city the centre of the movement became a Women's House, the meeting point of all the different groups. Following the example of the active squatters' movement of those days, the Copenhagen Redstockings in September 1971 occupied their first Women's Centre, while in Aarhus the movement persuaded the local authorities to rent a building to the movement at a token rent.

Discussions over the organizational principles were endless during this period. Several attempts to tighten up the loose structure were made, especially in the mid-1970s, but with little result. Coordinating committees were formed in each city, and each small group was to send a representative to the meetings of the committee. This structure never functioned well, partly because of the rotation principle, partly because of the general distrust in representative democracy. The plenum, open to everybody, remained the highest decision-making authority. A national organization of the whole movement was never created, partly because of the general fear of bureaucratization, partly because the biggest wing of the movement, the Copenhagen wing, always felt that it *was* the movement.

Many women were mobilized to activism in the movement. But the turnover of members and activists was very high. During this first period the ideological foundation of the movement was developed through extensive discussions, the reading of international literature and a rediscovery of the old socialist women's movements, especially the German ones.

Even if the movement was rather outgoing during this period, men and women from the New Left often accused it of concentrating on 'luxury problems' and thereby deserting the revolution and even working-class women themselves by focusing on sexual life, division of labour at home, self-realization and so on. Even during the first couple of years, several independent socialist women's groups were formed in opposition to the main ideology of the movement and in frustration over its diffuse organizational structure.

The Danish new women's movement participated in three large political reform movements during the period 1970–3: abortion; the campaign against EEC membership and equal pay. Although the demand for free abortion had been raised by many other groups all the way back to the 1930s, the new women's movement soon became the main actor in the abortion campaign, which succeeded in changing the rather liberal abortion law of 1970 into abortion on request by the law of 1973. Like all hospital services in Denmark, abortions are now performed free of charge, and the subsequent sick leave is paid by social security. The new women's movement organized demonstrations, hearings and actions in support of free abortion, partly in cooperation with other groupings.

The movement also participated in the campaign against Danish membership of the Common Market, the EEC. The main argument was that harmonizing legislation within the EEC would not, as the advocates of EEC membership claimed, better the position of women in the other countries, but would on the contrary drag Danish legislation down to southern European standards. The new women's movement was never a major actor in the campaign against the EEC, but it succeeded in getting the position of women on to the agenda of the EEC debate. The whole issue disappeared more or less from the movement after the referendum was lost in October 1972, when the Danish population, by a small margin, voted for the EEC membership, as opposed to the referendum result in Norway.

The third important political reform issue in which the movement participated during this period was the demand for equal pay. Women workers had made this demand for decades (a law on equal pay for public servants had been passed as early as 1919). At the beginning of the 1970s, however, the campaign for equal pay was intensified, partly because of the support from the new women's movement. In several cities, the movement formed 'equal pay committees' together with women from the trade union movement, the women's rights organizations and others. These committees arranged hearings and demonstrations. Not until 1973, following intensive pressure from women, did equal pay get into the general wage agreements of the labour market — and then, only in the restricted form of equal pay for work of equal value.

Equal pay was an example of successful, yet troublesome, cooperation between the new women's movement and working-class women. According to the ideology of the movement, working-class women constituted one of the most important, if not *the* most important, groups in the struggle for women's liberation. But the new women's movement never succeeded in recruiting working-class women, although several attempts were made, some of which were very naive (as when the branch in Aarhus invited all women from a large working-class area to tea — and one came!). During this period working-class women would usually dissociate themselves from the ideology and style of the new women's movement.

The new movement primarily mobilized young women (20–30 years of age), but special sections of 'Women over 40' were created within the movement in several cities. These sections attracted women who had often become radicalized after many years as housewives.

The movement became well-known through the mass media, but the message of the movement was often distorted to an image of man-hating, bra-burning women. However, the movement managed to reach out to a broader circle of women through its summer holiday camp on the island of Femø. This camp was started in 1971, and 500 women and children (boys under 13 were admitted) stayed at the camp for one week or more during the first summer. Every function necessary to run the big tent camp was carried out by women alone. This was a novelty and a symbol of a new independent womanhood. Apart from this, the camp gave hundreds of women who would never have approached the Redstocking centres an opportunity to meet and talk with other women. During the international week of the camp, feminists from many European countries came together. The very successful island camp of Femø has continued every year since 1971, and new camps have been established in other parts of the country as well.

The movement created another event that reached wider circles of women than those recruited as activists by the movement organization: the first feminist festival was arranged one weekend in August 1974, in a central park of Copenhagen. An estimated 30,000 people — women, men and children — attended the festival, to listen to the speeches and the all-woman bands and join in the singing and dancing. The lawn was encircled by numerous booths, in which women from various movement groups could display information about their activities and sell their pamphlets, snacks, teas and beer. It was a pioneer task and was received as such, because it was another proof that women could run a big event by themselves. After a few years no one paid special attention to this fact, but thousands of people continued to come to the festivals. In Aarhus the movement organized similar festivals from 1977. Eventually, however, this kind of event became a ritual and faded away.

Stage 2: proliferation and a new feminist counter-culture
No sharp distinction should be made between what is here called stage 1 of the movement, from 1970 to around 1974, and stage 2, from 1975 to around 1980. But the movement clearly changed gradually, although not according to any deliberate plan.

From the mid-1970s direct action by the new women's movement almost stopped. The movement gradually engaged more and more in a less dramatic, every-day kind of work, which created a new feminist counter-culture in opposition to the patriarchal culture. There was a proliferation of many new groups, some of which were closely connected with the movement organizations while others were more independent from them. Most of these new groups considered themselves part of the new women's movement at large, and were considered as such by the original activists.

The Women's Houses, or Women's Centres, of the big cities began to split into more specialized groups. The consciousness-raising groups were still an essential part of the movement, but were no longer the basis of it. In the mid-1970s several attempts were made to tighten up the diffuse structure of the movement, introducing formal membership and the like, but most attempts to regulate the structure were short-lived or ineffective. The division into many task-oriented groups was a way of getting things done. This meant that the general, overall movement organization gradually disappeared. Coming up to the 1980s, the Redstockings, previously identified as *the* movement, had become just one group among others in the enlarged Women's Centres of the big cities. The development did not come about according to any plan, it just happened. But it put an end to the passionate, almost daily, discussions about the ideology and strategy of the movement.

A geographical diffusion began to take place. The new women's movement spread from the big cities to a number of middle-sized towns in Denmark. By 1976, outside the five largest cities, ten towns had got their own 'women's group' or even a Women's House or Centre.

Outside the big cities, the new feminist activists usually did not call themselves Redstockings. They did not want to be identified with the media image of that man-hating, radical group. In their opinion, that would keep many women away from the local branch of the movement. The coalitions were usually broader in these towns than in the big cities. The creation of a Women's Centre in a town of, say, 50,000 inhabitants was usually the mutual endeavour of several women's organizations, not infrequently including the local branch of the traditional women's rights organizations, the Danish Women's Society. Because they had fewer resources, feminists in these towns had to stick together. Likewise, the New Left was never as differentiated in these towns as in the cities.

During this second period an autonomous lesbian movement was created. The many lesbian women within the women's movement felt they needed a forum of their own, within the movement at large. The split between lesbian and non-lesbian feminists, however, caused much dispute and confusion. Since the principle of the movement organization was 'If you want something done, go ahead and do it', the lesbian wing of the movement, which was very active, for periods came to represent the movement. This probably discouraged many non-lesbians from joining or staying in the movement organizations.

During this second stage of the movement, a new feminist counter-culture began to unfold. Some of these new initiatives will be mentioned in what follows.

The Women's Centres began to offer many courses, for instance in feminist self-defence, film-making and yoga. The courses for pregnant women were a big success; the idea was that pregnant women together in a group should learn about the changes of their bodies, about the principles of alternative, self-regulated labour — and should get some exercise. These courses were, and still are, very well attended, and the principle of giving women back the control over their own labour has had some effects on hospitals and midwives.

Counselling groups for women emerged in many places during these years. The counselling offered was free and was based on the principle of solidarity among women, rather than reducing the woman to a mere client or victim. Women were given practical advice, but in addition they were given an opportunity to join with other women in a group in order to get the strength to fight their own problems and the social causes of the common problems.

A new feminist magazine was published by the Redstockings from 1975. The organizations in various cities did have their own internal newsletters, but the new magazine was meant for women in general, offering an alternative to the commercialized and traditional women's magazines. The new magazine, *Kvinder* (Women), had a maximum circulation of 3,000–5,000. Unlike the US *Ms.*, *Kvinder* never managed to threaten the traditional women's magazines, of which the biggest ones have a circulation of 100,000–200,000 a week.

At the universities, women's studies developed as a challenge to the established university education and research, which had often neglected women, taking the male as the norm and standard of human beings. Since a large proportion of the movement activists, especially in the first years, were university students, women's studies at the university were and are regarded as part of the new women's movement by most participants. Usually it was women students and young women faculty members who started women's studies at the universities.

A feminist publishing firm was also established in this period. It published poetry, novels and also a very popular knitting book, *Hønsestrik* ('Chick knit'). Somehow, your knitted sweater would signal that you were a feminist or were married to one! Within the many newly established New Left publishing firms, women formed women's groups that put out feminist political literature. A new genre, the 'Report books', emerged. In these books, factory women, women in politics, women in clerical work and so on would describe their lives, thus making women's conditions of life more visible to others.

Perhaps the most important part of this new culture was the many novels now being written by women. The new wave of feminism gave potential women novelists the necessary self-confidence to write; it made women's personal and social lives a legitimate and interesting literary subject; and it created a large audience for these books. Danish novels as well as translated books began to sell in large numbers. Some of these writers considered themselves part of the new women's movement, some did not. But their books probably brought the new feminist ideas to a wider audience than any demonstration or political resolution could have done.

In 1978 a feminist folk high school was established in the buildings of an old inn in southern Jutland. Denmark has a long historical tradition of folk high schools (courses for adults living at the school for several months; no exams), and also has a very liberal law giving them economic support. Kvindehøjskolen (the Women's Folk High School) has been a success, and several hundreds of women and their children go there every year.

For the first time, women began to form their own music bands, film teams and theatre groups. They began to break the male monopoly of composing music and organizing performances. The first all-women bands were met with surprise and suspicion: can an all-women band really play properly? In general, a counter-culture on women's premises was being born — and is flourishing.

From the mid-1970s, the economic crisis hit Denmark, causing massive unemployment and cuts in public services. The new women's movement did not manage to form a joint protest, although women were hit especially hard by unemployment, with the cuts in the standard of day care facilities and the feminization of poverty – phenomena that were experienced in other countries as well. Now, when the new women's movement was needed the most, it did not respond. The reason for this was that no joint movement organizations or centre existed any longer; there was no joint ideology and no joint strategy. The constant proliferation of groups had done away with the previous diffuse, yet joint, movement organizations.

*Stage 3: decline of the Redstockings; new centres and
further specialization*

During the third stage, from around 1980 until today, the creation of a feminist culture continued. Further proliferation of new feminist activities took place. New centres emerged. Specialization and, to some extent, a professionalization of feminist activities mark this period.

The old core, the Redstockings, was becoming less important. Many women still label themselves 'Redstockings' although they do not belong to such an organization any more. In Aarhus, the Redstockings made the surprising move of closing the organization down in 1985. This caused extended discussions in the press about whether the women's movement was dead. The fact was, however, that the Redstockings in Aarhus had shrunk to just one office with only a few activists, within a Women's House of many specialized activities, in a city with several different feminist centres. In most cities, the centre of gravity has even moved away from the original Women's Centres and Women's Houses, although they still perform important tasks like counselling, education and courses. There is no longer any one major centre within the movement, but instead many specialized centres.

The general feminist struggle has been replaced by specialized feminist activities, most of which still consider themselves part of the new women's movement. The geographical diffusion of the movement continues. By 1985, women's centres and new feminist organizations existed in about fifty Danish towns.

Crisis centres began to emerge. In 1979, a large house in Copenhagen was occupied by women, and a broad coalition of women's oganizations managed to collect enough money later to buy the house; in 1980 the Danner refuge for battered women opened here. The house is also a Women's Centre of many cultural events. In this way, battered women are offered support not as victims, but as collaborators. It has, however, taken enormous resources to buy and run the house. Since 1980 additional crisis centres have been established in five or six other Danish towns and cities. This work has given feminist activists many experiences — good and bad — in dealing with the authorities and in building alliances with women outside the movement, for example women politicians.

Women's studies have developed further at the universities. Many books and articles have been written, many seminars and lectures held. At the same time, cutbacks in the universities' funding (all Danish universities are run by the state) threaten the future of women's studies courses. However, women's studies are now being institutionalized. After years of discussion about integration or separatism, centres of women's studies at the universities have been formed in recent years, with some public financial support. In 1985 the Danish parliament gave special support to women's studies (eight permanent positions plus research money). This support was a result of cooperation between women in women's studies courses and sympathizers among women parliamentarians.

The university curriculum has in fact changed somewhat as a consequence of the feminist criticism. So, where women's studies have proved most successful, a new problem will often occur: what happens when women's studies changes from revolt into curriculum?

Numerous other activities flourish. A Women's Studies Information Service, KVINFO, started in 1983 in Copenhagen. Several new women's studies magazines have emerged. The number of courses on women's literature, women's health, women's work and history, feminist philosophy and the like offered to the general public has grown very fast, and many new and independent centres of education have been built. Thanks to a very liberal legislation on public financial support to evening courses for adults, many feminists now have paid jobs (often part-time) teaching some of those courses.

The counter-culture of the new women's movement has developed still further. Women's art galleries have been established and many film, theatre and art groups have emerged. In Aarhus, a Museum of Women's History has been created — one of the first of its kind in the world. This and many other feminist projects are supported by public money (for instance, job creation money). The movement has learned how to raise money, without which no project would ever last more than a couple of years.

A general characteristic of all these new, and often more institutionalized, activities is the attempt to practise the principles of a horizontal organizational structure; rotation; the 'plenum' as the top decision-making authority; and working in groups. And, of course, all the activities are run by women.

Evaluation of the new women's movement in Denmark
Is the new women's movement dead?
In the mid-1980s people began to wonder whether the new women's movement was dead. 'Are there no Redstockings any more?', some would ask. Others stated that the 'women's movement' as such is finished. Women who consider themselves Redstockings argue that you cannot close down a movement: the women's movement, they insist, is still alive and active.

The conclusion to be drawn from my analysis of the movement's three stages is this: the new women's movement is not dead, but it certainly has changed during these fifteen years. It is still a movement; that is, no transformation into political party or a more established interest organization has occurred. The all-movement character remains, contrary to what is happening to the Icelandic women's movement, and for instance to the Green movement in many countries right now.

All social movements are in a constant process of change. This ever-changing characteristic makes it difficult to understand what is really happening to a given movement. The previously mentioned distinction between the movement at large, movement organizations and movement events is an appropriate tool with which to study social movement change.

The first years of the new women's liberation movement in Denmark were marked by lively discussions of ideology and experiments with organizing and ways of living, but it was the many direct actions of this period that made the movement generally known. When the movement ceased to create all these spectacular events, it became less visible. The mass media went for newer news. The movement, however, was not dead, but was now focusing on creating a counter-culture, which gradually managed to influence the culture of the country. Furthermore, some of the 'old' organizations of the movement declined. That was the case with the general movement organization, which was replaced by specialized activities. The old centres and the Women's Houses are now used for activities like counselling, self-help groups, education and so forth. New centres have been created, including crisis centres, women's studies centres, women's information centres and a Museum of Women's History, to name only a few. Without new centres, the women's movement cannot survive. Without committed activists, the movement cannot go on. All movements need some kind of organization and many committed activists.

New women are being recruited to movement activities as activists and sympathizers, although mostly they are women over 30 years of age. The younger women do not seem to become involved in feminist organizations any more, but rather seek other social movements like the peace movement and the ecology movement. The drive to challenge patriarchal society in order to change women's subordinate position is still living and in fact is spreading to many more women. But there is no joint movement organization or even a joint meeting point any more.

In general, I will argue that a social movement is still alive *if* new organizations and centres replace declining ones; *if* recruitment is continuing; *if* new resources are constantly being mobilized; *if* new ideas unfold; and *if* the drive to challenge the established society is still present. Empirical research must study all these aspects in order to determine whether a movement is actually fading away, or just changing.

These analyses of the Danish movement leave us with the question of whether it is still the same movement. As pointed out earlier, the new women's movement is neither the first nor the only feminist movement in Denmark, although it was no doubt the most radical and vivid of the feminist groupings of the 1970s and 1980s.

On the one hand, it is possible to argue that a distinct movement of 'women's liberation' still exists, because most of the ongoing and new activities still rest on the common base of a left-wing feminism, the ideology of liberation rather than equality with men in the given society, the small group of women as the organizational base, the idea of participatory democracy and cultural changes.

On the other hand, the gap between 'old' and 'new' feminism, and even between feminist women and other women, is no doubt narrowing. Both the traditional women's rights feminism and the new radical feminism have changed. Moreover, the new women's movement has managed to influence women in general — and to some extent men as well. Feminist coalitions are becoming broader and new alliances are being built.

Seen in a broader historical perspective, the period from 1970 until today represents a period of renewal and a high point in the long history of the women's movement. During the past one hundred years, the women's movement has lived through periods of enthusiasm, mobilization and visibility — and through periods of more quiet, dogged and less visible struggle, as in the interwar period.

The new wave of feminism in the 1970s and 1980s experienced many splits, internal antagonisms and rather bitter discussions. But in a longer historical perspective, these divisions will seem minor, and what will remain is the picture of a strong and radical new feminism, which changed the feminist movement as a whole.

Why did the new women's movement change?
Social movements are in a constant process of change. They are movements, not just organizations.

Brand et al. (1984:36–7) argue that the necessity of change in social movements follows from their low degree of organization and institutionalization, and also from an 'immanent logic of change', which makes it necessary for any social movement always to increase its mobilization and to escalate the conflicts in order to remain successful. The dynamics of this development lies in the interaction between protest strategies and the social–political reaction.

Jo Freeman goes further, stating that for social movements decline seems inevitable: 'Because they are an unpredictable combination of conflicting tendencies in an ever-changing environment, they inevitably decline.' The type of decline is not, however, inevitable, she continues. Some movements decline because the grievances that stimulated them are resolved; others are repressed successfully. Some fall apart because their resources disappear, the costs of participation become too high or internal bickering splits them into competing factions. Some disappear after having had a transformative effect on society; others may pass leaving no lasting effects (Freeman, 1983:277). All this, even the inevitability of decline, is true if viewed from a sufficiently long historical perspective.

The study of the change in the new Danish women's movement reveals several internal as well as external factors that have contributed to this change. The decline of the core organizations of the movement, the Redstockings, and the division into many specialized groups were probably inevitable, although unintended, consequences of internal factors, among others the organizational structure of the movement.

The enthusiasm that carried the movement through the first three or four years could not possibly last for ever. The ideologically based preference for the small-group structure meant that few resources were mobilized for organizational work. More than for any other social movement, the statement of Gerlach and Hine (1970:xvi) holds true for the new women's movement: 'a successful movement is the point of intersection between personal and social change'. Many women used the movement for personal change and resource mobilization, and after a short period in the movement went out to use these new resources elsewhere.

With the split of the movement into specialized activities, the ideological discussion of feminism and socialism slowed down. In a way, the movement was held together during these fifteen years exactly because it was not bound together into one organization. This atomization saved the movement from the fractionalism that has contributed to the decline of many New Left organizations. Whereas Miller (1983:296) argues that the participatory structure of the US Students for a Democratic Society (SDS) was fine for a small, cohesive group but allowed fractionalism to flourish as the group grew, and consequently killed the movement, the same principle of autonomy for all groups in the women's movement, and the proliferation of groups without any declared common ideology, in fact probably saved the women's movement from complete disintegration.

In her analysis of the Norwegian new women's movement, which, unlike the Danish, was split into two large factions, Runa Haukaa (1982) argues that conflict may in fact be very fruitful. Even if the conflict between the Norwegian small-group-based New Feminists and the Marxist Women's Front was considered destructive, this conflict, she argues, did bear fruit: it strengthened the offensive forces of the movement at large and furthered the ideological development of feminist theory.

In order fully to explain the development of the Danish new women's movement, I will add the aspect of *generations*. Biological age, and social experiences connected with age, have played an important role. The new women's movement started as a revolt by a new generation of women against patriarchal society — but also against the traditional women's organizations. Collective learning from one social movement to the next was quite limited in this case. And maybe it has to be like that.

The wrath necessary for a radical change of perspective is probably possible only by cutting the ties to all previous movements. Further, wrath as well as enthusiasm cannot be inherited, because it comes out of personal experience. Today, the women of the new women's movement experience this when they find themselves unable to mobilize the younger women to join movement organizations.

On a much more down-to-earth level, the question of biological age has influenced the development of the movement — and will probably do so for all women's organizations. The extreme fluctuation in membership of the new women's movement during the 1970s no doubt also had to do with the fact that the young women who had been active in the first years soon had children, or had to work hard to pass their examinations, and later to get a job. Consequently, many activists simply had no time for movement activities, even if they still felt part of the movement.

External factors also contributed to the change of the movement. The new women's movement emerged as part of the New Left in a period of reform and prosperity. From the mid-1970s the economic crisis made itself felt, causing massive unemployment. In 1973 the new anti-establishment right-wing party of Mogens Glistrup won a smashing victory and gained 16 per cent of the votes in the parliamentary election. The political and economic climate changed dramatically. The progress of the New Left stopped, and many New Left movements and organizations declined, including the student movement among others.

In fact, the new women's movement proved to be one of the most vital parts of the New Left — and also the part that insisted most persistently on the anti-hierarchical principles of organization.

The opportunities present in the 1960s and 1970s no longer exist. It is an irony of history that the New Left, and among them the new women's movement, did not succeed in making a large protest movement when, according to its own ideology, it was most needed: during this period the women's movement did not make any joint protest against unemployment for women, cutbacks in public services and so on.

These changes in the political and economic factors were bound to influence the strategy and ideology of the new women's movement.

The economic crisis and the success of the new political Right meant
that the New Left vision of immediate, radical, if not revolutionary,
change withered away. The feeling that we are changing history
remains in the women's movement, but the perspective has changed.
There is a new reformist trend in the movement. The socialist
revolutionary rhetoric of its first years is heard less frequently, except
among small Marxist groupings.

What is of vital importance for the study of social movements, and
even more for the particular movements themselves, is not so much
whether they continue to live, but whether they have had a significant
impact.

The impact of the new women's movement
Herbert Marcuse appraised the new women's movement as the most
important and potentially the most radical political movement of the
1970s (Marcuse, 1974). Now we are in the 1980s, and the movement
is not just 'potential' any more. Yet we are faced with many problems
in evaluating the effects of the activities of the movement over these
fifteen years.

It is an unquestionable success in itself that a movement, in fact,
emerged; that the frustrations and protests developed into such a
widespread movement which is still proliferating.

Second, it is important to note that, contrary to what happened in
the USA, no anti-feminist movement developed in Denmark. Anti-
feminist sentiments have no doubt grown out of the media image of
the movement as a bunch of man-hating radicals and by some of the
movement's actual actions. But feminist sentiments developed too.
Free abortion was introduced by law in Denmark in 1973, and the few
attempts to create an anti-abortion movement in Denmark have all
failed completely. Abortion is now a non-issue in Danish politics.

Raising the issues
The most important impact of the new women's movement has
probably been its influence on women and on public opinion in
general. No opinion data exist in Denmark to support this
hypothesis, but it is probably true that some of the movement's ideas
have reached every single person and family in the country. The
movement has no doubt contributed to changes in interpersonal
relations: the relations between women and men, and women's
relations with other women.

For most activists, being in the movement changed their personal
lives. The movement became an agent of consciousness-raising for its
activists, for sympathizers and also for many others. The disruptive,
imaginative actions of the first years soon made the movement
known all over the country. These actions aroused feminist

consciousness, but no doubt they also resulted in anti-feminist feelings. We know, for instance, that many women of the trade union movement disliked the disruptive actions of the first years, and many housewives of the older generation felt depreciated by the movement. Its cultural activities, which have flourished since the mid-1970s, have given more widespread acceptance to the movement, although these activities are less obvious — or maybe because of that! Parts of this counter-culture have in fact become an integrated part of the mainstream culture in Denmark. For some feminists this represents a positive sign of influence, whereas others are worried about the effect this integration might have on the movement and its original ideas.

   The new women's movement never considered the political parties or institutions the main target of its activities. Nevertheless, it has made an impact on the political parties, on the trade unions, on other social movements and on public policy. It has managed to raise new issues in public debate. Wife-beating, incest, clandestine abortions, discrimination against lesbian women, a women's control over her own labour, support for rape victims and other subjects previously considered women's private problems have now reached the political parties, parliament and in some cases also the local councils. Other issues have been put forward insistently by the new women's movement: the lack of child care facilities and the high fees for existing facilities, the feminization of poverty, the need for a six-hour workday for both men and women, the need to have male partners share the joy and burden of household work, the issue of equal pay, the suppression of women and women's lives from research and from curricula in schools. Many of the last mentioned issues have been advanced by other women's organizations as well.

   After being raised or fought for first by the new women's movement, other issues have been taken up by women and women's organizations who have then worked hard within the system to translate them into legislation and action. These women — politicians, public servants and members of other organizations — have met criticism both from the male-dominated political establishment and from women of the movement, who oppose the usual de-radicalization of the issues on their route through the political system.

The political parties

In Denmark, the ideas of the new women's movement were picked up primarily by the political parties on the left wing. After many disappointing experiences with the small socialist groupings and parties of the left, many movement activists joined the Socialist People's Party, which during the 1970s developed an elaborate programme on politics concerning women. Within the Socialist

People's Party an influential women's movement was created, which works according to the non-hierarchical principles of the new women's movement. The ideas of the movement have also made an impact on the Social Democratic Party and to a lesser extent on centre and conservative parties. The Progress Party — the now declining right-wing part of Mogens Glistrup — is the only party that openly detests everything the movement stands for.

During the 1970s and 1980s, extensive debates on women's position in society have been going on. The new women's movement has played a major role in starting this debate, but has not been the only actor on the stage. A growing number of women and feminists from other organizations and institutions have participated in this debate. It is more appropriate to talk in terms of the *interaction* between the new women's movement and other social forces than just of the *impact* of the movement.

The new 'state feminism'

As in many other countries, equality between men and women, previously a non-issue in politics (Dahlerup, 1984), reached the political agenda in Denmark during the 1970s and 1980s. 'Machinery' to work with problems of women's position has been set up in Denmark, in the form of the Equal Status Council (1975) under the prime minister's office, and in each county there is now an 'equality consultant' whose task it is to try to improve women's position on the labour market and break down the sex segregation of the market.

During the same period, several laws have been passed concerning women and the equality of the sexes. The new women's movement played a crucial role in the passage of the law of 1973, providing free abortion on request. A law concerning equal treatment on the labour market (1978) and a law prescribing equal pay for the same work (1976) were passed, with only little action on the part of the women's movement. In 1984, maternity leave was extended to six months, of which the father of the child may use the last part. A symbolic change of the marriage law was passed in 1984: now a woman will keep her own family name when married unless she explicitly states that she wants the name of her husband. The same goes for the husband. Previously, the law automatically gave the wife the name of her husband unless she explicitly stated otherwise.

This strengthening, although modest, of the official policy of equal status of men and women is not the result of work by the new women's movement. The movement has strongly criticized the equality policy and pointed to the shortcomings of this kind of politics, especially during an economic crisis. But the progress of the state policy on women has no doubt been furthered by a combination of the indirect impact of the new movement through its renewal of the feminist debate and the direct effect of actions by feminists working inside the political institutions.

Women's political representation has increased rapidly during the 1970s and 1980s in Denmark, from 5–10 per cent in the 1960s to 26 per cent women in the Danish parliament today and 23 per cent in the local councils at large (Haavio-Mannila et al., 1985). The women's liberation movement has never been particularly interested in getting more women into the male-dominated political arena, but again, the movement and the debate it created have indirectly affected the political parties and the voters so that they nominate and elect more women — and have influenced more women to wish to or dare to stand as a candidate. Other actors have been more directly involved in this increase, especially women in the political parties and the Women's Rights organizations.

Women's networks

One of the main principles of the new women's movement is that women should stop competing with each other, to the benefit of men only. Instead, women should work together in solidarity, in this way creating collective resources and strength as a group.

It is the merit of the new women's movement that women's groups, equality committees and so on have emerged in large numbers in recent years — in political parties, in trade unions, at universities and in various work-places. The general trend of the 1960s was to close down separate organizations for women — often in the name of equality.

The new women's movement stresses women's need to work together. And somehow it has been possible to reverse the previous marginalizing effect for women when they formed all-women's groups. Women are still marginal, but in many places women's groups have proved to be a strength for women as a collective. Their hard work within their own institutions, using their collective strength, will no doubt be an important future feminist activity (whether they call themselves feminists or state that 'we are not feminists, but . . .'), followed by all the demands they support on behalf of women.

In general, it is becoming less and less clear what can be defined as activities of the movement and what cannot. Many of the new initiatives that have sprung up during the economic crisis have been taken or supported by activists who work hand in hand with women who have never been active in the movement. Projects for unemployed women, support groups for single mothers, a new kind of folk high school (daytime) for women — all these projects constitute a continuation of the new women's movement, without actually being movement organizations.

Through the combined efforts of active women from the old and new feminist movements, from the political parties, from the bureaucracy, from the trade unions, informal networks of women are being established, networks of women at the grass-roots level and networks of elite women, often broader than the 'old boy' network they try to counterbalance. Carol Mueller (1983) has called this kind of network one of the most successful outcomes of a social movement, hereby providing resources for future mobilization.

Zald and Ash (1966) argue that, the more specific are the demands of a social movement, the shorter it will live. That is true. Movements like the abortion movement and the movement against nuclear plants live only until that particular issue is settled. The project of the women's movement is much more comprehensive: to change the subordinate position of women. This extensive project offers no quick or easy victory.

References

Brand, K.-W., D. Büsser and D. Rucht (1984) *Aufbruch in eine andere Gesellschaft. Neue soziale Bewegungen in der Bundesrepublik*. Frankfurt: Campus Verlag.

Cook, Alice, Val Lorwin and Arlene Kaplan Daniels (1984) *Women and Trade Unions in Eleven Industrialized Countries*. Philadelphia: Temple University Press.

Dahlerup, Drude (1984) 'Overcoming the Barriers: An Approach to the Study of How Women's Issues Are Kept from the Political Agenda', pp. 31–66 in Judith H. Stiehm (ed.), *Women's Views of the Political World of Men*. New York: Transnational.

Freeman, Jo (1975) *The Politics of Women's Liberation*. New York: Longman.

Freeman, Jo (ed.) (1983) *Social Movements of the Sixties and Seventies*. New York: Longman.

Gerlach, Luther P. and Virginia H. Hine (1970) *People, Power, Change: Movements of Social Transformation*. Indianapolis: Bobbs-Merrill.

Haavio-Mannila, Elina, et al. (1985) *Unfinished Democracy. Women in Nordic Politics*. Oxford: Pergamon Press.

Haukaa, Runa (1982) *Bak slagordene. Den nye kvinnebevegelsen i Norge*. Oslo: Pax Forlag.

Marcuse, Herbert (1974) 'Marxism and Feminism', pp. 279–88 in *Women's Studies*, 2. (Berlin)

Miller, Frederick D. (1983) 'The End of SDS and the Emergence of Weatherman: Demise Through Success', pp. 279–96 in Freeman (1983).

Mueller, Carol (1983) 'Women's Movement Success and the Success of Social Movement Theory'. Working Paper, Wellesly College, Mass.

Piven, Frances Fox and Richard A. Cloward (1979) *Poor People's Movements. Why They Succeed. How They Fail*. New York: Vintage Books.

Tarrow, Sidney (1983) 'Resource Mobilization and Cycles of Protest: Theoretical Reflections and Comparative Illustrations'. Paper to the Annual Meeting of the American Sociological Association, Detroit.

Zald, Mayer N. (1979) 'Macro-Issues in the Theory of Social Movements. SMO Interaction, the Role of Countermovements and Cross-National Determinants of the Social Movement Sector'. University of Michigan, CRSO Working Paper no. 204.

Zald, Mayer N. and Roberta Ash (1966) 'Social Movement Organizations: Growth, Decay and Change', *Social Forces*, 44: 327–41.

Index

Notes on contributors

Anne Batiot was educated in France, Canada and the UK. She taught politics at the University of Essex and at the Open University until 1983. She is now running her own business in Paris.

Drude Dahlerup is leader of the Nordic Council of Ministers project to reduce sex discrimination in the labour market. She has taught politics at the University of Aarhus and has published widely on women's political representation, on social movements and on the women's movement.

Maria Angeles Duran is Professor of Sociology and Director of the Seminario de Estudios de la Mujer at the Autonomous University of Madrid. She has been Visiting Professor at the Institute for Social Research at the University of Michigan. She has published several books in Spanish on women in society and the feminist movement.

Eleonore Eckmann Pisciotta completed her doctoral dissertation on the Italian Women's Movement. During the 1970s she has been active in the feminist movement in both Germany and Italy. She taught at the International Women's Studies Institute, San Francisco, USA, in Greece in 1982 and in Italy in 1986. She currently teaches at the European University Institute, Via dei Roccettini, San Domenica (FI), Italy.

Maria Theresa Gallego is Professor of Political Science at the School of Economics Autonomous University of Madrid. She has published several articles and chapters on the women's movement in Spanish and has been a participant in the Spanish Women's Movement since the late 1960s.

Joyce Gelb is Professor and Chair of the Department of Political Science at City College in New York and a member of the graduate faculty of The City University of New York. She is author of books and articles on problems of the powerless, including blacks and women. Co-author of *Women and Public Policies* (Princeton, 1982, 1986). The University of California Press will publish her forthcoming comparative analysis of feminist politics and impact in the US, UK and Sweden in 1987.

Pauline Conroy Jackson was born and educated in Dublin, Ireland. She is a graduate in Social Science of University College Dublin and in 1968 completed a Masters Degree at the London School of Economics and Political Science. She was active in the early women's movement in Ireland and in the anti-nuclear movement and is secretary to the Dun Laoghaire branch 'of the Anti-Amendment Campaign on abortion. She is currently a member of the University College Women's Studies Forum and preparing a Doctoral Dissertation on industrial sex segregation in Ireland. She has published several articles on the women's movement.

Riitta Jallinoja has done research on women, social movements and the family. Her publications include *The active periods of the Finnish Women's Movement* (dissertation), *Introduction to family sociology* and, together with Elina Haavio-Mannila and Harriet Strandell, *The Family, Work and Feelings*. She was a founder member of the Helsinki group, 'Female Researchers', and President of that association for the first two years, 1982–83. At present she is at the University of Helsinki.

Joyce Outshoorn is Senior Lecturer in the Department of Politics at the University of Amsterdam. She is author of *Vrouwenemancipatie en Socialisme de SDAP en het 'Vrouwenvraagstuk'* (1973). She is also co-author of *Lijfsbehoud. Tien jaar Abortusstrijd in Nederland 1967–1977*, (1977), editor of *A Creative Tension. Essays in Socialist Feminism* (1984) and author of *De politieke strijd rondom abortus in Nederland 1965–1984* (forthcoming).

Audur Styrkársdóttir graduated from the Social Science Department of the University of Iceland with a BA in 1977 and from the University of Sussex in England with an MA in social and political thought in 1980.She has published a book on the women's movement in Iceland in the years 1908–26 and is currently working on a project on women MPs and women's issues in the Icelandic parliament.

Virginia Sapiro is Professor of Political Science and Women's Studies at the University of Wisconsin-Madison. She is author of many books and articles on gender and politics including The Political Integration of Women: Rules, Socialization, and Politics (1983), Women in American Society An Introduction to Women's Studies (1986) and (edited) Women, Biology, and Public Policy (SAGE 1985).

Sirin Tekeli has researched mainly in the USA and France. She was docent at the University of Istanbul, Department of Political Science, from 1978, but resigned in 1981 as a result of the adoption of the new anti-democratic university law. She has published many articles in Turkish, English and French in scientific and popular journals and has been active in the organization of the women's movement in Istanbul. She has recently translated Andrée Michel's *Le Féminism* into Turkish.

DATE DUE